DANGEROUS
FRONTIERS

For Paula

DANGEROUS FRONTIERS

Campaigning in Somaliland and Oman

Bryan Ray

Pen & Sword
MILITARY

First published in Great Britain in 2008 by
Pen & Sword Military
an imprint of
Pen & Sword Books Ltd
47 Church Street
Barnsley
South Yorkshire
S70 2AS

ISBN 978-1-84415-723-5

A CIP catalogue record for this book is
available from the British Library

Typeset in 10/12pt Palatino
by Concept, Huddersfield

Printed and bound in England by
Biddles Ltd

For a complete list of Pen & Sword titles please contact

PEN & SWORD BOOKS LIMITED
47 Church Street, Barnsley, South Yorkshire, S70 2AS, England
e-mail: enquiries@pen-and-sword.co.uk
Website: www.pen-and-sword.co.uk

Contents

Maps

Preface

In my youth I had hoped that one day I might follow a career in the Indian Army. In the event I was disappointed in this ambition as, by the time I had reached the required age to apply, India had achieved independence. Nevertheless I was not denied a taste of the North-West Frontier style of soldiering which had fired my youthful imagination and about which I had heard from my father – two tastes, in fact, the second a quarter of a century after the first.

In 1948, as a newly commissioned – and remarkably raw – National Service subaltern in the Royal Fusiliers, I was fortunate enough to be posted to the Somaliland Scouts. Somaliland, in north-east Africa, was then a British protectorate. I enjoyed my service there so much that during my time in Somaliland I applied for a regular commission in the British Army. Some of my experiences during my two years with the Somalis are the subject of the first part of this book.

I resolved that one day I would return to the Scouts as Commanding Officer, a modest enough ambition but one in which I was thwarted – for the same reason which prevented my joining the Indian Army. In 1960 the Protectorate, together with Italian Somaliland, gained independence and became the Republic of Somalia. China and Russia commenced their jockeying for positions of power on both sides of the Gulf of Aden.

Eventually, however, I did have the opportunity to gain my second experience of frontier- style soldiering when I accepted the offer of command of an Arab regiment in a country that already enjoyed full autonomy – the Sultanate of Oman in south-eastern Arabia. At that time the Sultan's Armed Forces were engaged in a war against Marxist-inspired guerillas in the southern province of Dhofar. The second part of this book concerns my adventures there from 1972 to 1974.

I went back to Oman in 1982 and spent seven more years in Dhofar with the Oman Internal Security Service, during which I was able to witness the impressive progress that Oman had made following the war. By comparison, when I revisited Somaliland in 1995, I saw the devastation that decades of unceasing war and violence had wreaked on the country, its wildlife and, most sadly, its people. My impressions on returning to both countries are given in the Epilogue.

This book was written shortly after my return from Oman in 1974, while events there were fresh in my memory. Fortunately, much earlier, when I was in Somaliland, I had kept a diary and this helped me a great deal. I was able to give details – names of persons, places, and so on – which otherwise I am sure I would have forgotten.

I do not attempt to go deeply into political issues with either country, nor do I attempt to teach any lessons in military strategy. The book is simply a personal account of two well-separated periods of soldiering spent in hot and dusty lands. I hope that it reflects some of the happiness which I found during both.

James Bryan Ray
Hovingham 1980 and West Compton 2007

Acknowledgements

My appreciation to Pat Cheek for facing my terrible writing and, undeterred, typing the original manuscript in 1980.

My heartfelt thanks to my sister, Pamela, for reading through the manuscript and correcting numerous grammatical faults. Also to my children, Anthony and Julia, for their encouragement and support.

Thanks to those who jogged my memory on details of actions which took place fifty-seven and thirty-five years ago, and who struggled through the drafts making helpful suggestions en route. In particular, I am indebted to General John Graham and to Brigadier Malcolm Page for their advice on Oman and Somaliland respectively, to Colonel Nigel Knocker for his asssistance in writing about Operation Simba, and to Lieutenant Colonel Peter Worthy who kept me straight on the Jebel Regiment's operations. I am most appreciative to Lady Annette Creasey for her kind help.

My comrades in NFR – Angus Ramsay, Ian Gardiner, Peter Tawell, Tresham Gregg, Viv Rowe, Christopher Kemball, Charlie Daniel and Charles Ogilvie-Forbes have all made valuable contributions and suggestions. They were always at the sharp end.

Nicholas Knollys took many of the photographs between 'incomers' which illustrate this book. He was the fastest camera on the Hornbeam. My thanks to him too.

I am indebted to those electronic wizards, Gail and George Milne, who transferred faint typescript and ancient photographs to a disk.

To Henry Wilson, Bobby Gainher and Pen and Sword Books Limited, my publishers – thank you. I owe you all many drinks.

Finally, for Paula, Mary and Harriet, who have made my life joyful and everything worth-while; no words can express my love and gratitude.

PART I

Somaliland 1948–1950

Chapter 1

Awareh

'The last time your tribe – the Dhulbahante – ate a man was only twenty years ago,' said the soldier Hassan Haji lying in his blanket by the flickering fire.

'Liar!' shrilled the smaller blanketed bundle, Suliban Ahamed. 'Liar! Like all your clan. It was the Esa who ate that man.'

'Dhulbahante,' replied Hassan, flatly. 'Everyone knows.'

I sat up and scratched my dusty hair. I was weary of the story. Every night Hassan teased Suliban spitefully with a reference to it and every night Suliban faithfully leapt at the lure – to Hassan's huge satisfaction.

'Shut up both of you – and let's get some sleep'.

We had been patrolling on foot for two days and had covered 40 or so miles, showing the tribes that the soldiers were ready to intervene in any fighting over the dwindling wells – fighting which, despite our efforts, all too often flared up. Our task was made more difficult because of controversy over frontier lines.

Boundary disputes are notoriously complicated, but those concerning the parched wedge of semi-desert and thorn scrub lying on Ethiopia's eastern frontier with Somalia are especially intricate. The Ogaden (see map) is roughly triangular in shape and, although falling within Ethiopia, it is peopled by Somali-speaking nomads who recognize no boundaries other than the limits of their ancient grazing lands. A welter of treaties, agreements and grazing rights signed among Britain, Ethiopia, Italy and Somalia since 1894 have resulted in frontier lines on maps, which are either straight, or follow some well-defined geographical feature – but certainly pay scant regard to tribal movements.

The northern third of this wedge is known as the Haud, a plateau rising to an average height of around 4,500 feet. It is partly waterless rolling plain but where there is permanent water the vegetation is

3

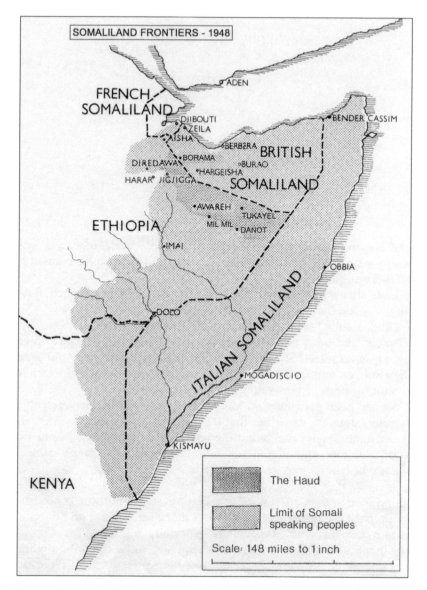

SOMALILAND FRONTIERS - 1948

ADEN

FRENCH SOMALILAND

DJIBOUTI
ZEILA
AISHA

BENDER CASSIM

BERBERA

BRITISH

BORAMA
DIREDAWA
BURAO
HARGEISHA

HARAR JIGJIGGA

SOMALILAND

AWAREH
MIL MIL
TUKAYEL
DANOT

ETHIOPIA

IMAI

OBBIA

DOLO

ITALIAN SOMALILAND

MOGADISCIO

KISMAYU

KENYA

The Haud

Limit of Somali
speaking peoples

Scale: 148 miles to 1 inch

dense – thick bush, with acacia, juniper and fig trees. It is also one of the four areas in the world where frankincense trees are found. In the Ogaden itself there are a few good permanent waterholes.

Grazing is good after the spring and autumn rains, and the Somali tribes, numbering up to 3,000 nomads, herding their camels, goats and sheep, move in from the north and east. Some of these later move on south to the Ogaden wells under a reciprocal arrangement with the Ogaden tribesmen, who wish to export their stock through the Northern Somalia port of Berbera on the Gulf of Aden.

Whilst the grazing is rich and the levels in the wells high, the Somali warriors mix happily with the clansmen of the Ogaden. The age-old camel-watering songs of the Habr Yonis, the Aidagallah and the Arab tribes can be heard at the wells of Awareh, Mil-Mil, Danot and Wal-Wal as they have been heard down the centuries.

> They (the camels) are all here, ready,
> They belong to us.
> How splendid and useful they are
> And they are standing ready.
> I set my foot (on the well),
> Oh Master of the World,
> Oh God the Just make our task easy.
> You will be cooled
> Come forward slowly
> Put your mouth to it with blessing,
> it is devoid of evil.
> Your shrivelled bones
> are now moist and full again.
> When they are standing ready,
> and the clansmen are all present,
> none must leave till all are watered.*

After the rains, as the grazing withers and as the surface water in the Haud dries under the impact of the searing sun, the tempers of the tribesmen rise – rise, it seems, in inverse proportion to the sinking of the levels in the Ogaden wells. Inevitably and annually the quarrelling begins – fuelled by now-remembered insults and jealousies, woundings and killings from the past. Camels are looted and the fighting starts, small in scale at first, but later involving whole *rers*, or tribal sections.

In the days following the Second World War, and before Somali independence, the Haud was administered by Britain, before being returned to Ethiopia in 1955. A District Commissioner, answerable to the Governor of British Somaliland in Hargeisa, listened wearily to the many complaints of murder, camel looting and tribal squabbles, and despatched his *illaloes* to bring in offenders, collect taxes and seize camels as appropriate. If the fighting escalated and things became tense he could call on the company of Somaliland Scouts stationed in the Haud to help keep the peace.

* Andrzejewski, B.W. and Lewis, I.M., 'Camel Watering Chant' (Anonymous), *Somali Poetry*.

Peace in the early 1900s had been harder to keep, mainly due to the activities of the followers of one who aspired to become the Mahdi of Somaliland, Mohammed bin Abdullah Hasan (known to the British as the 'Mad Mullah'). He fought the British for twenty-one years and was a formidable and cruel adversary.

In 1900 the Somali Levy was raised, strengthened by Indian troops, the first locally raised unit to campaign against the Mullah. Later the Levy was designated 6th Battalion King's African Rifles, but was disbanded when the British administration withdrew to the coast at Berbera. However, the Mullah raided Berbera and the administration realized that to defend the area they needed to occupy the hinterland. A Camel Corps Constabulary was therefore raised in 1912 commanded by Richard Corfield, a political officer who had a military second in command, Lieutenant Gibb. The Camel Corps fought well and successfully against the Mullah but suffered a heavy defeat in August 1913 when Corfield and thirty-five of the Corps were killed. It was decided to convert the Corps to a military unit and this was raised in 1914. Included among the British officers seconded to the new Corps were one Captain Ismay of the Indian Army, later General Lord Ismay, and one Captain Carton de Wiart of the 4th Dragoon Guards, later Lieutenent General Sir Adrian Carton de Wiart VC.

Much later the Camel Corps fought under the British flag against the Italians in the Horn of Africa. During this campaign Captain Wilson of the East Surrey Regiment, seconded to the Corps, was awarded the VC. The end of the Camel Corps was a sad one, however. On the night of 5 June 1944, just after the Corps had been converted to armoured cars, and before departing on active service, the volatile and sensitive Muslim soldiers mutinied against their British officers. The Camel Corps askaris were disarmed, disbanded and told to go home – a dishonourable end for a brave force.

A year earlier a number of Somali infantry companies, which had originally been raised to blockade pro-Vichy French Somaliland, had been organized into a battalion and designated 'Somaliland Scouts'. After the War the Scouts, with the Camel Corps gone, were the sole remaining unit left to garrison the Protectorate as foot soldiers – not camel-borne – with British Army trucks to cover the dusty tracks. It is a curious thing that, although officially no Camel Corps trooper was to be enlisted in the Scouts, the foot drill and bearing of many a potential recruit was of a remarkably high standard.

'T'isn't my fault if I dress when I 'alt – I'm back to the Army again!*

* Rudyard Kipling, 'Back to the army again'.

6

In the autumn of 1948 the company of Somali Scouts on detachment in the Haud was D Company, of which I was a member. We were based at Awareh, one of the few watering places and therefore an important centre and confluence of camel trails.

Awareh Camp was well laid out and about half a mile from the *magalla* (town) and wells. It was tented, the *askaris* (soldiers) living in '180 pounders', eight to a tent, and there were four bigger marquee-style tents, three for the officers living quarters and a larger one for the officers' mess. Neat rows of whitewashed stones demarked the soldiers' lines, the motor transport and petrol areas, the compounds for the officers' ponies and the burden camels, and the parade square. The whole camp was surrounded by a *zariba* (thorn fence) to keep out unfriendly nocturnal visitors – both human and animal. About a quarter of a mile away was a smaller *zariba* containing 200 or so camels which had been seized by the Scouts from time to time as fines on the tribes for camel looting or fighting.

In a small compound close by, the District Commissioner (DC) lived and held court. With him in his mud-brick house he kept a sensuous and beautiful Somali woman as housekeeper, an arrangement that would, no doubt, lessen the force of his argument with the tribal chiefs – especially those of the woman's clan.

What sort of people were administered by the DC? The Somalis are a strikingly handsome race, the men being tall and lean with well-defined features betraying their Galla extraction. Many are up to 6 feet and the young warriors appear even taller as they grow their hair long and dye the ends with henna. At the time I was there they wore a one-piece robe often dyed ochre, and carried at least one spear, with sometimes a selection to include weapons for stabbing and others for throwing. Some tribes – like the Esa and Gadurbursi – also carried round leather shields and huge curved knives called *bulahwis* which were used to disembowel, very messily, their opponents. The Esa warriors filed their teeth to sharp points and in addition to their deadly proficiency with the spear were skilled in the use of a sling as a weapon. These they wore wound round their heads, forcing the shock of hair even taller.

The Somalis are natural warriors and love fighting; they are fiercely brave and do not fear death. When wounded they rarely whimper but accept their fate because 'God, who is generous, wills it.' They love intrigue and can be devious in the extreme, yet they have poetry deep in their souls and Somali verse is hauntingly beautiful and evocative, speaking of war, love and camels.

Somali women are renowned for their beauty of features and graceful carriage; they are straight backed and slim, with classically fine features. Yet the lot of the Somali woman was, and in many cases still is, cruel and hard. As a young girl her genitals are partially sewn up so that her eventual husband is guaranteed a virgin. It is his job to 'open' his bride with his knife, thus ensuring a ghastly wedding night for her that could reduce her enjoyment of the sexual act thereafter. Like many nomads they age rapidly, their once taut breasts sagging and their voices sharpening. In common with some other Muslim races, however, Somali women, although apparently totally subordinate to the male, are in reality often the power – and certainly the voice – behind the scenes. The ancient harridan tottering in her rags on crabby feet behind the camel train – who eventually must drop to die in the dust – wields power in her tribe. Having dropped, that same woman will be left until a halt is made at nightfall. One or two men will take a camel from the hobbled herd and retrace the weary miles to collect her light corpse and, having loaded it on the beast, return to the sleeping camp. In death, she rides a camel to her destiny – two rough stones in a parched wilderness, one at her head and one at her feet.

But we must return to D Company sitting in the sand in Awareh in 1948, close to the DC reaching for his whisky brought to him by his Somali beauty, all wondering when the tribes would fight.

From my point of view I found life remarkably pleasant. I liked and respected my Somali soldiers and was fascinated by the lifestyle of the nomads. Add to that the fact that I enjoyed the heat, the country was teeming with game and I was nineteen years old, and it can be seen why I was not complaining. Even as a very impoverished subaltern, my personal staff in those days was impressive. It was headed by Mohammed Usuf, my bearer, known as 'Little Ears' for obvious reasons; unfortunately, as I was to discover, there was very little between those ears! A *'chokra'** Suliban Ahamed, aged twelve, who nominally assisted Mohammed, but in effect ran derisive rings round him. Suliban cooked for me when I was away from the Company. My soldier orderly was Hassan Haji, a handsome man and a good tracker and hunter; he was proud, and a great womanizer. Lastly, Abdi Farah, another soldier (ex-Camel Corps) who was my syce. Abdi, who was forty years old and lived for horses, looked after my grey pony, Borro, and also helped me buy a spirited chestnut stallion from the Jibril Aboker tribe. He was as upset as I was when it later died of horse sickness. (The Jibril Aboker are famous for their horse breeding and dealing – had they detected a sickness in the fleet and beautiful

* Bearer's assistant.

Saharadide which prompted a hasty sale? It was more than possible). Abdi was my principal friend in Somaliland and we exchanged letters for years after I had left.

In early September, when D Company arrived in Awareh from Hargeisa the capital, the wells were full and many hundreds of camels watered there daily. There was plenty for all and it was sufficient to keep an eye on things during our early morning or evening rides, and by the occasional 'flag' patrol by a platoon of Scouts.* We spent the mornings training and improving the soldiers' infantry skills; more often than not a shooting party went out in the afternoon. Although we had our own herd of Somali fat-tailed sheep we relieved this diet with guinea fowl or venison. The long-necked Gerenuk gazelle abounded, as did Spekes and Sommerings gazelle, oryx and greater kudu. The rabbit-sized dik-dik – smallest of all the deer – thrived and was a favourite addition to the soldiers' stew. (Even such a minute specimen had to have its throat cut like all other game in order to be *Hilal* and fit for Muslims to eat.)

Towards the end of September, however, the odd inter-tribal squabble had already broken out, and while the situation was generally calm, all the indications were that the tribal temperatures were going up. As expected the DC issued an order forbidding the carrying of spears in the *magalla* at Awareh or by the wells, and asked for a platoon of D Company to be detached to Mil-Mil 20 miles away. This was a sensitive spot which commanded the routes into the Ogaden and through to Ethiopia. He and Reay Girdwood, D Company Commander, then went into a huddle over a bottle of gin and emerged with a PLAN. The detachment at Mil-Mil would remain while the bulk of the Company would stay quite properly at Awareh wells – but a platoon would move further south to Danot on the boundary of the Haud with the Ethiopian administered Ogaden. Another junction of camel trails, Danot had fairly permanent water and had been the scene of recent and increasing inter-tribal murders and fights.

Returning unsteadily ⸞ ⸟n the DC's camp – legs working busily without disturbing or creasing in any way his enormous starched shorts – Reay explained the new deployment to Nick Cochrane, the other British officer in the Company, and myself. I was to take 4 Platoon to Danot with a Signals and MT detachment. Having set up a camp near the wells, I was to patrol vigorously and show the flag. Any tribal fighting or camel raiding was to be investigated immediately, but the

---

† i.e. Showing the flag. A body of armed soldiers to show military strength and discourage trouble

District Commissioner must be kept fully in the picture by radio; his approval would be needed before any punitive measures were taken.

I liked the sound of it all very much indeed. 'There is no doubt,' said Reay, reaching for the gin, 'that we ought to have a drink, as we won't be together as a company again for a bit'.

Chapter 2

Danot

We left Awareh for Danot in the morning of 24 September 1948, about twenty-eight of us in all. We rode in a 15cwt Bedford truck and two 3-ton trucks tightly jammed with askaris and their kit, plus a small flock of fat-tailed sheep for our fresh rations. The Somalis were glad to be off and sang happily, beating the sides of the trucks in time to their songs, aided and abetted by the bleating sheep. It was a noisy departure which must surely have disturbed Reay and Nick clutching their reeling heads over breakfast and gazing uneasily at fried eggs and sandgrouse breasts. (We prided ourselves on living well in D Company.)

A hundred and twenty miles east-south-east and then due south for another 50 miles, each truck threw up a plume of thick choking dust and the heat increased as the day wore on. We wound our puggarees around our mouths and faces, but the dust got everywhere – eyes, mouth, nose, ears – a situation which was, of course, quite normal.

We drove through the tiny villages of Darkendalaq, Daror and Tukayel. These villages consisted of one or two mud buildings, including the inevitable coffee shop, and a huddle of *ghurgies*. These dome-shaped huts are the customary Somali nomad dwelling. They are fashioned from a framework of curved wood covered in matting that can easily and swiftly be dismantled and loaded onto a camel.

Around Awareh the low-crouching thorn bushes were sparse in the sandy soil; the flat-topped acacia trees were widely spaced and the broad expanses of hills were readily recognized landmarks for miles. Giban Libah – the Lion's Tooth – a jagged rock in the wastes near D Company camp, served as a finger post for the traveller for hour after hour; and on this day of our departure it seemed it would never disappear below the hazy horizon behind our trucks.

11

Nearing Danot, however, the bushes became thicker and thicker, and the soil changed from yellow ochre to a remarkable red colour. Pillar-like termite hills, many topping 12 feet, pointed red fingers to the sky and visibility was restricted to yards in this amazing landscape. It crossed my mind that it must have been fashioned to suit the Somali raiding bands (*shifta*) which were rumoured to be operating in the area.

The sun had swung down behind the thorn bush by the time we ground wearily into a wide valley containing the Danot wells and on into the *magalla* itself. The village was as mean as the others we had passed through that day, but we could see many *ghurgies* grouped near the wells and hundreds of camels moving to and from the water, the wooden bells round their necks clacking musically. Surprisingly, as we stopped by the coffee house in a swirl of dust, an English voice hailed me, and a dark-haired, heavily tanned figure with a black up-brushed moustache emerged from the deep shadow of the doorway. It was Captain Fitz Ambler, immaculate in his neatly wound puggaree and beautifully pressed khaki-drill uniform. In his briefing Reay had not mentioned – perhaps he hadn't known – that a patrol from A Company of the Scouts was already in Danot. And here they were!

At this point Sergeant Mohamoud Egeh murmured in my ear that the soldiers, less a vehicle guard, would appreciate a drink of camel's milk and magically they melted away leaving me with Fitz. Evidently the A Company patrol had been in Danot several days. Following a number of inter-tribal incidents Fitz and his soldiers had been ordered to establish a presence until my platoon arrived – a presence that Fitz Ambler could certainly establish, on his own! He had been in the country for years and there were many stories of his prowess – and of his capacity for pink gin. Curiously, on this occasion, he had chosen to house himself and his men within the Danot village itself, which was handy but not too tactical. However, he was the first to recognize that it wasn't the best permanent spot to be and he recommended a place outside the village which he thought would be more suitable.

Mohamoud Egeh gathered the soldiers and in the fast-fading light we found a promising campsite; the askaris swiftly cut thorn branches with their pangas and built a *zariba*. By the time it was finally dark our tents were pitched within the prickly fence and cooking fires were flickering. I bought an extra sheep in the *magalla* for the platoon's evening meal to celebrate our arrival and, leaving the askaris clapping time to their singing, I returned to the coffee shop for dinner with Fitz and a pink gin. Or two.

The following day Fitz and his patrol left and before the dust plume marking their departure had dispersed, we were hard at work improving our camp. It was about half a mile from the village and our first task was to clear the bushes for a hundred yards or so outside the *zariba* to give fields of fire for our weapons. There were one or two flat-topped acacia trees within our perimeter and these we converted into cool and airy huts known as 'wobs'. The tree's foliage forms a natural circular roof and we placed long branches all the way round to build walls between this roof and the ground. More branches were then woven into the framework to thicken it up. One of these wobs we used to supplement the soldiers living accommodation and another housed the radio operators and their set, with which we had made immediate contact with Awareh (by Morse code as the range was too great for voice conversation.)

My tent was pitched in the corner of the *zariba* furthest from the camp entrance, opposite the vehicle park and petrol drums. I could thus keep an eye on comings and goings. In the centre of the camp was a small compound containing our sheep, amongst which, mysteriously, a few goats had now appeared.

Over the next few weeks we improved our living conditions and security, allotting some time most days to this task. Mohamoud Egeh was a stern but fair taskmaster who was well supported by the three corporals – Ardan Abdi, Ibrahim Hussein and Hassan Farah. Lance Corporal Ismail Warsama, in his oily dungarees and gleaming teeth, was in charge of the trucks.

Our main task was, of course, to patrol, and we did this most days on foot, sometimes with burden camels to take our heavier equipment and vital water. We kept a sharp eye on the Danot wells, often the presence of a section of soldiers preventing inter-tribal squabbling over the water developing into fighting. We used the same water ourselves and it took a bit of getting used to, being brackish and brown in colour. I found when I strained it through a handkerchief that a deposit of tiny white wriggling grubs remained! I laced it well with water purification tablets which made it taste even worse, but after a hot day's patrolling through the thick bush it served to quench the thirst.

Whenever possible we drank camel's milk, the staple diet of the nomad who can live on it and literally nothing else for months. At villages which we patrolled through, or where we stayed overnight, we were always offered gourds of this, which we accepted gratefully. But ... those gourds! Of ancient origin they provided their own unique flavour to the milk – a little to do with the smoke of cooking fires and a lot to do with the fact that camel's urine was often added to help preserve the milk through the hot days! In Danot Mohammed Usuf sent Suliban, the *chokra*, to collect my milk fresh from the camel in a rice tin, and it tasted delicious.

Throughout my time in Somaliland I tried hard to learn the language, not an easy one. Soon I was able to make myself understood and when I could not my venerable and well-named interpreter, Hersi Gas, was always ready to help.

Several times a week I took out a shooting party to provide meat for the soldiers and to supplement our fat-tailed sheep and new goats. Usually Abdi Midgan accompanied us. The *Midgan* tribe provide many skilled craftsmen – metal and wood workers as well as hunters and trackers. They are of low caste and, rather like the Untouchables of India once did, also do the jobs of cleaners and sweepers, which tasks are beneath the dignity of the warriors (and soldiers). Abdi Midgan cleaned the camp and, in addition, was a marvellous hunter. I remember him taking my party through extra thick bush to suddenly present Cpl Ibrahim Hussein with a perfect and close view of a magnificent oryx stag. This stood as high as a fourteen-hand pony and was almost as sturdily built. Its curving horns seemed to go on for ever. Ibrahim brought it down cleanly with a single shot through the heart and it provided meat and an excuse for dancing for everyone in camp that night.

On the first of October a tribesman walked into the camp, spear across his shoulders, and asked to see me. He came from Massara, a tiny *qarya* (village) about 5 miles away, and wished to report the theft of camels by men of the Ogaden, *Rer* Ibrahim section. I collected a patrol together and we went with the man back to his village.

Squatting under an acacia tree with the village headman, I exchanged the usual greetings. 'Ma nabut ba?' (Is it peace?) I asked. 'Wa nabut!' (It is peace) the headman responded. We then came to the subject of the camels. He confirmed they had been stolen and went on to say that the warriors of the *Rer* Ibrahim carried rifles in addition to their spears. Unlike his tribe, the Aidagallah, he added shiftily, who possessed no arms like that. I told the headman that he would be very pleased to hear that my soldiers would shoot any man seen carrying a rifle – this was the law of the land and would obviously include any of the *Rer* Ibrahim. I added that I was mightily relieved to learn that the Aidagallah possessed no rifles, because, of course, the law would apply equally to them too. However I now had the Chief's assurance on this point – as I was sure he would confirm? The old man's eyes darted here and there, settling like a locust on one spot before taking off once more for a fresh destination. He mumbled into his beard, hawked and spat.

I sent a man to the *qarya* of the *Rer* Ibrahim to instruct their Chief to visit me at Danot Camp the next day, and gathering the patrol, we returned as darkness fell, suitably refreshed with camel's milk (of a very well-preserved vintage).

The next day my messenger returned. Yes, he had gone to the Chief of the *Rer* Ibrahim, and yes, he had given the message. Where was the Chief? All the Chief had said was, 'Go away or you will be shot.' Clearly I could not allow this response and I told Mohamoud Egeh to prepare a patrol to leave with me before dawn the next day.

At four-thirty in the morning we were ready. Sergeant Mohamoud Egeh, Corporal Adan Abdi, seven askaris (none from the Aidagallah tribe) and three *illaloes* from the detachment permanently stationed in Danot. We piled into the Bedford and, without lights, drove 15 miles along the Massara track before swinging cross country towards the *Rer* Ibrahim village. About a mile and a half short of our objective we left the truck and went quietly forward on foot. We had no difficulty in locating the village, even in such thick country at night, because of the grumbling and bubbling of the *Rer* Ibrahim camels. As we approached, dawn brightened the horizon and I could gradually make out the shapes of bushes and the silent figures of the soldiers on either side moving with their long tireless strides. With a sudden clarity I realized that I was totally happy and would not exchange my present position with anyone.

We stopped within a hundred yards or so of the *ghurgies* and the soldiers melted silently into the shadows of the bushes. I sent the head *illalo* to locate the Chief, while I told Mohamoud to position the soldiers round the village to prevent anyone slipping away.

The *illalo* returned to say that the Chief was not in the village – whether or not he had wind of our arrival it was impossible to say. Leaving the cordon of soldiers intact I went into the circle of round huts taking Mohamoud and Corporal Ibrahim Hussein with me. Ignoring the shrill screaming and abuse of the women, I addressed the men of the tribe on the evils of camel looting and the carrying of arms. We then made a thorough search of the village but found no rifles. A quiver of poisoned arrows came to light which I confiscated – but otherwise nothing.

I walked over to where a handful of the *Rer* Ibrahim elders were sitting in the shade of a large thorn tree, away from the shrill-voiced women, and squatted with them in the dust. I gazed round at their proud, cruel faces and saw the derision behind their eyes. Their rifles were all hidden safely in the bush, their Chief was also safely concealed and only their old and barren she-camels were left in the village in case this pale-faced youth and his soldiers would take them as a fine. Surely there was a lot to be amused at, and later the story could be told – embellished. And told again, and again.

'Listen, old men!' I said heavily. 'My purpose today is only to warn you; so I will have achieved what I want to do. What will you achieve today?' A good story for the telling, I thought bitterly to myself.

I warned them as they squatted on their horny heels that should I hear of any camels looted by the *Rer* Ibrahim in the future I would take all their stock for the Government – all their stock, not the useless old she-camels now in the camp, but the young milking females, the bulls and the calves. Any man seen carrying a rifle would be shot, I continued. They looked at me, the contemptuous-eyed old men who had been involved in camel raids and fighting every year of their adult lives, and murmured politely, 'Go in the light of God.'

For me it was a significant, if unsuccessful little operation; it taught me the importance of achieving surprise and a lot more about losing face – and the significance that Muslims attach to that. That day I had failed to achieve surprise and I had lost face.

Following our visit to the *Rer* Ibrahim *qarya*, I stepped up our activity and every day patrols left the camp so that there wasn't an area within 50 miles around Danot which wasn't covered. I recall that during the next three weeks in October there were no inter-tribal incidents, and I like to believe that this peace was not unconnected with our efforts. There were nevertheless some memorable high spots. First and foremost it rained – buckets of it – constantly. For two days it poured down, accompanied by dramatic sheet lightning and distant rumbling of thunder like tribal drums. The wells at Danot were filled and the tension in the air lessened. I stretched a groundsheet to catch the clear sweet water and hoarded it in my own container.

Secondly, the great lion shoot took place. There were many lion in the area, and every night we could hear their unmistakeable and unforgettable coughing roars. One day a small pride of the black-maned Abyssinian variety had padded past my patrol no more than a few yards away. We were not surprised therefore when we heard that sheep were being taken from a neighbouring *qarya*. With Corporal Adam Abdi, my orderly Hassan and two askaris – Ibrahim Abdi and Farah Matan – I went to the village and we staked out a young goat close to where the lion had taken the last sheep. We concealed ourselves in the bush with torches and rifles and I felt very confident that we would shoot our great cat. But we had reckoned without the hospitality of the locals! A steady stream of men moved to our hiding place from the village carrying gourds of camel's milk and baskets of roast meat. It was the fasting month of Ramadan when Muslims did not eat or drink by day, but were allowed to break their fast after the sun had gone down. My personal tally was four pints of milk and several pounds of goat. Subsequently there was further movement as pressure built up and it became urgent to make room for more milk. Any visiting lion would surely have been trampled to death, and certainly would have had to take its place in the queue to get anywhere near the goat. Bloated and tired we returned to Danot at dawn. No lion – but a monstrous meal.

Thirdly, a snake appeared in the new wob I now used as my dining room. It was about 4 feet in length and light grey in colour, with black diamonds on its back. I managed to shoot it, after several attempts, with my revolver. Abdi Midgan, who found the whole incident most amusing, dried the skin to make me a beautiful belt, which, unfortunately, as the days passed, began to smell so violently that I eventually 'lost' it when Abdi was looking the other way. Whether the snake was poisonous or not I never discovered, but I was to see many similar ones at Danot.

Then the DC visited and took me on a tour of his parish. I told him of the *Rer* Ibrahim incident and my patrolling programme and, as he left in his battered truck, realized that he was the first European I had seen or spoken to for over a fortnight.

Three days later Reay arrived for a two-day visit over the Muslim holiday of Eid al Fitr. We sighted the new moon to mark the end of Ramadan that same evening and fired rifles and flares in the air to celebrate – God is Great! Reay had brought a sack of sugar and tea, and three sheep for the soldiers – that night the dancing and singing reached fever pitch. He told me much later that following his visit he had become worried that I had 'gone native'. He had noted uneasily the way I had cut the throat of a gazelle I had shot, muttering the appropriate Somali blessing over the meat. (What he had forgotten was that everything I shot was shared by my Somali soldiers – and it was essential that it was rendered edible for them as strict Muslims.) Reay's uneasiness had apparently increased when he later saw me sharing a bowl of rice with the soldiers and chatting to them in Somali. My behaviour, he thought, was definitely very rum. Very rum indeed!

During this interlude I was taught by one of my soldiers how to ride a camel. We held a grand sports day to include running, jumping and spear throwing, and, despite the daily mepacrine tablet which we all took, we had our first cases of malaria amongst the askaris.

In the third week of October several inter-tribal incidents occurred and I was kept busy investigating these, and sending reports to the DC, or taking what action seemed to me to be necessary. The *Rer* Ibrahim featured once more by announcing that the wells at Massara were exclusively for the use of Ogaden tribes – not even the Government could water there! But the Government could, and did. Regularly for the next few days, we filled our water drums at Massara instead of at Danot, and ensured that the Aidagallah and Habr Yonis also drank their fill under the haughty noses of the *Rer* Ibrahim.

Near Massara the recent rains had left a clear shallow lake and it was our custom to stop there for a cool swim before returning to Danot in the evenings. Had someone murmured 'Bilharzia' at the time, I would probably have thought they were referring to a new officer for the Scouts. Now I wonder if that water had been swarming with deadly little snails!

One day we were told that a man of the Habr Yonis *Rer* Suguleh had been killed by a Bah Dhulbahante warrior and that both sections were preparing for battle. The Habr Yonis *qarya* was at Warrenleh some 40 miles away. I decided that I must – like Fitz Ambler – establish a 'presence' in Warrenleh as soon as possible, and so early the next day I left for the area taking Corporal Ibrahim, my orderly Hassan and four soldiers. The remainder stayed at Danot under Mohamoud Egeh in case of trouble at the wells or elsewhere.

In the early afternoon we arrived in Warrenleh, after a hundred-mile detour because of the lack of suitable tracks. The majority of the Habr Yonis *ghurgies* were grouped round the well, but the *Rer* Suguleh village was some miles on where no vehicle could go. We spent a night by the wells with the Habr Yonis sharing their camel's milk and their mosquitos. The following day my party split into two and we visited all the neighbouring *ghurgies*, including those of the *Rer* Suguleh, and spread the word that the Government would act swiftly and firmly against any war parties. Corporal Ibrahim, in charge of the other party, confirmed my feeling that the rumour of trouble between the *Rer* Sugulah and Bah Dhulbahante had been exaggerated and that certainly the former appeared to have no intention of exacting vengeance for the murdered man – yet. So after gathering as much information about the killing as we could we returned to Danot and tapped out a report to the DC in Awareh. He would arrange the necessary investigation of the affair with his *illaloes*.

News came in over the next few days of various armed raiding bands from a variety of tribes and we were busy following up these reports, but without any contacts. On the last day of October a man walked into my tent and flung a bloodstained garment on the ground. It belonged to a murdered girl and, visiting the *qarya*, I saw that she was very young – in her early teens – and had been shot through the stomach. It was a tiny entry wound, but the bullet had made a terrible mess of her back on its way out.

The husband was to blame, said the village headman. The girl had been unfaithful to him and had run away to this village; he had followed and shot her. Another report for the DC and I later learned that the husband had been picked up by police many miles away in the Protectorate.

These murders were not strictly military business. It was up to me to report them as fully as possible and then leave the follow-up action to the civil authorities, i.e. the DC – who was not all that civil when he complained in flowery language of the number of such cases on his books . . . and each day several more . . . and each sparked off others. An eye for an eye.

Our vigorous patrolling was, however, paying off, and it seemed that our warnings of terrible retribution for those fighting or camel looting were, to some extent, being heeded. Several times our intervention was swift enough to prevent trouble between opposing clans. The DC went as far as to say – by Morse key – 'Well done'. Even Reay indicated later that for someone going round the bend I hadn't performed too badly.

And all the time the real trouble clouds were gathering much nearer to Awareh itself. Fighting near there did break out on several occasions, and the number of deaths began to mount. With a platoon at Mil-Mil and another at Danot, D Company was left with only two at Awareh itself – and in what looked likely to be the main trouble area. A redeployment was obviously necessary and the DC and Reay did not take more than a bottle to work it all out.

Mil-Mil was important because of the routes into the Ogaden and there had been one or two nasty skirmishes there already. The detachment had to stay. Danot on the other hand, was pretty quiet – I like to think entirely because of my platoon, but probably the real reason was that a number of tribal sections had moved closer to Awareh to support their clansmen there. The Danot platoon, it was decided, must return to Awareh.

On 4 November we struck camp, carefully placed Corporal Hassan Farah and Private Elmi Ali, both with raging malaria, in the back of the Bedford and started out along the dusty tracks.

Nothing of great importance in the Ogaden scene had occurred during the six weeks of the Danot detachment, but the many small experiences which made up our lives there combined to make the period a significant one for me. I believe also that it was an unparalleled way of learning the trade of a soldier. I had greatly enjoyed my independent little command and I was very sorry to be leaving.

Chapter 3

Tribal Troubles

As we shuddered over the corrugated tracks the hazy bulk of Giban Libah shouldered its way over our horizon and served as our direction post thereafter. Twenty miles short of Awareh a Bedford 15cwt truck, with its canvas canopies removed from cab and body, stood in the fast-lengthening shade of an acacia tree. Beside it was a familiar squat figure carrying a 12-bore shotgun in one hand and a brace of vulturine guinea fowl in the other; it was joined by a second figure also carrying a gun. Reay and Nick had combined an evening shooting trip with welcoming the return of the Danot detachment.

We covered the remaining miles in fine style, racing along like dusty-tailed comets, sometimes, where the track disappeared in the sand, two or three vehicles abreast. The askaris started singing and clapping as the camp came into sight and the thoughts of the *magalla* and its hidden delights loomed large. The girls in the Awareh brothel would be kept extra busy during the next few days.

The quarter guard turned out as we approached the guard tent at the camp entrance. It consisted of three smart soldiers under their NCO, all in their best uniforms, puggarees and *kullahs*, highly polished leather bandoleers (ex-Camel Corps), shirts, shorts, long puttees and leather sandals. The guard presented arms as we passed and the bugle boy Hussein sounded D Company call followed by the General Salute.

A surprise awaited the returning soldiers. Reay had arranged for huts to be built in neat rows alongside the camp, huts with strong wooden frames and covered with dried grass. These were the married quarters and wives and children had walked in from Hargeisa or their tribal vlllages. Now the women lined our route through the camp shrilling the ululating cry which is used to urge the warriors into battle, or in celebration – in this case 'Welcome Home!' The married men from Danot, murmuring fervent praises to God, slipped quietly away to inspect their new homes and did not reappear again that day, or the next day which, being *Jumaa* (Friday) and the Muslim holy day, Reay declared a holiday.

While we had been in Danot a gymkhana had been held in Hargeisa, the capital of the Protectorate. Each company of the Scouts had entered a team and there were also competitors from the Police, Gendarmerie and Civil Administration. Despite the difficulties involved in being a hundred miles away in the Haud, D Company was determined to enter. There were no tarmac roads in the country at that time and moving horses in makeshift boxes along the evilly rough tracks risked injury and was not practical. The syces therefore walked the ponies to and from Hargeisa, taking several days for each trip. In my absence I had given permission for Abdi Farah to ride Borro in the team and he had done particularly well. On 11 November the little party of ponies and syces arrived back in Awareh, dusty, but all very fit. Grinning hugely, Abdi gripped my hands and enthused about his own performance, Borro's speed and agility, the gymkhana generally and my return – in that order.

I was delighted to have Borro back and rode most mornings and evenings, sometimes with Reay and the syces, more often on my own. Thus I got to know the trails around the *magalla* and the wells, and also those radiating out from the town for several miles. These rides also proved valuable in assessing the movement and numbers of the tribesmen in the area and the quantity of camels at the wells. Perhaps the most useful aspect of all was that I could go some way to finding out the mood of people in Awareh by their responses to me. It is rather indicative that the Somali greeting is in the form of the question: '*Ma Nabut Ba?*' (Is it Peace?) It is normal to reply in the affirmative: '*Wa Nabut*' (It is Peace). (I suppose a flung spear or drawn knife is the reply when it definitely is NOT!). Normally on my rides those I greeted shouted 'Wa Nabut' happily, the young boys saluted and the girls giggled and hid their faces. Sometimes, however, the reply was mumbled, or backs were turned and I drew my own conclusion that on that day – for some reason – perhaps all was not well in Awareh. Temperament does perhaps have its assets – although I would not have been able to apply this sort of gauge with, say, the inscrutable Chinese!

Most of November passed without any major incidents. We kept up a high rate of patrolling and arms searches, the latter with little success. I remember that General Chater, the Colonel Commandant of the Somali Scouts, visited us on one day and we paraded smartly for him in our best uniforms. Shortly afterwards tempers flared in Awareh over a tribal feud and the whole company marched through the town, with

Reay grandly at its head on Ainib, his bay pony. That same night a number of shots were fired over our camp and Nick and I raced out with some soldiers, but in the darkness the chances of finding anyone were very slim indeed, and we didn't.

Towards the end of the month a fire – no doubt started under a cooking pot – flared up in the married lines. Two grass huts were burnt but luckily the wind was in our favour and no others caught alight. The wife of Sergeant Hashi Jama had a very badly burnt arm, but thankfully no one else was hurt. Apart from this the quarters were a great success and enhanced life in Awareh for all the soldiers – not just the married ones. Spurred on perhaps by the thought of such a home, Mohamoud Egeh, my Sergeant in Danot, took his first bride and I joined the celebration party in the married lines. This took the form of a Somali dance, the men in line facing the women, and all whirling and singing to the rhythmic clapping of hands. An impressive cloud of dust built up through which one could just make out the leaping, whirling figures. They kept it up for most of the night refreshed by great draughts of camel's milk. In the early hours I crept away to my tent, but could hear the high provocative singing of the girls for hours afterwards.

One morning at the end of the month the DC sent a message to say that about 400 armed and hostile Ogaden horsemen were reported to be at a place called Shilasse, some 20 miles away. Nick and I took two platoons with rations, water and ammunition for three days and set off with the DC for the area. In order to mask our intentions we took a very roundabout route, made even longer by the thick bush country, and camped about 2 miles short of the low hill which was our destination.

At dawn the next day we broke camp and, having left our vehicles and the majority of the soldiers at the foot of the hill, climbed to a vantage point from which we could see many miles in all directions. To one side were the scattered *qaryas* of the Ogaden clans, and to another flank were visible the *zaribas* of the Habr Awal and Habr Yonis tribesmen.

The DC sent his *illaloes* to seek out the tribal chiefs and summon them to a meeting that evening. Surprisingly all three turned up and aired their grievances at some length, which were a string of complaints about camels looted and men murdered over the past months. The DC gave them their heads before sternly lecturing all three and reiterating the Government's position: to allow no large-scale fighting which it would suppress with force. And so on. Grumbling, the chiefs gathered their robes and their escorts round them, and stalked away to their respective clans.

22

From our hill the next morning we watched our ration truck, accompanied by its plume of dust, thread its way towards us, grinding its way for miles across the plain. In addition to the dates, *jowari*, ghee and fresh meat, it bore a message from Reay – he would like to come to Shilasse to see the situation for himself, but I would have to return to look after the rest of D Company in Awareh for him to do so. The situation there was also quite tense. So back I went over the bone-shaking miles to Awareh where, pinkly, Reay was impatiently waiting to be relieved; he briefed me rapidly, and departed.

Abdi saddled Borro for me and I rode into the *magalla* where much of the talk was about the tribes gathering at Shilasse, but things seemed relaxed in the town and by the wells. I returned and ate an enormous meal, enjoying the facilities of the Mess at Awareh – all to myself!

Early next day I took a platoon in a 3-ton truck on a short patrol round the town. As we approached a hut a woman darted across the track right in front of our wheels, the driver slammed on his brakes, but too late. When I carried the woman into the hut she was already dead. It was the first of many times that I was surprised at the Muslim calmness in the face of the death of someone close. 'God is generous,' said the woman's husband; and that was all. (He was subsequently paid the necessary 'blood money' by the Government, otherwise it might *not* have been all!)

Many years later in Oman I found exactly the same impassiveness in the comrades of soldiers who were killed. '*Allah Kareem*' (God is Generous), they would say – and I invariably remembered that woman in Awareh.

That same afternoon the *illalo* Sergeant Major, who had been left at Awareh in the DC's absence at Shilasse, came hurrying into the camp. He told of armed men who had fired at his small patrol that morning at Quoray, 20 miles away in the opposite direction to Shilasse. I hastily assembled a platoon and we tumbled into the standby vehicle. This truck was already loaded with enough ammunition, water and food for one platoon for three days, and stood by the guard room at all times.

We made good time along the Hargeisa track to Quoray and, leaving the vehicle under guard, advanced in extended line. Hassan Haji and the *illalo* Sergeant Major were the first to sight a group of men carrying rifles running through the bush, and soon we all saw them moving across an open gravelly plain. I called on them to halt but received a couple of shots in reply and a fine turn of speed. I ordered the platoon to fire on them but the range was great by this time and I very much doubt if anyone was hit. At that point a group of horsemen, waving rifles, bore down on us from a flank and we switched our fire to them.

In a great swirl of dust they swerved to one side and raced off after, and then past, their running fellow tribesmen.

Rather wishing I had more than the twenty-odd men with me, we loped off in pursuit. The Somalis have a wonderfully ground-consuming trot which they can maintain for hours. Luckily, being built on the same stringy lines, one of my very few assets is to be able to do the same. Thus I managed to keep up and for two hours we chased those elusive *shifta*, yet only saw them the once and then not again. What we did see, for miles, were tracks of men and horses – many of them. Hassan estimated a hundred at least, all heading the same way as our quarry. As dusk fell we knew we had no chance of finding the fleet warriors and started back for our vehicle, walking at first, but back to our lope when we heard distant shots from the direction of the truck. On arriving there we found the body of an Ogaden *Rer* Ali warrior who carried on a cord round his neck a silver-plated French hunting horn – often used by the tribesmen for rallying their war parties. He had been shot by a group which had then been engaged and driven off by the Corporal and two soldiers I had left with the vehicle. We later discovered that this group belonged to the Aidagallah tribe, as were the men we had been chasing. We took the Ogaden body back with us to Awareh, where I placed it in the DC's compound. After making their reports the *illaloes* would hand the body over to the Ogaden tribesmen for burial.

In the town things were noisy. News travels very fast in Somaliland and warriors from the Ogaden were shouting for vengeance against the Aidagallah. Women were shouting and shrilling, and the few Habr Awal (pro Aidagallah) tribesmen there were fingering their spears sullenly. I gathered the headmen and forbade any gathering of people in the *magalla* that night. Later I told D Company Sergeant Major – Isman Said, a delightful old warrior – to take a platoon on a march through the centre of the town. Periodically during the night I fired 2-inch mortar parachute-illuminating flares over the town. Whenever we heard shouting one of these flares produced a startled silence and these, together with our patrolling, just about kept the lid on a pot which was very much on the boil. At three in the morning I saw the lights of a vehicle dipping and flickering as it bumped its way towards the camp. Reay had seen my flares from Shilasse hill and, intending anyway to return at daybreak, had made an early start. Luckily he approved of my action and felt that we might have averted a big clash between the Aidagallah and the Ogaden tribes. The DC, who also returned that morning, agreed.

Some skirmishing was going on somewhere, however. Four more corpses – two Aidagallah and two Ogaden – joined the one already within the DC's compound that day, brought in by their own clansmen. During the next few days the number of warriors killed and wounded on both sides increased – results of skirmishes well out of the way of our patrols. Feeling was very high and this was reflected by an electric tension in the town and round the wells at Awareh.

Two days after Reay's return I took a patrol before first light to Shillasse where I joined Nick and his patrol. We walked for 15 miles, visiting the neighbouring villages and, we hoped, discouraging any fighting. On the way back to our hill my patrol spied a tribesman who was watching us from the cover of some bushes. The observer, seeing himself observed, darted away, but was caught by two askaris. He was from an Ogaden tribe but refused to talk to us at all, and was sullenly silent when we asked him where his village was and where he was going to. I knew there was absolutely no way in which we could get any information out of him so I let him go, but retained his razor-sharp spear as a fine for his lack of co-operation.

When I returned to Awareh I found that an extra platoon had been sent to us from Hargeisa as reinforcements and, the next day, we were visited by Major Humphrey French, the Second in Command of the Scouts, and Lester Morgan, the Adjutant. Over lunch Humphrey explained that the grazing area would be officially closed at about Christmas time, and the British Somaliland tribes would then be required to move out. Up to then, however, we could expect trouble. We listened attentively. Humphrey French was a very experienced officer in Somaliland having served in the Somali Gendarmerie before the Scouts. He was also a very popular and charming person, who was to succeed Oliver Brooke as Commanding Officer in due course, although we, and he, did not know it at the time.

For me one of the enjoyable times of day in Awareh Camp was bath time! An essential piece of tent furniture for all the British officers was half a 44-gallon petrol drum cut lengthways. This made an admirable bath, providing large stones were placed round its sides to prevent it rolling over! Mohammad Usuf supervised the ritual of filling the bath which involved Suliban darting to and from the mess tent with bowls of hot water. It was a luxury we could only afford in Awareh where there was plenty of water.

That night, after Humphrey French and Lester Morgan had left, I sat in my bath, knees nearly on a level with my shoulders and thought about the last few weeks. It seemed to me that we had been running hither and thither with our patrols in a very disjointed way. Whenever we or the DC heard of a likely trouble spot off went a patrol to investigate and perhaps contain the trouble, before rushing off in the opposite direction to the next possible crisis – and so on. Yet there had been no major conflict so perhaps our popping about, appearing and reappearing, might be doing the trick. In any case what was the alternative with our tiny force in such a huge tract of country? Sit still in the middle and wait for the big one? Definitely not as that way many people would be killed in the smaller skirmishes and there certainly *would* be a big one. No, perhaps we were doing the best thing – holding a central reserve in Awareh and responding to all the indications of possible trouble with our patrols. Nevertheless, bearing in mind the present tension and the inescapable fact that tribal fighting was a way of life in the Ogaden, I felt sure that we would see a major engagement despite all our efforts.

I climbed out of the bath and Mohammad pulled out the bung. The water flowed into the little channel in the floor and on under the tent wall to the mess garden, where our tomatoes were coming along very nicely indeed.

The next day, 6 December, Nick and I visited the wells at a spot called Mer-Mer close to Shilasse. The Ogaden warriors had been denying the Habr Awal and Habr Yonis clansmen the water and had pitched their *ghurgies* on every side of the wells. It was a very obvious potential trouble spot and we decided that the best thing to do would be to order the Ogaden to move their huts 5 miles back from Mer-Mer. Surprisingly, they agreed to go, albeit with ill grace. We waited while they made their preparations, and I was intrigued to note that it only took about an hour to dismantle a *ghurgie* and lash it onto a camel – not bad for moving house and all one's worldly possessions.

News now came in from Regimental Headquarters by radio of a brush which an A Company patrol had had with armed *shifta* close to the Ethiopian border and about 50 miles from Awareh. The patrol was commanded by John Gilbert, a very recently arrived subaltern whom I knew. It appeared that Gilbert's patrol had killed several *shifta* and were now in a dangerous situation as the area was swarming with armed men. The Commanding Officer of the Scouts, Oliver Brooke, felt that it was quite on the cards that Gilbert's few men would be overwhelmed. He had decided therefore to call the patrol in, but Gilbert's radio had unfortunately chosen this moment to break down; he could neither send messages nor receive them. D Company was ordered to send a platoon to find Gilbert and his men and bring them in to Awareh, the only snag being that the exact location of the patrol was not known, nor could it be verified by radio.

At this time Reay was in Hargeisa, but the reinforcement platoon commander, Malcolm Page of B Company, remained at Awareh, thus releasing me to Hunt the Gilbert.

Off I went in the standby vehicle with the standby platoon, 30 miles along the Mil-Mil track and then across country for three sun-blistering and bumpy hours, until we hit the Dagahbur trail and headed towards the Ethiopian border. By the time we reached the general area of Gilbert's patrol it was dark. One of my soldiers knew the area and guided us to a well. It was nearly dry and the water very dark and muddy, however it was a lucky find as we had used up a good deal of our original water during the day due to a leaking radiator. We were in very close country and knew that there would be tribal *zaribas* close to the well. Indeed we could hear camels grumbling and, once, men shouting in the distance. The soldiers built a remarkably thick *zariba* in a remarkably short time and I posted double sentries. We lit several fires and wrapped ourselves in our single blanket against the usual cold of the desert night.

We were all awake, chilled, at dawn and there was enough water for a small cup of tea each. As it grew lighter we saw a couple of *ghurgies* a few hundred yards away and standing near them two young boys looking after their goats. I took Hassan Haji and we walked over towards them, but they ran off, obviously very frightened. There were no men anywhere to be seen, but an old woman and a young unmarried girl with braided hair were hiding in one of the huts. Hassan took the girl by the arm and spoke softly to her. No, she had no idea where the menfolk were; no, she didn't know anything about any soldiers in the area, or at least she didn't think so. Hassan pressed her arm gently. 'Tell us about the soldiers. We know and you know they are near here. No one will realize that you have talked to me.' The girl looked over her shoulder – the crone was out of sight. She nodded towards a small flat hill and pointed with her tongue.* Hassan let her go, rather reluctantly – she was a fine-looking girl.

It took us no more than an hour to reach the hill in our already steaming truck and sure enough, as we approached, we saw a group of askaris who led us up to their position. John Gilbert had sited his platoon well and it would have taken a great deal to have dislodged him from his natural defensive position. Nevertheless he was pleased to see my soldiers and to receive the orders which I relayed. It had been a very uneasy period for him while his radio had been out of action. He had been involved in a brisk exchange of fire with the *shifta*, who had taken a number of casualties; luckily his own men had escaped any injury. Since then his position had been approached by increasingly large armed bands, but they had not attacked. He had done well but

* A method often used by the Ogaden people to indicate direction as it is not so obvious as pointing with a finger.

was naturally pleased to be moving out. We lost no time in loading all the B Company equipment, the soldiers leapt aboard the trucks happily and we headed back towards Awareh. The extra platoon was to prove a bonus for D Company at exactly the right time.

Back once more in my tent I kicked off my *chaplis* (sandals) and shouted for Mohammad and a bath. The tent flap was pushed aside and a dignified figure stood before me in a spotless white tobe. *'Nabut, Sahib,'* he said and gravely extended a hand. I knew him at once – Abdullahi Hassan of the Aidagallah, one of the most respected bearers in the Scouts. I had seen him last in the Officers' Mess at Hargeisa. 'I am your new bearer. Mohammad Usuf has returned to his village.' And that was that. On his last trip to Hargeisa a thoughtful Reay had told Abdullahi that I was not pleased with Mohammad Yusuf, and here he was – engaged! Abdullahi stayed with me for the next eighteen months and never once did I have cause for complaint. Like Abdi Farah, he was in his forties and a man of great presence. I became very fond of him.

Reay, Nick and I celebrated John Gilbert's return that night and the pale light of dawn was brightening the sky as we left the Mess for our own tents – unsteadily.

In the case of a general 'stand to' for the whole company, Hussein the bugler was required to sound the alarm and it was to these urgent notes that I awoke the next morning. Abdullahi had laid out my uniform and, as I struggled into it, handed me a mug of tea. Outside was a scene of tremendous activity – soldiers running in all directions, trucks revving and Reay scurrying in the direction of the Mess shouting for Nick, John and me. 'Trouble expected at the wells,' he said tersely, making grand inroads into fried eggs and devilled kidneys. He gave us our orders for approaching the wells and our deployment once we were there. As he finished this muffled briefing we heard the sound of shots from the direction of the town and lost no time in getting the Company mounted into the waiting trucks. We rattled off and shouted out our orders to the askaris in the back as we drove along.

Approaching the wells we saw large crowds of tribesmen and a great flurry of activity. There were scores of camels milling about and several horsemen herding them away from the wells with shrill cries – we were witnessing large-scale looting, or rather an attempt to loot. Skidding to a halt we threw a cordon of soldiers round the tribesmen, while one platoon deployed to block off the camels and the would-be rustlers.

Suddenly one horseman broke away from the rest, thundered off through my platoon and headed towards the *magalla*, shouting and firing his rifle. I dived back into my truck and told the startled driver to set off in pursuit. With a grin splitting his face he did this with a will and as we roared off several soldiers swung aboard too, including Hassan Haji I was pleased to see. It was a marvellously exhilarating feeling as we accelerated away and started to gain on the horseman who, for some reason, was riding in a wide arc; we kept to as straight a line as we could hoping to head him off. Gradually we drew alongside the warrior, who we could now recognize as an Ogaden clansman. He gave a startled look over his shoulder and the askaris in the back of the truck hooted and shrilled.

Had I been Errol Flynn or Stewart Granger I would have dived gracefully from the speeding vehicle and brought the man off his horse with a flying rugger tackle. As it was I pondered and wondered what to do as we lurched along beside his fast-tiring pony. We might still be going now, but at last I closed my eyes, waited until we were as close as possible and launched myself sideways in an inelegant sort of pounce. By some lucky chance I caught the horseman a glancing blow with my shoulder and he fell to the ground. It should have been he who was winded, but of course it was me. I lay on my back incapable of movement while the warrior propped himself up on an elbow and gazed at me in total amazement. Perhaps he was as frightened as I was. Anyhow my truck performed a dramatic turn and rocked to a halt in a huge cloud of sand, out leapt the askaris and collared my tribesman – another candidate, but this time a live one, for the DC's compound. It turned out that he was one of the ringleaders of what was to be a raid on the Habr Awal, Habr Yonis and Arab stock at the wells.

More of the Ogaden war party were arrested by the askaris at the wells and we rounded off the day with a search for arms in a suspect neighbouring *qarya*. That evening the DC appeared in our Mess. Silently he placed a bottle on the table. 'I want you to have this one on me,' he said. 'Today D Company prevented not only large-scale camel looting, but a fair amount of slaughter too.' We settled back comfortably in our chairs. It promised to be a yet another long session.

Chapter 4

Closing the Grazing – and a Hyena

The DC sent news the following day, Friday, 10 December, that once more there was an unusually large number of tribesmen watering their stock at the wells, and as he felt there could be more trouble he asked for two platoons to position themselves by the water. Hussein performed delightedly in ascending notes on his bugle and soldiers ran towards the vehicles from all directions. Some from the married lines were wearing white tobes, but flung bandoliers across their chests and clapped *kullahs* on their heads as they hurried along. I jumped into the first vehicle, John Gilbert leapt into the second and off we went, the askaris laughing and shouting as we rattled down the familiar track.

The area round the wells was jammed with camels – several thousand of them. The DC, who met us on arrival, thought that a number of tribes were 'filling up' before heading back to the Protectorate, anticipating the closing of the grazing area at Christmas.

I had thought that the days had long since departed when infantry soldiers formed squares, but John and I decided that it would be the ideal formation for these circumstances and we did just that – my platoon on one side of the wells and his on the other. Having fixed bayonets first, we marched our men into their positions, faced them outwards and stood them ease. At each corner of the squares we positioned our light machine guns, also facing outwards. Very impressive the soldiers looked too, and from this formation we could keep careful eyes on every side.

Taking Hassan Haji, I strolled through the groups of tribesmen as they watered their stock. They were predominantly clansmen from the Aidagallah, Habr Awal and Habr Yonis so the DC could have been right with his filling-up theory. But I also noticed groups from the Ogaden, heard the mutterings and saw the looks full of hatred between those clansmen and, particularly, the Aidagallah. It was just as well we

30

were there and we remained until evening when all the camels had been driven back to their *zaribas*. The lid was back on the simmering pot.

Reay arranged for a platoon to be present at the wells throughout the next day, as there seemed to be no lessening of the numbers watering there. He and I rode down on our ponies at noon and spent some time helping the Arab tribe rounding up the odd recalcitrant camel, galloping backwards and forwards in fine style. At about midday two RAF fighters appeared and made several low passes over the wells – Oliver Brooke had arranged for a little extra flag showing. We were busier than ever after that in our cowboy role as a number of camels took grave exception to this intrusion and cantered away complaining bitterly.

Some time during that night a most unusual thing happened. A hyena, on his nocturnal prowl near the wells, fell down one of the main waterholes, and couldn't climb out again. There it remained, about 20 feet down, howling and whining, and generally being very unhygienic in our water supply. The Awareh headman asked for our help when we arrived at daybreak so I took some askaris and we peered at the beast dimly splashing about at the bottom of the pit. Glowing evil eyes glared back. What on earth were we to do? Uppermost in my mind was the thought of rabies as hyenas are well-known carriers of the disease and there were many cases in the country. If we shot the beast and it bled into the water, what then? But how to get it out? No sane man was going to enter the pit with that mad satanic beast leaping and howling, and exposing its fearsome teeth.

Finally we hit on a plan by accident. One of the soldiers had tentatively lowered the leather bucket used for hauling water down towards the animal. With a frightful snarl it leapt up, seized the rope in its teeth and dragged it down. A couple of askaris pulled back and, joined by two more, lifted the hyena a few feet. Then its armoured jaws sheared through the rope, and it fell once more to the bottom, yelping and splashing.

This gave me an idea and I sent Hassan back to camp for a length of chain. By this time the Askaris were enjoying themselves greatly and were intrigued by the problem. They shouted with laughter when I explained my plan. Yes, they said, it might work. Hassan soon returned and we tied the chain to the end of the rope in place of the bucket. One soldier then stood by with a shorter length of rope fashioned into a noose. Hassan loaded his rifle and waited. Three men gingerly lowered the chain on the end of the rope and the hyena, on cue, seized the end. Even he couldn't bite through the tough iron links. Hand over hand we hauled him up towards the lip of the well, the beast swinging round and round. The idea was for the soldier with the looped rope to lasso one of the animal's legs when it was in range, and Hassan would shoot it. With luck, we could then lift the dead beast clear, but timing was going to be the important factor. Three times, as that frightful face neared the top of the well, it released the chain at the last moment and crashed to the bottom again. Incredibly it still continued to seize the chain when we tried again.

The fourth time we muffed it. The great head was level with the top of the well, the noose was cast and, slightly too soon, Hassan fired. It was a good shot through the brain but the noose had missed. Down to the bottom crashed our hyena once more; it would not be seizing the chain again. The worst had happened as it steadily bled into the water!

I called for a volunteer to descend into the well and tie the rope round the dead creature. Everyone, still grinning, looked at Hassan – he of the premature discharge. Reluctantly, Hassan volunteered. As we lowered him down the soldiers yipped and howled like the hyena. Was it quite dead? It really touched their sense of humour, but not Hassan's, and it was a long way down for him. Luckily the beast *was* dead and we hauled it out. The askaris suggested leaving Hassan for a little while longer, but I could not treat my orderly like that!

I had no idea that a hyena could be so large. It lay, sodden, fearful and frightening in appearance from the front, but made grotesque and slightly ridiculous by its dwarfish hindquarters.

We sent an urgent signal to Hargeisa and a doctor appeared the next day with a specialist party to clear the well and test the water. In the meantime we used the remaining waterholes – rather uneasily as they were presumably all linked underground. And what about seepage? Luckily no one contracted rabies. For Hassan Haji the episode dragged on and the joke wore thin. For weeks afterwards wherever he walked in the camp he would hear the weird rising cry 'Whooo-oop' of the hyena – from behind a bush, or from inside a tent, followed by giggling. The joke wore very thin indeed for Hassan, but the others loved it.

On Sunday, 12 December we heard about armed men in the Shilasse area yet again. We already had a platoon under Sergeant Mohamoud Egeh on the hill itself and so I took a section of eight askaris and some *illaloes* and, leaving my vehicle under a guard, set off across country on foot – the chances of surprising anyone in our truck would have been nil. As it was we had no luck on our feet either and saw no one.

On our way back to the Bedford we found the body of an Ogaden *Rer* Ali warrior. He had been killed recently and apart from being shot through the chest had been stabbed twice through the throat. I had seen similar ghastly wounds before and knew how they had been inflicted – by a spear.

The Somalis hold their stabbing spears with the right, or master, hand at the butt, in an overhand grip. The other hand, palm uppermost, holds the shaft about a third of the way up from the haft, the spear head inclines upwards and the idea is to thrust towards the opponent's neck. The jaw forms a convenient shelf to stab against. And here was a typical recipient of such treatment. I left a guard with the body and returned to Awareh. Later that day we returned with the DC who collected the body while I again patrolled the area on foot. We saw no signs of trouble.

The next day, Monday, it was my turn to go to Hargeisa for supplies. I took with me Abdullahi Hassan and Hassan Haji. Jama Ismail drove the truck and Corporal Farah Ismail, who was going on leave, came too. Hargeisa was about a hundred miles along a graded, but heavily corrugated track. Well shaken, but in high spirits, we reached the capital at about noon, I left my overnight kit with Abdullahi in the B Company Officers' Mess and drove into the *magalla*. Corporal Farah and Hassan slipped smoothly away, Farah to his two wives living outside the town, Hassan ... well Hassan had an appointment too.

Most of the shops in Hargeisa were owned and run by Indian traders and contained an amazing assortment of goods. In the same store I bought a tilley lamp for my tent, yards of white drill cloth for a new uniform for Abdullahi, biscuits by the tin and dozens of items for D Company. I was in a tailor's shop next door buying some shirts when a Gadurbursi warrior strode in. He was a young man, well over 6 feet in height, lean and straight. His hair was dyed with henna and worn very long as was then the fashion with his tribe. He wore an ochre-coloured *tobe*, a *bulawhi* at his waist, and he carried a stabbing spear and shield. 'Is it peace?' he murmured. It certainly was! The Gadurbursi pointed silently to a jacket hanging by the window, a loud-checked jacket, with heavily padded shoulders and brilliant lining. The shopkeeper helped him into this ghastly piece of clothing and the warrior examined himself in front of the full-length mirror in the corner of the shop – the god-like figure was transformed into a music hall joke. Don't take it! I willed. Don't take it ... don't. But he did.

Betty Morgan, the Adjutant's wife, had asked me to tea in her bungalow that afternoon. She was one of the very few British wives in Somaliland, and a wonderfully warm and charming person. We had toast and cake, and it could have been Sussex. After tea Lester had arranged ponies for me and we both played polo in a scratch team against B Company. Lester, an experienced player, was the mainstay of the side as Number 4 (the back). As a novice I was playing in the Number 1 position, enjoying it hugely, but not scoring goals. We lost convincingly. Alas Lester, a fine soldier and personality, died a few years after that game. He was a great loss.

That night there was a dance at Hargeisa Officers' Club and Ron Harris, a civilian friend of mine, introduced me to a nurse who was visiting from Aden, and suggested we might like to go. The nurse was keen and Ron lent me his Dodge pick-up truck. In the early hours I drove her back to the hospital where she was staying. She was thirty and knew exactly what she wanted; I was totally gauche and didn't. I remember that I stopped the Dodge and, leaving the engine running, leapt out and opened her door, saying jovially, 'Well thanks. Jolly nice evening. Goodnight'. She leaned forward and switched off the engine. 'Don't be silly,' she said. 'Come here.'

The next morning I completed my work in Hargeisa, dropped off some patrol reports for Humphrey French and headed back for Awareh with Abdullahi and Hassan. Jama Ismail drove carefully. We were a fairly fragile and silent bunch.

The day after my return, 15 December, Reay, John Gilbert and I were invited to lunch with the DC in honour of a visiting Ethiopian Army general, Walde di Georgis, a close relative of Emperor Haille Selasse. Evidently the General was, ostensibly at any rate, interested in shooting lion. In fact, I believe he was there to investigate the shooting of Ethiopian subjects, Ogaden tribesmen, by one of our patrols, which made it tricky. We had a curious lunch of Ethiopian dishes in deference to our guest, washed down with neat gin. Neat gin – good God!

A new Officer for D Company, Michael Dickinson, appeared the next day, having arrived from England that week, and was brought down to Awareh from Hargeisa by Humphrey French. This kindly and understanding man reduced the shock of entering the deep end which Michael must have felt when he saw Awareh, and his fellow officers! Anyhow, he took it all very well.

The lid finally lifted from the inter-tribal pot under the pressure on 17 December. It was inevitable, I suppose, with feeling running so high between the Ogaden tribes and those of the Protectorate, as I had thought earlier in my bath. We heard the shots during the morning so Nick and I each took a platoon and headed along the Shilasse track towards the sound of the increasing rifle fire. After leaving the track and setting off across country, we soon came across a wounded man. He was from an Ogaden tribe and told us of a big battle between his clansmen and those of the Aidagallah and Arab close by. He guided us a mile or so to the scene of the fight. It was a memorable sight. The opposing warriors were drawn up facing each other and, as was customary, the riflemen occupied the front rank of each side while behind them massed the spearmen. The two sides were about 300 yards apart, but were gradually converging, firing as they advanced. When a rifleman fell a spearman leapt forward, seized his weapon and pressed on with the others.

Sergeant Mohamoud Egeh and his platoon from Shilasse hill were already present on the far flank and, as we watched, he fired several 2-inch mortar rounds into the gap between the two closing sides as a very blunt warning to keep apart. There was immediate confusion, with tribesmen milling about, the riflemen in the front trying to move back and the spearmen behind continuing to push them forward.

Nick and I took the opportunity to move in as near as we could and I told Hashi Mohamed, my Platoon Sergeant, to shout to the tribesmen to disperse or we would shoot the ringleaders. In the confusion I doubt very much if we could be heard, but although our intention was plain to all, the opposing warriors once again started to move towards each other shrilling their war chants. Our platoons fired at individual targets and a number of tribesmen fell. Mohamoud Egeh recommenced firing mortar bombs into the gap between the sides and, suddenly, it was all over. The warriors broke away and disappeared into the bush leaving the field to us.

Mohamoud Egeh was the man of the hour – undoubtedly his initiative had prevented widespread slaughter. Had the two sides met in hand-to-hand combat there would have been many slain. As it was we now had the unpleasant task of collecting the remaining dead in one of the 3-tonners. There were eighteen in all, some bearing the familiar stab wounds but some of them shot by us. The total number of tribesmen who died that day will never be known, however, as most were carried off by their own clansmen.

Nick and his platoon remained with Mohamoud Egeh at Shilasse that night, while I returned to Awareh in the 3-tonner with its grisly cargo. As I drew into the DC's compound Michael Dickinson, the new officer, met me and peered into the back of the truck. The deep end deepened, but he took it very well. The DC called for tribal representatives from the *magalla* and the dead were finally identified. Four Aidagallah, eight from the Arab Tribe and six of the Ogaden. Luckily it was quite even. Yes, the lid had indeed lifted from the pot, but had been quickly clapped back on again before it could boil right over.

Early next day Reay took Michael to Shilasse, where things now appeared to be quiet, leaving me to look after the Company in Awareh. My old friend the *illalo* Sergeant Major visited me shortly after Reay had left and, sure enough, things were uneasy in the *magalla*. The war leader of the Ogaden tribes rejoiced under the rather sinister name of Ugaz (Sultan) Mohamed. He was a notorious man and I had heard a lot about his exploits. Evidently he had arrived in Awareh with a group of horsemen and was even now inflaming the passion of his fellow tribesmen in the town, calling for war against the Aidagallah and other tribes from the Protectorate.

I went into the town and it was certainly a sight to stir the blood. The mounted warriors were circling round waving their spears and singing their war songs; the Ogaden tribesmen had flocked to them and were stamping and howling the responses. A cloud of dust covered the scene – it was no place for the Aidagallah. Standing on one side was the Ugaz himself looking pretty satisfied. An *illalo* had indicated the great man to me and I walked over. I remembered the contemptuous looks of the old men weeks ago at Massara and saw it again now in the Ugaz eyes. He was a tall man, over 6 feet, and with an impressive paunch, which was unusual with the nomads who looked upon it as a sign of wealth.

After our murmured polite greetings I told the Ugaz that the Government held him and only himself responsible for any fighting involving his tribes. Furthermore, I said I would make sure that I was present with the soldiers at the scene of any future battle or camel looting and would not hesitate to shoot those responsible. And then came my telling card. 'As we did yesterday,' I said, 'at Shilasse.' His eyes shifted from mine – I would stake a good sum that he had been there the day before, urging on his clansmen. 'Remember, you are responsible. I know it and I will remember.' And so, with absolutely no face lost, I turned on my heel and left him. The singing continued defiantly for a while but soon the Ugaz gathered his horsemen and left. My fingers were well crossed. We had a peaceful night.

Abdullahi Hassan woke me at seven and said, 'Listen.' War songs in the *magalla*? I groaned and cursed the Ugaz. Abdullahi told me that they were not Ogaden songs I could hear. They were fine songs, sung for good reason – Aidagallah songs, his tribe. So it seemed to be turn and turn about at Awareh, and I wondered who was doing the bookings.

Reay had returned so he and I took seven soldiers and drove hurriedly to the town. A slightly different stage was set. A hundred or so Aidagallah were grouped in a circle round their chief, Sultan Abdullahi, whom I knew. The singing was wild and was accompanied by the usual hand-clapping, leaping and whirling. On one side were scores of women urging on the men with their high-pitched shrilling. Reay told me to speak to Sultan Abdullahi. I told him that it was the Government's wish that he dispersed this crowd immediately and stop his warmongering. 'Go quickly – like they went quickly yesterday at Shilasse.' Had Abdullahi faced the Ugaz at Shilasse? Very possibly. In any case he had heard all about it and he agreed to disperse.

The Aidagallah warriors leapt into battered trade trucks and drove off beating the sides of the vehicles and waving their spears, the women's ululating cries ringing in their ears. But the stage farce continued and that evening a group of Ogaden horsemen reappeared briefly, eager to have the last word.

With all the rabble-rousing, inflammatory singing and warlike posturing over the last two days we began to think that perhaps Shilasse had not been a good enough lesson after all. It came as a great surprise, therefore, when we heard on Monday, 20 December that the Aidagallah, together with the Habr Awal, Habr Yonis and Arab nomads, were all on the move out of the Haud and back to the Protectorate. They were beating the gun and departing just before the grazing area was officially closed. It set us wondering. After all the singing and shouting had there been a battle somewhere? Certainly not in our parish, and surely we would have heard about one anywhere in the Ogaden, wouldn't we? Anyway it was true – the tribes were moving and we could relax.

The next morning I rode north along the Hargeisa track. In front of me I could see a hazy smudge of dust hanging in the air and tinted red by the rising, strengthening sun. As I drew nearer this sandy cloud became supported by tiny figures which soon grew into the shimmering shapes of people, goats and camels – hundreds of them plodding steadily northwards. The men walked with their spears across both shoulders, behind their necks, with their hands drooped over either end, totally relaxed for their long trek. They walked with total economy of effort, heels dragging in the sand. The women walked in small chattering groups, pulling their head-cloths over their faces as I approached, some with small babies on their hips and most with tiny children trailing along behind.

The young boys herded the sheep and goats, whistling and throwing small stones to keep the movement going. As I drew level with some of these small herdsmen they shouted greetings; a number stamped their feet and saluted smartly.

There were numerous strings of burden camels, their loads including the upward-curving frameworks of *ghurgies*, matting and covered bundles of household goods. The camel herds included many young calves.

In April they would be back for the spring grazing, and with some old scores to settle. D Company would still be in the Haud when they returned, but in the meantime, it looked as if it was going to be a good Christmas. I turned and cantered back towards Awareh.

Interlude

I remained in Awareh until August 1949 when I visited Nairobi for a course of instruction and leave. I stayed with the King's African Rifles at Langata, just outside the city and by the National Park, and had the time of my life. I found Nairobi very colourful with a vibrant night life, an ideal place for a subaltern on leave. In those days the white hunters propping up the famous Long Bar in the New Stanley and in the Norfolk Hotels were the genuine article. They were larger-than-life personalities and outstanding raconteurs. All in all it was a splendid holiday.

On my return to Somaliland I was sent to the Depot of the Scouts at Borama, about 70 miles north-west of Hargeisa near the Ethiopian border. The town had been established in 1921 by the British Administration because of the number of complaints about Ethiopian 'tax collectors' from across the border seizing Somali livestock. The Depot served two purposes: the training of Somali recruits and a military presence in the area.

The Commander at Borama was Major Clarke – inevitably 'Nobby'. He was a delightful and efficient soldier with a generous and kindly nature, who was intensely popular and held in great respect by the Somalis; I learnt a great deal from him. His wife Edum was a tiny Welsh woman with the heart of a lion. She was a trained nurse and did a lot of work in her spare time in the small hospital at Borama. In the absence of a doctor, she often exceeded her nurse's brief and many who would have died survived as a result. I watched her once as she tackled a leg amputation, but left her to it after a few very long moments. I think it was the noise of the saw which appalled me more than the sight of it cutting into the bone.

Early in 1950 the ending of my duty with the Scouts coincided with the arrival of the 1st Battalion the East Surrey Regiment in Italian

Somaliland. It had come from Salonika in order to reinforce the British Garrison in Mogadishu during the handover to Italy, which country had been nominated as trustees of the country for the United Nations. I received a signal in Borama saying that before I could be considered, and reported on, for a regular commission it was necessary for me to serve with 'white troops'. All my service as an officer up to that time had been with Somalis.

The Surreys were in the Home Counties Brigade Group to which the Royal Fusiliers also belonged. The War Office therefore considered that it would be more economical to send me down the road to Mogadishu rather then despatching me back to England to join the Royal Fusiliers. I would do six months with the Surreys who would then provide my confidential report.

(Later, when I had completed my six months and passed the Regular Commissions Board, I transferred my first choice of regiment to the Surreys. I knew all the officers in the Battalion and had settled in to life in that friendly Regiment. I was lucky enough to be accepted.)

Arriving in Somalia I joined C Company which was stationed in Villaggio about 60 miles north of the capital. It was strange to be operating with British soldiers for the first time in conditions which were so familiar to me, yet strange to them. I recall that on a two-day patrol to show the flag in the villages my platoon took most of the hours of darkness on the first night to build a *zariba* which any enterprising tortoise could have leapt with ease the next morning. Being the wonderful soldiers they were those cockneys soon learnt! They were tickled pink too when I chatted up the locals and we were royally entertained within the village stockades.

It wasn't all plain sailing for me on joining. My unusual Somaliland Scouts attire caused a certain amount of mirth and some rather caustic comments from the Commanding Officer, Lieutenant Colonel John Metcalfe. He had a habit of baring his teeth when annoyed and, thinking he was smiling at me, I smiled back. It was a mistake! Colonel John was a magnificent CO, later to become a major general.

After C Company had been relieved in Villaggio by a company of Italian infantry, we moved to Mogadishu and provided the Escort to the Colour on the final parade of British troops in the city on 1 April 1950, which the soldiers referred to as an 'appropriate date'. The Union Jack was lowered and the flags of Italy and the United Nations fluttered in its place. We marched the Colours onto a lighter and moved out across the harbour to the waiting troopship, the *Empire Test*. It seemed a fitting end to my experiences in the country which was to become the Republic of Somalia ten years later.

For the next twenty-one years I was an orthodox infantry soldier alternating periods of duty with the Battalion (which I always enjoyed) and the Staff (which I sometimes did not). During this time the Surreys were amalgamated twice. First with the Queen's Royal Regiment to become the Queen's Royal Surrey Regiment; then with the remaining regiments of the Home Counties to become the Queen's Regiment. I was fortunate in remaining for more than my fair share of this period in the sun – in Libya, Egypt and Cyprus (twice). I also spent a year in Northern Ireland during the start of the 'troubles' in 1969 and 1970.

In 1971 my wife and I were on holiday with our children in a Danish friend's summerhouse on the Baltic coast when a telegram arrived. It posed a question: did I wish to be considered for command of the Northern Frontier Regiment of the Sultan of Oman's Armed Forces? Silently I handed the cable to my wife. Her face fell, but she said, 'You'll have to go. You'll never forgive yourself if you don't.'

And so I went.

PART II

Oman 1972–1974

Chapter 5

Bid Bid

Have we not made
the earth
a home for the living
and for the dead?
Have we not placed high mountains upon it
And given you fresh water for your drink?

Koran
Sura 77. Those that are Sent Forth
(Translation by N.J. Dawood)

'You will find the work pretty taxing and there is hardly one single aspect of the nation's life and development which you do not get personally involved in. And you only have a small number of British officers to help you run your battalion. Also, there are the threats to the Sultanate to see off militarily; of these the war against the Chinese-backed "People's Army" in Dhofar is by far the most serious. But our campaign there entered a new phase on 2nd October; SAF [Sultan's Armed Forces] is back on the *jebel* in strength and all is going well. We are getting a kill ratio of about 10:1 which is satisfactory. But it will be a long slog as the terrain is massive and formidable and the enemy well equipped. I believe your years here will prove to be the most challenging, interesting and rewarding of your whole career.'

Thus wrote Brigadier J.D.C. Graham OBE, Commander of the Sultan's Armed Forces (SAF) to me when I was learning Arabic in Beaconsfield in the autumn of 1971. (Bill Kerr, a fellow student on the course, and also bound for SAF, commented when he read about the ratio of ten to one, 'Fine – providing you're not the one!') I flew to Oman the following

43

February and, during the next two years, found the Brigadier's predictions to be true.

Nowadays there is an international airport at Seeb, just outside Muscat, which can take all shapes and sizes of jet aircraft, but this was not opened until after my arrival in Oman. My flight out therefore involved staging overnight in Bahrein's Gulf Hotel, before boarding a small Fokker Friendship aircraft, which hopped like a flea along the northern seaboard of the Arabian Gulf, calling at Dohar, Abu Dhabi and Dubai before heading for the mountains of northern Oman.

Ancient Muscat, the capital, and its larger and more recent sister city, Muttrah, the commercial hub, are ringed by craggy peaks, and the entrance to the harbour is guarded by two picturesque sixteenth-century Portuguese forts: Jalaali, which was the city jail, and Merani – one on either side. The airstrip, for it was no more than that, was squeezed in between the mountains in the (then) almost empty Ruwi Valley and guaranteed an interesting approach run via these coastal forts.

February is in the middle of the seasonal rains in northern Oman and I noticed some very impressive black clouds sitting on the Muscat peaks. We banked steeply and lost height, and at the same time the rain started in force, dimpling the steely sea. The aircraft slipped between the two majestic forts, rocking in the turbulent air currents. It seemed to my nervous eye that both wing tips were scraping the mountains when suddenly we were safely down, tyres squealing and the engines in reverse. The doors were opened to reveal the airport buildings which consisted, in the main, of a *barusti* hut,* unsophisticated to say the least. David Insall, a Captain on contract to Sultan Qaboos bin Said al Busaidi, Sultan of Oman, was there to meet me. David was on Brigadier John Graham's staff and smoothed my way through 'customs' – a smiling Omani policeman, who shook me warmly by the hand and welcomed me to Oman, while chalking the appropriate hieroglyphics on my suitcases. An old friend, Vyvyan Robinson, one-time Gurkha and now commanding the Frontier Force in Dhofar, was also at the airport and, as it turned out, was my fellow guest that night in the bungalow of Slim Horsford, the Assistant Defence Secretary. Slim lived close by the dramatic white fort which housed SAF Headquarters in Bait al Falaj on the outskirts of Muscat.

The next day – the clouds gone and the skies clear – I met Karl Beale, the Commanding Officer of the Northern Frontier Regiment (NFR), from whom I was to take over. Karl, as in my case, was seconded from the regular British Army to SAF. His parent regiment

---

*Hut made of palm fronds covering a wooden frame.

was the Parachute Regiment and he had a background of service with special forces. Karl had won a Military Cross as a young officer and was in Bait al Falaj that day having received the Distinguished Service Medal from the Sultan for his work commanding NFR in Dhofar. With him was Fergus McKain-Bremner who commanded the Muscat Regiment and who also had just been decorated by Sultan Qaboos. We accordingly celebrated this happy double event in the bungalow of Tony Best, the senior staff officer at SAF Headquarters concerned with operations and training (GSO 1). Also present and wielding a glass was the substantial figure of Richard Anderson. Like Tony, a contract officer, Richard had been in Oman for many years and was slyly known by the Omani soldiers as 'the Drum'. He was the appropriate shape and, it must be admitted, he did bang and boom.

Later that day Karl and I climbed into his Landrover to drive the 50 or so miles to Bid Bid where NFR was stationed. He introduced me to Mohamed Salim, his driver, and to his Baluchi radio operator who both greeted and welcomed me with dignity and courtesy.

It was a bumpy journey into the Interior, along an unsurfaced road between the splintered brown hills. Many of the sharp peaks were capped with little watchtowers once used to give warning to the locals of approaching – and perhaps hostile – travellers. The road we were using was the main route to the Buraimi oasis on Oman's border with Abu Dhabi, and passed through Bid Bid, Ziki, Nizwa and Ibri, skirting the main massif of northern Oman, the Jebel Akhdar (the Green Mountain). This *jebel* (mountain) soars to 10,000 feet and in 1957–9 was the scene of fighting between the Sultan's soldiers and tribesmen loyal to the Imam of Oman, Ghalib ('Lord of the Green Mountain'). The final assault on Ghalib and his force was spearheaded by D Squadron of the SAS which stopped off in Oman on its way home from the Malayan Campaign .

At the time of Karl's and my journey to Bid Bid no European other than SAF officers and Omani police were allowed to travel into the Interior without a written permit. Consequently the tribes and the villages were totally untainted by tourism and the children unspoiled. The colours of the mountainous landscape varied, in sun and shadow, from browns to ochre and orange, contrasting with the brilliant green of the palm trees and village gardens in the wadis. Just before reaching Bid Bid we crossed a wider-than-usual wadi, splashing through a thread of water in its centre. On either side were mud buildings, and watchtowers sat on a variety of surrounding peaks, all at different levels. This was the village of Fanjr with the high *jebel* named after it serving as its dramatic backcloth; in the waning sun it was a deep ochre, almost orange colour.

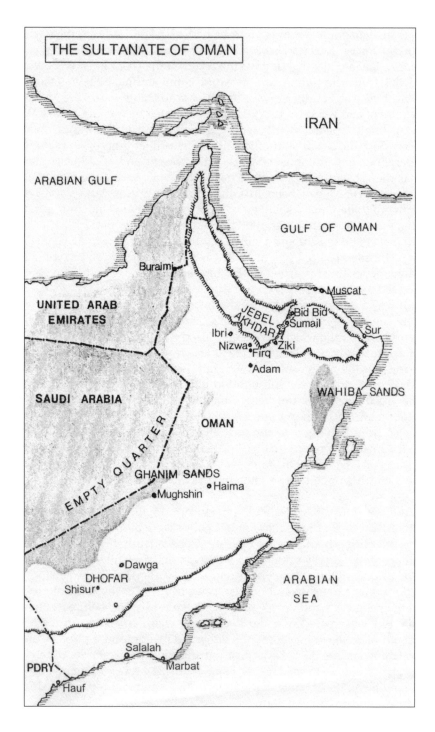

THE SULTANATE OF OMAN

IRAN

ARABIAN GULF

GULF OF OMAN

Buraimi

Muscat

UNITED ARAB
EMIRATES

JEBEL
AKHDAR
Bid Bid
Sumail
Ibri
Nizwa
Ziki
Firq
Sur

SAUDI ARABIA

Adam

WAHIBA SANDS

EMPTY QUARTER

OMAN

GHANIM SANDS

Mughshin
Haima

Dawga

DHOFAR
Shisur

ARABIAN
SEA

Salalah

PDRY

Marbat

Hauf

46

We left the main track and rattled down a narrow rock-strewn trail which wound between huge boulders towards the low white buildings of NFR camp. 'This road,' said Karl, 'helps keep too many visitors at bay – I haven't pressed to have it regraded.' At the camp entrance a Baluchi sentry presented arms smartly as we passed, and then waved and shouted welcomes to us, a huge smile on his face. We drew up at a tiny white house within the camp perimeter and on the edge of the Fanjr Wadi. It commanded a breathtaking view of the *jebel* standing in its emerald-green fringe of palms and gardens. 'This is your *bait* [house],' said Karl. 'Adequate, not luxurious, but the view's all right.' It certainly was.

The next day Karl started to hand over NFR to me. 'I'll give you the facts about the Battalion but I'm not going to tell you a thing about how to run operations in the Dhofar War,' he warned me. 'That, you'll find out for yourself, and, like me, you'll play it the way you think best, I expect.'

The Battalion was organized on British Army lines, with three rifle companies and a Headquarter Company which contained the clerks, cooks, drivers and administrative soldiers. Also in Headquarter Company were the Mortar Platoon (six 81mm mortars), the Reconnaissance Platoon, mounted in Landrovers, and the Assault Pioneers – our domestic sappers who could lay and lift mines, build wire fences and blow things up. Lastly, but certainly by no means least, was the happy band of ancients – the donkey handlers, a marvellous group of old greybeards who cared for and led the animals which carried our heavy weapons, ammunition and equipment over country which vehicles could not manage, or where a clattering helicopter would jeopardize our security. (Up to about 1970, before helicopters were available to SAF, casualties were evacuated from the *jebel* by donkey. Sometimes such journeys took several jolting hours, a terrible experience for a wounded man, as some British officers serving with SAF could testify if pressed).

There was a total of twelve British officers in NFR, of which half were on contract and half seconded from the British Army. The former were selected by interview and were required to have previously held a British Army commission for a minimum of three years. The British were distributed three to each rifle company and three to Battalion Headquarters – myself, Arthur Brocklehurst the Second in Command, and the Adjutant.

The remaining officers were predominantly Omani plus several Baluchis, and included Abdul Qadir the Quartermaster, a Pakistani, Khadim Hussein the MTO, and Medhi our superb Indian Medical

Officer. As more Omanis were commissioned and others rose in rank the number of expatriates were reduced in proportion.

The non-commissioned officers (NCOs) and soldiers, numbering some 700, were about two thirds Omani and one third Baluch. The men from both nations made excellent soldiers. It was essential that their British officers got to know them well as the two races differed considerably in temperament. Good communication with them was therefore essential, and although some spoke good English most did not. Arabic was the language common to all and it was important that the British learnt it. The seconded officers attended a language course at the Army School of Languages in Beaconsfield before travelling to Oman; those on contract made it their business to learn early in their service. By speaking it every day most British were soon able to manage in Arabic, and some became fluent.

I found the Omani soldiers to have a natural courtesy and dignity, and an abundant share of pride. They could exhibit great courage when properly led and proved this in many an engagement with the enemy, earning many decorations for bravery. However, if they felt that a plan of action was a bad one they were not frightened to say so! We recruited most of our Omani soldiers from northern Oman, many of whom appeared very young on enlistment, but since no records were kept of exact dates of birth in those days, we were never too sure of exact ages. All developed physically during their first months of military training and army rations. I thoroughly enjoyed serving with them.

Some of the Baluchis had settled in Oman and had taken Arab wives, but most were mercenaries – soldiers for cash. Having purchased an expensive trip from Baluchistan across the Indian Ocean, many had first tried to obtain jobs 'up the Gulf' in the United Arab Emirates, but had failed to find the easy employment they had been promised by the shady shipping firms in Karachi. Springing from a warrior race the job of soldiering was a natural one for them to fall back on, and they had drifted down to Oman where Baluchis had traditionally served with SAF. The Baluchis were not therefore fired by any patriotic fervour as were many Omanis, and one could expect a more orthodox and perhaps a more careful approach by them. This is not to say that they were not brave. Many a Baluch soldier was decorated for gallantry and too many of mine in NFR were buried in Salalah having fought bravely and died in the Sultan's cause.

Although most of NFR were at Bid Bid, C Company was detached at Ziki (also known as Izki) another 50 miles along the road from Muscat in the Wadi Sumail – one of the few routes through the massive *jebel* range to the desert beyond.

After four days spent handing over to me Karl was due to return to England and, on leaving the Officers' Mess after breakfast on his last day, we found that the route to the main gate and his waiting Landrover was lined with soldiers. All were carrying their rifles which, as Karl moved between them, they fired joyously into the air – round after round, a crackling fusilade which continued for the full five minutes which it took to complete the route. It was an Omani farewell to a departing Qaa'id* which contravened all rules of safety and would have given a British Army RSM a fit! I saw soldiers seizing Karl's hand with one of theirs whilst firing their rifles generally skywards with the other. I thought, uneasily, that those rounds had to come down somewhere, and tried to resist the peculiar urge to hunch my shoulders and grit my teeth against the shock of a falling bullet from above. What a way to go! I could see that Karl was very moved despite his easygoing manner; he had a strong rapport with his men as they now demonstrated by the seizing of his hand as he walked by and the ringing cries of 'Fee amaan illah' (Go in the security of God) and 'Allah Ma-ak' (God be with you) – a warm and noisy demonstration. I found out later that the firing of rifles by soldiers on such occasions had been banned by Headquarters SAF – fruitlessly, I'm glad to say.

Of the four infantry battalions in SAF at that time, two were in Dhofar engaged in the fight against the rebels, and two in northern Oman. Every nine months or so the pairs changed over. NFR was due to return to the south in early May and so I had three months to get to know my battalion and, most importantly, to learn as much as possible about its officers, their strengths and weaknesses, their skill as infantry leaders and their understanding of their men, their humour and their hates.

I was fortunate as far as the prominent personalities in NFR were concerned. As a battalion it had earned a rugged down-to-earth reputation and had established an excellent fighting record. New officers were inclined to adjust to this image, and quickly. They became very professional in close-quarter battle shooting, and in controlling and adjusting the fire of our own 81mm mortars, the 25-pdr guns of the Oman Artillery and the rockets of the Strikemasters of the Sultan's Air Force. They also took pains to improve their Arabic.

Arthur Brocklehurst, the Second in Command, had been in Oman for a number of years and spoke the language well. He had a close understanding of the soldiers and understood the tensions which could arise between the Omanis and the Baluchis – and how to smooth things over. He was invaluable to me and his past knowledge of the Dhofar

* Leader. The Commanding Officer of a battalion was known as 'Al Qaa'id'.

jebel was to prove an added bonus. Arthur had originally served in the Parachute Regiment, but had found his right niche with SAF. Slight in stature he was burnt dark by the sun and on the *jebel* wore a black beard which made him indistinguishable from the soldiers. He took great delight every time he was mistaken for an Omani by visiting officers. Arthur was a man who appeared happier with warrior tribes than with his own race and was one of the few who had spent time with the nomads in Baluchistan. He was fiercely loyal to NFR and had scant regard for anyone unfortunate enough not to be in it!

A Company was commanded by a Royal Marine, Bob Hudson, who had Simon Hill of the Parachute Regiment as his Second in Command. In the same company was David Nicholls, another Marine. Tresham Gregg of the Royal Tank Regiment had B Company and he was assisted by Graeme ('Smash') Smyth-Piggott and Robin Barton, both on contract. C Company was headed by Peter Tawell of my own Regiment, the Queen's, with Christopher Kemball, a Greenjacket, as his Second in Command. They were shortly joined by Charles Ogilvie-Forbes, on contract.

Headquarter Company had an Omani commander, Saif Ali al Hawseneh. Saif was a delightful character and a very much respected figure in NFR. He was a fine soldier and on his last Dhofar tour had been awarded the Sultan's bravery medal. Saif was probably in his mid-thirties and generously built, which was unusual at that time for his race. He had a wonderful sense of humour and an infectious laugh. I can illustrate best his great sense of fun and joy of life by a story about dates.

The Hawseneh tribe live in the Wadi al Haseneh which is renowned for its date groves, and Saif brought baskets of delicious fresh dates to Bid Bid from time to time. Some of these appeared in a bowl on the table in the Officers' Mess and were a welcome sight. Behind my bungalow was a young and rather struggling date palm which produced mediocre fruit of a rather unhealthy hue. (The tree was nourished by my bath water which might have contributed to this). One day a sample of these lesser dates appeared in a second bowl on the Mess table, next to the Hawseneh one. A carefully printed notice was placed on each. One, on the perfect and beautifully succulent fruit, stated 'Al Hawseneh Dates'. On the bowl of meagre offerings the notice read 'Al Qaa'id's Dates'! Saif was in his usual seat at the table at dinner that evening struggling to keep a straight face. But his smile refused to be smothered and broke through in a brilliant expanse of teeth and crinkling damson-coloured cheeks. He roared as I examined the cards and compared the two bowls. He spluttered with mirth throughout the meal, laughed out loud over his coffee and he was still chuckling as he eventually left for bed.

In Saif's company was another giant personality, squeezed into a more spare frame. A wiry, quick-moving man with hawk-like features, a neat black beard and the most devastating twinkle in both eyes – the Reconnaissance Platoon Commander, Mohamed Said al Raqaishi. Promoted to Second Lieutenant after his last Dhofar tour, Mohamed – or Raqaishi as he was generally known – had been decorated for bravery as a sergeant platoon commander. Like all the Omani subalterns at that time he had earned his promotion by his performance in the field – or, more properly perhaps, on the *jebel*. Raqaishi was unique in 1972 being the only member of his tribe in the Sultan's Army. There was a reason for this. During the Jebel Al Akhdar campaign in 1957–9 some of the Raqaishi fought for the Imam against the Sultan, since when there had been a marked reluctance on behalf of the Raqaishi to serve in SAF, and little effort by the Army to enlist the young men of the tribe as soldiers – with this one exception, and he was worth a whole platoon. I was to get to know Raqaishi extremely well and it pleased me greatly when he eventually became the first Omani Commanding Officer of NFR. He retired as a Brigadier, but I suspect his happiest days of soldiering were those he spent within his own regiment.

Captain Mahanamba Medhi, late of the Indian Army Medical Corps, was our doctor. Known to all as Medhi he was probably the most universally loved and respected man in the battalion. He was from Assam in the extreme north-east of India, according to some reports a wild land peopled by fierce people. Medhi was anything but fierce in appearance – on the contrary, he had a most pleasing face with kind eyes, a large man with a large heart. Karl had told me how this gentle giant had patrolled ceaselessly during the last tour in Dhofar in order to be able to give immediate aid to those wounded. I was to see for myself his physical and his mental strength a little later. At Bid Bid and Ziki Medhi had organized clinics for the locals and every morning there were many brightly clothed women squatting outside the medical centres, some clutching naked babies to their bosoms.

One officer I only met fleetingly at this stage, as he was on his way for a spell of duty with the *Firqa* in Dhofar; Johnny Braddell-Smith, a contract officer from Eire who spoke excellent Omani Arabic with a delightful brogue. Johnny liked to give the impression that he was a 'hard man' who was only interested in the cash but, strive as he might, he failed to conceal the affection and understanding he had for his men. They made no effort to hide the respect they felt for him. He had a faraway look in his eyes and although he would hotly deny the thought, there was quite a lot of the poet in this tough mercenary.

51

He was an excellent soldier and returned to NFR from the *firqa* after about eight months; he was a great asset.

While I was busy taking over and getting to know NFR, 70 miles further up the same road into the interior Bill Kerr was doing the same thing with the Muscat Regiment (MR). Bill, of the Royal Highland Fusiliers, had been my fellow student at Beaconsfield and was relieving Fergus McKain-Bremner at Nizwa. MR was due to move to Dhofar at the same time as NFR and we would take over from the Desert Regiment and the Jebel Regiment who would return to Bid Bid and Nizwa respectively. I found it useful and enjoyable to share mutual problems with Bill and we visited each other's *baits* to compare notes over a glass of whisky from time to time.

I particularly enjoyed visiting Nizwa. At that time it was a fascinating and totally unspoilt Omani town, the mud-brick buildings clustered round and dominated by a massive fort. Portuguese cannon peered over the ochre battlements and ancient cannonballs lay in the dust outside the walls. I picked one up which was about the size of a croquet ball and very heavy. 'Keep it,' said the *Wali* (Headman) 'and remember Nizwa.' I did, and still do. Only a few years earlier prisoners had been thrown into the oubliettes and left to starve to death in this same fort. The only access to these frightful pits was through a grill sunk into the floor of the fort and through which filtered a meagre supply of air and light. Nizwa fort had many a bloody tale to tell up to and including the Jebel Akhdar War.

The main attraction at Nizwa was the magnificent covered *suk* (market) where the silver- and coppersmiths, fruit and vegetable sellers, gunsmiths and butchers, together with many other assorted vendors, noisily plied their trades. It was a wonderfully colourful and busy place, thronged with fascinating people: tall, white-robed Omanis wearing their headcloths wrapped round their heads in the Omani style; Bedu from the wastes near Ibri in saffron-coloured dish-dashas, bandoliers stuffed with enormous bullets round their waists and ancient Martini-Henry rifles over their shoulders; black-robed Bedu women wearing beaked masks of a rather frightening aspect, other girls shyly peering through their veils or shawls, perhaps one provocative, khol-lined eye visible as a sample of their hidden beauty; old women and equally ancient old men, white bearded and bent, many with blind blued eyes as a result of the all-too-common trachoma, caused by dust and flies. Nearly all the men wore in the front of their belts a khunja – the Omani knife in an ornate curved scabbard; some of these were beautifully chased in silver and the hilts of the knives set with stones.

Bid Bid had no *suk* to match Nizwa and was, in comparison, a very small village indeed, clustered round its own fort wherein lived the

Wali who features later in this account. Fanjr, close to NFR camp, boasted a small market but compared to Nizwa it was very subdued and simple.

The Regimental Sergeant Major of NFR was a stalwart old Baluchi soldier who rejoiced in the unusual name of Dad Mohamed. (For a long time I had thought this to be his nickname, but this was not the case). Soon after my arrival Dad approached me on the question of my orderly. He explained to me that I needed a man who must be a good smart soldier but also one who had experience on the *jebel*, and who would accompany me on operations. After several false starts with men who clearly would not do – either they would have driven me mad or I them – Dad produced a wild-haired tall Baluchi soldier known to all as Jebali (mountain man). I liked the look of him and the humour lurking in his eye, and took him on. He proved to be a cheerful rogue and accompanied me everywhere I went, loping along behind with his rifle on his shoulder, muzzle forward in the usual SAF fashion.

Jebali had rigid views on tea, as I learnt to my cost when he brought me a cup as he woke me at 5.30 on his first morning. It was a deep rust colour and thick with sugar.

'How many teaspoons of tea do you put in the pot, Jebali?'

He looked stern. 'Five,' he said and then, after, a pause, 'heaped.'

'Too much . . .' I started and then my voice faltered and trailed away as he leant forward from his supervisory position by the door.

'Five,' he said earnestly, 'I always put five. I like it strong,' he added and left.

At four that afternoon he brought me a pot of the same rich brew and, returning to collect my laundry, caught me as I was flushing half the pot of gravy-like fluid down the lavatory pan. I was about to top it up with hot bath water, which, despite his scandalized presence, I then proceeded to do, no doubt trembling visibly. Jebali was shocked to his very core.

'Strong tea is *good* for you,' he announced.

'Two spoonfuls only,' I countered.

He leapt into action, 'Four is the minimum.'

'Two and a half,' I bartered.

We settled for three and Jebali, with very ill grace indeed, left muttering. The tea improved markedly, but I needed to remain on the alert as, over the weeks, it showed a tendency to increase surreptitiously in strength unless checked.

Gradually I got to know the Battalion, its personalities and its capabilities. The period in northern Oman was a busy one. Forty or so recruits were being trained at Ziki – replacements for casualties during the last Dhofar tour and for those who had ended their service with

SAF – and the companies, having had leave, were improving their tactical and weapon skills. We ran courses to train new mortar teams and assault pioneers, for potential NCOs and for recently joined officers to learn how to direct artillery and aircraft fire. Behind all the training was the knowledge that we would shortly be putting all we had learnt into practice in Dhofar. Everyone, no matter what their rank, had to be proficient in the basic infantry skills.

Years before, as a recruit, I had been taught how to detect an enemy rifleman who was firing at you by the 'crack and thump' method. This, briefly, involved noting the time lag between the 'crack' of the bullet cutting the air over your head, and the 'thump' of the rifle. A trained ear could gauge the precise direction of the firer and also the range to him. I now relearnt this skill practically with NFR, out in the Wadi Mansah near Bid Bid. Riflemen had been hidden at varying ranges and angles, and these fired over our heads. One by one we indicated where we believed the firer to be. Most of us were dramatically inaccurate at first, but improved steadily. This method of training would not have been allowed in the British Army where there are strict safety rules about overhead fire from weapons without tripods, but it was typical of the realism in our training in SAF. The risk we ran on the *jebel* if we were unable to bring down swift and accurate fire on the enemy far outweighed, in our view, any risk we now took of an accident during our 'crack and thump' demonstrations. We did, nevertheless, take rather a lot of care in selecting the riflemen who were to fire over our heads!

Every soldier was taught how to react when he did come under accurate enemy fire – diving to the ground, rolling rapidly to one side and then squeezing off two quick aimed shots before rolling again to a new position and repeating the dose. The business of winning the initial firefight was of paramount importance in low-level operations in Dhofar. The enemy were mostly equipped with Kalashnikov assault rifles with thirty-round magazines and it was their custom to fire off as many shots as possible in the first few seconds of a contact. In rocky country, with the rounds screaming off the ground and ricocheting from boulders, it was a heart-stopping thing to be surprised by an enemy group. Instant reflexes in producing accurate return fire was what we strove for from our soldiers, whose FN rifles could not fire automatic. So we experimented with single-point sights (bought out of his own pocket by Arthur) and became efficient in our close-quarter battle ('CQB') routines.

We practised ambushes and anti-ambush drills by day and by night, often with live ammunition and patrolled over the harshest country we could find so that all of us became hardened to carrying a heavy rucksack, three full water bottles, one 81mm mortar bomb, a rifle (or general-purpose machine gun) and ammunition.

Most of all, perhaps, we learnt about the importance of ground in operations in mountainous country, where it was generally the case that those on the higher ground had the advantage. To be caught in the open with the enemy above you could prove fatal. Movement, therefore, often had to be either at night or, if by day, in sufficient strength to be able to provide 'rolling piquets' on the high ground flanking any force advancing on lower ground.

All in all there was a lot to do – but we all understood the reason for our training. If we worked hard, we certainly played hard too, and there were plenty of opportunities for people to let off steam, either in the sporting and social events we organized ourselves or, in the words of the Marines amongst us, on 'quiet runs ashore' to Muscat (or in the case of our Omanis back home to their tribal areas).

The rains, which had sometimes cut us off from Muscat as the water rushed from the hills and along the Wadi Fanjr, died away and over the next few months, the temperatures gradually rose. After one or two cases of heat exhaustion among the newly arrived, we all became used to working in temperatures around 100 degrees in the shade (later it would go up to 110 and beyond). The reason why we carried three water bottles became clear to all. A lesson I had learnt in Somaliland years before served me well: water is vital – make it the first consideration when planning operations; without adequate arrangements for resupply the plan is doomed. Another similarity with Somaliland occurred to me: I was beginning to enjoy myself – enormously.

After I had been in Oman a short while, Brigadier John Graham invited me to Bait al Falaj for a briefing on the Dhofar War and for lunch afterwards. I left Bid Bid early in the morning in my Landrover, with Mohamed Salim driving. In the back were Abdullah 'the Silent', who was my new radio operator, and a grinning Jebali savouring the thought of a visit to Muttrah and some of its more shady delights. In accordance with SAF standing orders all three were armed. Jebali sat with his rifle held between his knees, while Abdullah's and Mohamed's weapons were clipped to the Landrover frame within easy reach.

The sky was shot with the first pale streaks of dawn as we rattled over our evilly-surfaced camp track to join the graded road to Muscat. Once on this Mohamed drove fast to negate the jolting caused by the corrugated and potholed surface until we reached the Wadi Fanjr. There had been recent rains and the brown water in the valley was hub deep on our wheels as we drove cautiously through, exhaust bubbling merrily as we did so. In the village we could just see through the early mist a funeral cortege winding along the stony path to the graveyard, the shrouded corpse on the shoulders of the men, who chanted a dirge to the wailing accompaniment of the women. It was an eerie sound and sight in the half light. A little further on we picked up a grey-bearded tribesman who was walking in our direction, rifle over his shoulder and held by the muzzle in his right hand, *dishdash** hitched up to reveal skinny calves. We shouted the traditional greetings.

'Peace be upon you.'

'And on you peace.'

'How is your health?'

'Fine, praise be to God. And yours?'

'Fine also, praise be to God. What is the news?'

'There is no news, praise be to God.' (i.e. No deaths, no killings etc.) And so on.

He was a Bedu from the country west of the Wadi Mansah near Adam, where the gravelly desert wastes levelled out before giving way to the rolling sand dunes of the Rhub al Khali (the Empty Quarter). These dunes stretched south to Dhofar and west for mile after eye-aching mile, into Saudi Arabia. Our passenger complained about the collapsing price of camels, resulting from the advent of the new roads and the trucks to drive on them. He told us that one vehicle could lift in a day a load which a whole camel caravan would take a week over. The value of his stock, he added bitterly, had been cut by two thirds and the price was still dropping.

As the sun cleared the horizon and hung – a red globe – in the cool morning, Mohamed asked permission to pray, and we pulled in to the side of the road. He, Abdullah, Jebali and our Bedu stood in a row facing south-west, towards Mecca, and went through the ancient routines, changing their postures together as the mumbled prayers progressed: standing first, then inclining forward from the waist, hands on knees, before kneeling and placing their foreheads on the ground and then sinking back on their heels; foreheads on the ground again and back on the heels for a spell; finally standing up once more.

We drove on quickly, through the fast-warming day to Bait al Falaj and breakfast.

* Shirt-like garment reaching to the ankles.

Chapter 6

A Briefing and a Visit to Dhofar

The briefing took place in the operations room deep within the massively walled fort of SAF Headquarters. The Intelligence staff first explained the unique Dhofar landscape before taking me through the background to the conflict and the current situation.

The rocky coastal escarpment comprises the Jebel al Qamar (literally 'Mountains of the Moon') in the west, Jebel al Qara in the centre, opposite the provincial capital Salalah, and the Jebel Samhan in the east. This whole escarpment, with its precipitous cliffs facing seaward, leaves little room for a coastal plain, which is reduced in the main to a narrow strip. There are two exceptions: one in the extreme west at Sarfait, where the scarp edge is a little further back from the sea, leaving a narrow band of broken country covered in thick bush. The other is at Salalah where the town stands by the sea, on the edge of a crescent-shaped plain which takes a great bite into the steep cliffs of the Qara. The whole of the Dhofar *jebel* is riven by sheer-sided wadis which run generally from north to south, presenting formidable obstacles within the mountains to those attempting to cross them. Moving inland, northwards, the plateau gradually levels out and the wadis become increasingly more shallow until their courses are eventually only discernible by a few scattered thorn bushes trailing their irregular path to the horizon across the flat gravelly plain. This plain is replaced at last by the seemingly endless rolling sand sea of the true desert, in this case the Rhub al Khali – the Empty Quarter.

Gavin Pike, one of the staff, then pointed out the main settlements and places of significance from Habarut and Sarfait on the western border, the frontier with the Yemen, to Sudh in the east. He drew my attention to the 'Midway Road' linking Salalah to Thamarit. 'It's possible to drive from Muscat to Thamarit,' he said, 'but beyond there, where the road winds through the Jebel al Qara, the vehicles are often

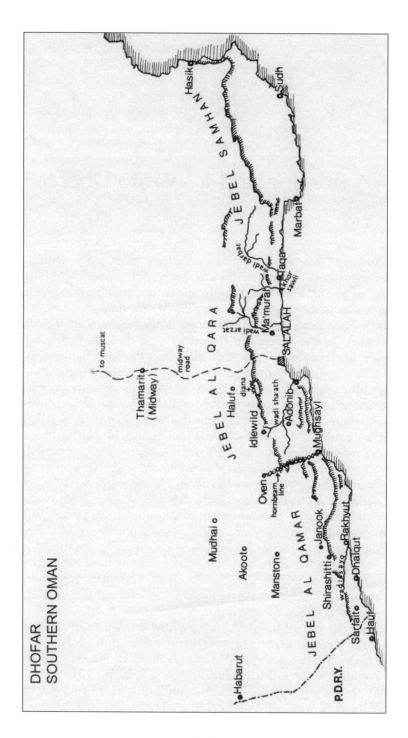

DHOFAR
SOUTHERN OMAN

JEBEL SAMHAN

Hasik
Sudh
Marbat
wadi darbat
Taqa
Khor
sawli
Ma'murah
wadi arzat
SALALAH
JEBEL AL QARA
to muscat
Thamarit
(Midway)
midway
road
Halufo
djana
Idlewild
wadi sha'ath
Adonib
Mughsayl
Oven
hornbeam
line
JEBEL AL QAMAR
Janook
Rakhyut
Mudhai
Akoot
Manston
Shirashitti
wadi sayq
Dhalqut
Sarfait
Haut
Habarut
P.D.R.Y.

58

ambushed and it necessitates a major road-opening operation before we can get stuff through to Salalah; so we normally do a lift by air over the hill – there's a good airstrip at Thamarit.'

Ancient Dhofar (most probably the 'Ophir' mentioned in the Bible, Gavin added) was famous for its frankincense which was sent to countries throughout the Arab world, for the Omanis were great sailors and traders. It was also sent to India, and even as far as Rome. Today the frankincense trees are a familiar sight in the province, but the lucrative trade has long since ceased. Centuries ago the Salalah plain was the granary of the Arabian Peninsular – the waters from the *jebel* fed an irrigation system which, until the war now being fought, transformed the plain into a verdant fertile crescent, from which cereals and green produce were exported by camel caravan and dhow, following the old frankincense trails and sea routes.

The reason for the plentiful frankincense trees, the once lush produce of the plain, the thick coconut groves by the sea, and for the incredible grassy stretches and jungle-like patches on the seaward slopes of the jebel is, in a word, monsoon. The south-west monsoon strongly affects India, but is unique to the Dhofar coast in the Arabian Peninsular. Rains blow in from June to September each year, nourishing the crops and encouraging the thick growth on the mountains. It is a period of mists and mosquitoes, and of water spilling down the mountain slopes and into the steep-sided wadis. During the monsoon movement on the *jebel,* although possible, is a slow and dangerous business for men, camels and donkeys alike – ideal conditions for those sitting and watching with loaded rifles; difficult for those picking their way uneasily over the slick rocks, peering through the clammy mists and wondering where the enemy are. Sometimes, in the Dhofar War, it was the Sultan's soldiers who sat in ambush waiting for the *adoo*** camel trains, with their vanguard of agile riflemen; at other times it was the *adoo* who patiently waited for a heavily laden SAF patrol to clamber along the wadi sides. In those months clear of the humid monsoon, Dhofar was dry and hot – although not quite reaching the blistering heat of the summer months in the north, where the shade temperatures remained steadily over 110 degrees and sometimes the mercury touched 120 degrees or so.

The varied climate had affected SAF operations considerably, Gavin continued to explain. In the past the tendency had been to patrol vigorously in the dry months and, rather like the soldiers of mediaeval times, postpone operations during the monsoon. Now the new thinking was to continue on the *jebel* through the monsoon, thereby, with a little

---

*Enemy. Always referred to thus by SAF.

luck, denying the *adoo* the chance to build up their forward supplies and making stand-off attacks on Salalah plain through the swirling mists.

It was ideal country for insurgents. The rocky escarpment and plateau, cleft by the wadis, provided good cover even when bare, but clothed with thick bushes – particularly on the *jebel* north of Salalah, the principal target – it provided good routes and hides for a sure-footed hill fighter. Add to this the bonus of mist in the monsoon and conditions to limit the government's troops activity, then the advantages to the guerillas were greatly enhanced.

It is not surprising that an area which differs so much from the rest of Arabia should be inhabited by a unique people, Gavin told me. The Dhofari *jebel* tribesmen (*Jebali*) bear little resemblance to Northern Omanis in appearance, customs or language. They spring from Galla forebears, probally stemmed from the horn of Africa, and are dark skinned, sharp featured and very lean. Many of the men wear their hair long, sometimes shoulder length, and they are fond of black clothing, which often consists simply of a *wazr*.* The *Jebalis* are wonderfully agile on the mountains and can race barefooted at an unbelievable speed over the sharp rocks. They live in curious round huts, built from the rocks so easily available, and graze the cattle, which provide their livelihood, on the pastures which are a bonus of the monsoon. These mountain people speak a guttural language which has no written form; many of them cannot understand Arabic. Their lives are hard, and they are constantly under threat from the elements, disease and hostile tribes. This cruel existence is reflected in their natures. Philosophical about death, they can be unpredictable and temperamental, and can be, of necessity perhaps, single minded to a degree in their struggle for survival.

I was then told who the *adoo* were and what they were trying to achieve. In 1962, when the father of Sultan Qaboos – Said bin Taimour al Busaidi – was the Sultan, the 'Dhofar Liberation Front' came into being. An offshoot of the Arab Nationalist Movement, it was supported by Egypt and Iraq amongst others, and its aims appeared to be separatist. Up to 1968 the Front proved fairly ineffective and enjoyed little support in the province. Then, however, significant changes occurred. The original leaders were liquidated and a new headquarters was set up in Aden, recently liberated from British rule, and now the capital of the People's Democratic Republic of Yemen (PDRY). The new, international organization called itself the 'Popular Front for the Liberation of the Occupied Arab Gulf' (PFLOAG), which lengthy title summed up

* Sarong-like garment, similar to the Indian *lungi*.

its Marxist aims. Russia, and increasingly China supported PFLOAG by supplying arms and cash via Aden. Every fighter carried Mao Tse Tung's 'Little Red Book' in Arabic translation and was taught to reject the Koran.

The switch in support resulted in little change as far as the fighter on the *jebel* was concerned. Some tribesmen who had been converted to the PFLOAG cause now attended training cadres in Russia or Peking. The next batch of Kalashnikov rifles and PMN anti-personnel mines would be labelled in acryllic script or Chinese characters; Katushka 122mm rockets might be delivered to Aden by a Chinese merchantman, or by a Russian ship, which perhaps had called earlier at Mozambique with a similar cargo. But to the Dhofari guerrilla it mattered little where the supplies came from – as long as they continued to be available.

In subsequent years the PFLOAG title was changed to the Popular Front for the Liberation of Oman (PFLO). It would, however, be naive to believe that this meant that those backing the Dhofar War would not turn their attention further up the Gulf should their aims ever be achieved in the Sultanate.

I was curious to know how a Muslim could reconcile his religious views with Marxist ideology, and Gavin explained how this could only be achieved with difficulty, and very often extreme pressure. Later this was illustrated to me by a Dhofari who told me his story as we sat on the high *jebel* one night and tried to keep warm in the bitter *shimaal*.* This man had joined the *adoo*, fought against SAF and his conscience, and tried to reject and forget the Koran. He had finally surrendered himself in Salalah, and returned to Islam and the Sultan's side.† He now worked independently of the *firqa* forces as a scout and guide for SAF, his knowledge both of the mountain trails and of the *adoo* proving of immense value.

'Ismaa!' (Listen!) said this man. 'The shuyueeyeen [communists] take the *Jebali* youths from their parents and set out on a long trek of several days walking and hiding, through the wadis and over the mountain ridges – always heading west. Opposite Sarfait they stick to the coastal plain away from the escarpment and cross the border to Yemen. They are heading for Hauf, the coastal town which is the forward head-quarters of PFLOAG and the indoctrination school for Arab youth.'

The guide continued, 'When the youths ask for water their guards reply with a question: is it God who provides or us? It is not until the boys admit that God has not provided the water that they are allowed

* Literally 'North' but also the nickname of the cold wind which blew in winter months from that direction.
† Known as 'SEP' (Surrendered Enemy Personnel' in military parlance.)

to drink. Some hold out for several days. The survivors have renounced their God by the time they reach Hauf. Not all finish the journey. Those who have refused to deny God do not see Hauf. At the school they will be taught the ways of the shuyueeyeen; they will forget God for ever. But for older men it is different,' the guide explained, 'they can never escape the knowledge of God.'

I have heard the story of how the *adoo* took the young Dhofari boys to Hauf many times since, but I remember it best from that wild windy night on the Qara *jebel*.

To return to my briefing at SAF Headquarters. The Operations staff officers took over to explain to me matters of their concern. First they dealt with the enemy's method of operations.

PFLOAG was concerned with winning over as many Dhofaris as possible to its cause, and did this by exploiting any existing anti-Government feeling to the full, and also by direct and blatant intimidation. There were cases where those who had refused to toe the party line were hurled over the escarpment to their deaths.

In the earlier days of the struggle, up to 1971, the Front achieved considerable success in its recruiting efforts. After all – living the hard life they did, often on the edge of starvation, with no sign of help from the Government – what had the *Jebalis* to lose by trying the new way? There was no sign, they said bitterly, of the roads, wells, schools and hospitals so long promised by Sultan Said bin Taimour. A steady stream of tribesmen attended the training cadres in Peking and returned to fight in the mountains that they knew so well.

Most of the enemy attacks on Salalah and the coastal towns were made at long range using the heaviest weapons they had, either 80 or 81mm mortars, Shpargen heavy machine guns or recoilless guns. The monsoon was a favourite time for such stand-off attacks, as the mists enabled the *adoo* to descend from the *jebel* unseen and move forward on the plain to within range of their target. More often than not this was the RAF base in Salalah, which also comprised a small civil airport. For such an operation the enemy would divide the attacking force into three: a forward protective screen of perhaps a dozen riflemen; a carrying party for the heavy weapon and ammunition; and a further group of riflemen to move with and protect the carrying party. Travelling with the group would be a political commissar.

For purpose of operations PFLOAG had split Dhofar into three areas which roughly equated to the main *jebel* massifs: the Western Area (Jebel al Qamar), the Central Area (Jebel Qara) and the Eastern Area (Jebel Samhan). An *adoo* command set up in each area loosely controlled the operations of the various *adoo firqas* and groups. A separate unit (The 'Ho Chi Minh' Unit) was tasked to handle the resupply. This took the form of camel trains, heavily guarded, which crossed the PDRY border below the scarp at Sarfait to deliver its supplies to the PFLOAG forward dump at Shirashitti (see map on page 58) in the Western area. Here the foodstuffs, ammunition, medical stores and all the requirements for the fighters were stored in vast caves, which were proof against the Strikemasters' Sura rockets and which were kept heavily guarded by a strong force. From Shirashitti supplies were sent forward to the Central and Eastern Areas as they were required. Normally they were loaded onto camels or donkeys, but sometimes the stores were manpacked in order to slip more silently past the SAF patrols and ambushes. However they were carried they were always heavily guarded by groups from the Ho Chi Minh Unit. It was difficult to estimate the total number of enemy on the *jebel*, but a figure of 2,000 PFLOAG hard core, aided by up to 3,000 *Jebali* armed men, were the figures given by the staff. The numbers fluctuated considerably, as extra fighters would be brought in from Hauf for specific operations.

Up to 1971 then, considerable numbers of *Jebali* tribesmen joined the rebels. After that the numbers dwindled and an increasing number of the enemy came down from the *jebel* to surrender themselves and their Kalashnikovs to the Sultan. They were then enlisted into the government *firqa* forces and returned to their tribal areas to fight for the Sultan. The main reason for this switch in allegiance was a change of Sultan. In 1970, in an almost bloodless coup in Salalah, Sultan Said bin Taimour was deposed by his son Qaboos bin Said. Almost bloodless, but not quite. The old Sultan was wounded during the excitement and the *Wali* of Dhofar, Shaikh Braik, was also hurt. The deposed Sultan was flown to London, where he remained until he died some years later.

Sultan Qaboos swiftly proved himself to be a more democratic ruler than his father was, and more in touch with the feeling in the country. Roads were built, wells dug and the long-promised schools and hospitals started to appear. These improvements were not restricted to Muscat and Salalah, as was first feared would be the case, but extended to the Interior and even to the Dhofar *jebel* too. Radios and cars, hitherto banned, were on sale, and some archaic and harsh laws were relaxed. A new, more understanding ruler was in power and efforts were being made to ease the hardships of the people. The word spread – on the new radios and, more importantly, by those who had seen the new developments at first hand. At the same time a new weapon was used in the war against the rebels: Psychological Operations – 'Psyops'. The word was spread by SEPs to their clansmen with PFLOAG that life was improving under Sultan Qaboos, and urging them to return to their age-old faith – God and the Koran. The number of SEPs increased and the government *firqa* forces swelled, but the dedicated communists fought on even more bitterly. Nothing would divert the hard-core *adoo* from their aims.

Finally the briefing switched to the Sultan's forces within Dhofar: the Dhofar Brigade. The main elements of the ground forces were the two infantry battalions – at the time of my briefing the Desert Regiment (DR) and the Jebel Regiment (JR). Despite their names the former was operating on the *jebel* and the latter responsible for safeguarding Salalah and the coastal towns. In addition there were two units permanently stationed in Dhofar: the Dhofar Gendarmerie, recruited from local tribesmen, and the Baluch Guard, shortly to be renamed the Frontier Force and composed entirely of Baluch soldiers on contract.

Directly supporting these troops were the Oman Armoured Car Squadron (eight Ferret scout cars and eight Saladin amoured cars), and the Oman Artillery. The latter consisted of three troops each of three 25pdr guns, plus a troop of two 75mm pack howitzers, and finally the 5.5in troop containing two elderly, but much respected last-war veterans of that calibre. (One of the 25pdr troops was stationed, on rotation, at Rostaq in northern Oman to train recruits and to support the two battalions there in any internal security operation which might be necessary.)

The irregular *firqa* forces comprised a number of units, each limited to a maximum strength of seventy of the same tribe, but who would normally achieve up to a total of twenty or thirty 'in the field'. They usually operated within their own tribal areas. They carried FN (Standard NATO) rifles and *jaish** radios, but wore their own clothing. These *firqa* were trained by the SAS Squadron on rotation in Dhofar and known as BATT (British Army Training Team). The SAS normally split into four-man teams, thus covering a number of different *firqas* and tribal areas. Each team included a medical orderly who played an important part in winning the hearts and minds of the *Jebalis*.

The SAS, from past experiences in Borneo, Brunei, Aden and, indeed, on the Jebel al Akhdar in northern Oman, knew the value of Psyops in a campaign such as Dhofar. It was their commanders, in conjunction with the Commander of the Dhofar Brigade and his staff, who masterminded the scheme whereby schools and hospitals were built and wells bored at the very first opportunity in those areas which were freshly liberated from PFLOAG control. Sometimes work was started before the area was totally clear of *adoo* – a risk well worth taking as the local tribesmen were anxious to see the project continue. In those areas

* Arabic for Army.

support for PFLOAG was inclined to wither – abruptly! There is no doubt that this 'hearts and minds' philosophy was a prime factor in the eventual successful outcome of the campaign.

The ground forces, regular and irregular, were supported by the Sultan of Oman's Air Force (SOAF). This comprised three squadrons: Strike Squadron of twelve BAC Strikemaster aircraft, which although cruelly slow by modern standards, were very manoeuvrable, and ideal for Dhofar. They could twist their way at low level along the wadi beds and deliver either a Sura rocket or perhaps a bomb weighing up to 540lb into the laps of the surprised *adoo* squatting in their cave or under a tree. Transport Squadron contained eight Skyvans, two Caribous, four Beavers and three Viscounts (the last named used for the haul from Muscat to Salalah). Finally, Helicopter Squadron had four Augusta Bell 206 Jet Rangers and eight of the larger 205 choppers, each of which could lift up to fourteen fully equipped soldiers, or a fair quantity of live goats for fresh rations on the *jebel*.

Salalah Airport was guarded by a ring of forts. These were nick-named 'Hedgehogs' and were constructed out of metal 'burmails'* filled with sand. They were bullet and grenade proof, and had withstood attacks from *adoo* groups from time to time. These Hedgehogs were manned by Dhofar Gendarmerie who were responsible for their local protection; each one also contained a surveillance device for detecting movement on Salalah plain by night. (It was claimed that a trained operator could always distinguish between animals and men – but a few camel corpses discovered at dawn did take a little explaining away on the odd occasion). The surveillance equipment was manned by British Royal Artillery observers, from the so called 'Cracker Battery', who could direct the fire of either the RAF Regiment detachment 81mm mortars or the Oman Artillery guns on to likely targets. The Hedgehogs were linked by a barbed-wire fence and anti-personnel mines. They were a very effective outer ring of defences and warning system, not only for the airport but also for Salalah town itself.

The Sultan's Navy in 1972 was modest: the *Al Said*, the Sultan's well-armed personal motor vessel, which was taken into military use when appropriate; SNV *Dhofar* (a logistic ship); three fast patrol boats and an inshore squadron of two 'booms', the *Muntasir* and the *Nahr Al Bahr*. These last two were a form of motorized dhow and were interesting craft to sail in (especially in the monsoon).

---

* 44-gallon petrol or oil drums. The word 'Burmail', in common use in the Arabian Gulf, is derived from 'Burmah Oil', which company was among the first to use such containers.

The aims of Sultan Qaboos in Dhofar were two-fold. Firstly to win and retain the hearts and minds of the Dhofari people by showing evidence of government long-term help – especially on the *jebel* – and to encourage those who had defected to the rebels to return to the ways of Islam. Secondly to defeat the remaining hard-core *adoo*. This could be achieved by establishing a series of blocking positions across the massif west of Salalah, in order to prevent further supplies and ammunition reaching the Central and Eastern areas. Operations could then be undertaken to mop up the remaining enemy groups east of this line.

Later, over an excellent lunch, Brigadier Graham told me that NFR's area of responsibility would be Salalah Plain when I went to Dhofar, but the Regiment would also get involved in operations on the *jebel*. 'You've heard of the blocking positions established west of Salalah,' he said. 'It's called the "Leopard Line". It's pretty effective but there's no doubt that *adoo* groups can slip through – the terrain is so massive and troops are too thinly spread. But it's been proposed that if we can establish a position here then we really are in business,' and a forefinger stabbed the map at Sarfait on the PDRY border. 'The enemy supply trains, as you've been told, slip through between the Sarfait scarp and the sea – it's very thick and rugged country. The Desert Regiment are planning an operation – we're calling it "Simba" – to establish itself on the scarp at Sarfait and then exploit down to the coast, via this jagged hill here.' Again the forefinger pointed. 'With any luck we can then sew up the whole *adoo* resupply right on the border.

'Nigel Knocker, CO of the Desert Regiment, is planning Operation Simba from his battalion position at Akoot,' went on the Brigadier. 'Go down and see him when you do your recce of Dhofar. I expect one or perhaps two of your companies will get involved in the second phase – exploitation to the sea. You'd better also take a look at the Central and Eastern *jebel* and, by the way, don't forget you'll personally be responsible for the safety of Salalah and the plain.'

After the briefing I sat rather thoughtfully in my Landrover as Mohamed drove me back to Bid Bid that night. One way or another I had quite a bit to think about.

Years later Brigadier Graham (now a Major General) confided in me that initially he was not totally optimistic about the ease of the Sarfait Operation. However, with the decline in support from the United Kingdom and many other factors he decided, with Colonel Hugh Oldman, the Defence Secretary, and others agreeing, that the Sultanate had to carry out a bold stroke to win Arab interest, sympathy and support, without which SAF could not have continued the campaign.

The launching and maintenance of Operation Simba gave him great anxiety. In the event all turned out well.

In the third week of February I flew to Salalah in order to see Dhofar for myself, and to be able to put the detailed briefing I had received into perspective. It was a two-hour trip in a Viscount of Transport Squadron and, as we approached the Jebel Samhan, the pilot invited me into the cabin. 'You get a better view from up here, Colonel, and I can point out various features to you.' It was an example of the friendly and thoughtful attitude of SOAF pilots which I was to encounter again and again.

After we left the mountains in the north we flew over 600 miles of yellow gravel and sand desert, bright in the sun. The graded, but unsurfaced road was visible below us for most of the way; sometimes, through the soft patches, it split into dozens of tracks as individual vehicles sought the best route. These eventually converged once more as the going improved. 'That's Thamarit – the huddle of huts is the airstrip. This is where road freight from Muscat is loaded onto Caribous and Skyvans to continue to Salalah – the road south is often ambushed.' I'd remembered hearing about it in Bait al Falaj, and here it was – a straight track heading for the hazy mountains. Gradually the ground below became more and more rugged and I could see areas of pasture dotted with fig trees and deepening wadis which became great clefts in the brown, rocky *jebel*.

Suddenly and dramatically the ground fell sharply away and the Viscount bucked and yawed in the disturbed air – we were over the escarpment. Below us was a brilliant blue sea, wonderfully clear, washing the sands of the coastal strip. I looked back at the scarp – it was a breathtaking sight. The mountain ridge was sheer, with bushes and stunted trees somehow clinging to its face and riven by deep wadis; for all the world as if some vast axe had attacked the edge of the *jebel* smashing gigantic wedge-shaped cuts into that rocky surface. It was a savage piece of country, and an awesome thought to imagine fighting over it. Perhaps the pilot knew what I was thinking for, as he reached the coast and banked east along it, he said, 'Sooner you than me down in that – I'd prefer to be up here! That's Sudh by the way . . . and there's Marbat.' They were two coastal towns with some fishing boats drawn up on the beaches, the latter boasting two forts which could be clearly seen from our aircraft.

We could now see Salalah Plain and its coastal fringe of coconut palms. From the air a network of lines criss-crossing the plain showed up clearly – they were the irrigation channels (*falaj*) now dry. 'The *adoo* blew up the *falaj* where it leaves the *jebel*, and so all the gardens and crops on the plain have withered and died,' the pilot commented. Then, 'You can see the hedgehogs clearly – some of them a long way out in the plain halfway between the airstrip and the *jebel*'. He banked steeply and lined up on Salalah runway as he began his aproach run. During the following week I saw a lot of the *jebel*, and of Salalah Plain. I spent two days with the Desert Regiment (DR) at Akoot, and accompanied the Commanding Officer, Lieutenant Colonel Nigel Knocker, to have a surreptitious look at Sarfait from a Jet Ranger helicopter – surreptitious because Operation Simba was due to be launched by DR in about seven weeks' time and, even now, Paul Mangin of DR was making a reconnaissance on foot of the area with a group from the *Firqa* Tariq bin Zaid – local tribesmen.

Akoot was subject to frequent stand-off attacks by *adoo* heavy weapons, but it was an impregnable battalion position with strong stone sangars on the high ground surrounding the camp. The Officers' Mess was a marquee with a strong stone protecting wall surrounding it. (Unfortunately this did not prevent a fatal officer casualty when it was hit by a lucky – or unlucky – round from an enemy recoilless gun.)

In Salalah I stayed with Lieutenant Colonel Peter Worthy, the Commanding Officer of the Jebel Regiment (JR), in Umm al Ghawarif Camp. JR was involved in patrolling on the Plain and also in the blocking positions on the Leopard Line. I made a number of helicopter flights to the Jebel Qara to see this line for myself and, after a couple of trips, began to get used to the stomach-churning feeling as we 'sycamored' down in tight spirals from high altitude to vulnerable *jebel* landing pads. (The helicopter never waited, it would be too attractive a small-arms target, but immediately took off and returned later to pick me up.) It was good to see Major Mike Ball of my own Regiment in one such position, and I remember his excellent knowledge of the situation, and the detailed and highly informative briefing he gave me.

I climbed into the Viscount for the flight back to northern Oman, having learnt a lot in a short time, and with two main lingering impressions. One was the formidable size of the *jebel* and the ruggedness of the country – everying was much bigger than I had imagined. The second concerned the professionalism and enthusiasm of all those I'd spoken to, at all levels, and, directly linked to this, my own growing confidence in SAF and in the outcome of the conflict.

Mohamed and Abdullah were waiting in my Landrover at Muscat Airport and we were soon heading for Bid Bid in the waning light. It was dark as we approached our camp and the sentry shouted, 'Who is it? Who comes?'

'*Al Qaa'id*! *Al Qaa'id*!' shouted Mohamed and Abdullah in unison, and I recall Mohamed glancing at me and grinning at that moment.

The sentry put up his rifle and opened the gate. 'Peace be upon you', he said. 'How are you?' and shook me by the hand. 'What is the news from Dhofar?' he asked.

Mohamed muttered, 'He is supposed to salute.' But I preferred my welcome home.

That night Arthur Brocklehurst, Saif Ali and Medhi called at my *bait* for a *loomi* (fresh lime drink) and to find out the latest news from Dhofar. I was beginning to feel a part of NFR.

Chapter 7

Fuddles and a Move to War

Jebali would not clean my lavatory! This was normal as such a job was beneath the dignity of a Muslim soldier – there were special sweepers of low caste for this, but not at Bid Bid. At Bid Bid, those people who had lavatories – the officers – cleaned their own! My technique was to apply a generous helping of Harpic, close the eyes and swiftly follow up using the lavatory brush rather like a swizzle stick. It needed such curious treatment to coax the inadequate drains into accepting any contribution whatsoever. For the soldiers it was simpler. Around the camp a line of small red flags was positioned in selected areas, about a hundred yards out from the barbed-wire perimeter fence. After dusk, or earlier if pushed, soldiers strolled out beyond these flags to perform. Not the place for an evening walk. Although such sanitary arrangements sound horrific they were surprisingly hygienic – thanks to the sun and hooded crows. A lavatorial note to strike, but another small aspect of life I remember from Oman in the 1970s.*

After I had been in Bid Bid for about two months the *Wali* invited me to his fort for a *fuddle*! This is a slang word used by SAF derived from the Arabic expression '*Tafuddle*' of which there is no real English equivalent; possibly 'Be so kind' or 'After you'. It is accompanied by a gesture indicating 'You go first'. For instance, an Arab will indicate a chair for you and say '*Tafuddle*'; he uses the same word when he opens a door for his guest, or offers food. Thus, when we were asked to an Omani house we referred to it as a '*fuddle*'. Anyhow, the *Wali*, Sheikh Yahya bin Immam al Beni Hinnah, indicated that I should visit, and so I assembled an appropriate retinue and we packed into my Landrover – myself, Arthur and his orderly, Hamid Salim the Assistant Adjutant,

---

* It is different now. All permanent camps have modern 'arrangements'.

Mohamed my driver and, of course, Jebali and my radio operator Abdullah.

Bid Bid village was then a cluster of mud houses and palm-leaf huts grouped round the fort over which on this day the red green and white flag of Oman fluttered bravely. The *Wali*'s son met us and conducted us through the heavy iron-studded door in the outside wall into the courtyard, which was cool, with a couple of palms and a fragrant fig tree. Up some steps we trooped, past the *Wali*'s armed guard, all fiercely bearded and bristling with weapons, into a long airy *majlis** – a room completely open on the courtyard side and lined with windows in the outer wall, through which we could see a brilliant green panorama of lucerne, gardens and palms. A soft breeze played through the room which was unfurnished save for some carpets on the floor, and a row of pegs for our weapons. Before entering the *majlis* we removed our shoes, and it was at this stage that I noticed a large hole in the toe of my sock.

Sheikh Yahya greeted us courteously. A striking man in appearance – grey bearded and sharp-featured with kindly but shrewd eyes – he was aged about fifty-five and was dressed in a white head cloth, *dishdasha* and camel-leather sandals. Round his waist was a colourful bandolier stuffed with bullets, and he wore a *khunja* (curved knife) in a silver and gold sheath over his comfortable stomach.

After the customary ritual of greetings we sat on the carpet, our backs to the wall and our feet tucked under us. I was glad to be able to hide my offending sock in this way. Sheikh Yahya sat by me and his son handed round small coffee cups before offering coffee from an enormous copper pot. I deferred and gestured for Yahya's cup to be filled first as was customary ('*Tafuddle*'), but gave in gracefully when he insisted. After three cups drunk noisily with relish I shook the cup and protested vehemently when offered more again as custom dictated. A tray of dates was then placed on the floor and we moved into a circle round it, right hands working busily squeezing out the stone and popping the dates into the mouth, left hands tucked firmly out of sight – to have used this would have been a major breach of etiquette. After the dates, more coffee, then a huge bowl of custard for which we were all armed with tiny spoons. This was followed by tea, heavily laced with cardamom, and a communal bowl of the delicious fudge called *halwa* – delicious, but messy with the fingers. No Omani meal was complete without *halwa* and I developed a taste for it in the next couple of years. Finally biscuits, with Sheikh Yahya sorting out the chocolate ones and pressing them on me.

* Meeting room. Also used to describe an assembly or conferring group.

This was not a main meal or there would have been goat and rice, but was more of a light snack – after all it was about ten in the morning. It would have been unthinkable for the *Wali* not to have offered his guests food.

Before we had started to eat, Sheikh Yahya had murmered the customary grace, '*Blismallah Ar-Rahaami Ar-Raheem*' (In the name of God, the Compassionate, the Merciful), and afterwards he rounded off things nicely as he threw back his head and a mighty belch rumbled forth.

The *Wali* was a splendid host and attended to his duties well, despite interruptions by an elderly official who lurched in from time to time and mumbled inefficiently into the Sheikh's ear. Once he shuffled back within minutes, as he had forgotten what he had been told, and received a short but lethal admonishment from his chief.

Then to a spot of business. 'In Fanjr village,' said Yahya gravely, 'the people complain of the soldiers' corruption. They are using a certain house where there are two women. I have even had a letter of complaint.' Arthur had already got wind of this and had briefed me carefully on the matter beforehand. The two women were notorious and energetic prostitutes who enjoyed a roaring trade, and sometimes dispensed disease with gay abandon.

'*Walaahi ya Salaam, ya Sheikh* [My God Oh Sheikh], how kind of you to bring this shameful fact to my notice. Shame on the owner of the house for lowering the high morals of the village and for corrupting the country's fighting men; of course you will already have arranged for the house to close, I'm sure?'

Yahya smiled and met my eye. 'There are difficulties,' he murmured. 'Let us see how it develops.'

No doubt the girls are still hard at it, in the house in Fanjr which has been a brothel since everyone's grandfather can remember. After a decent interval we asked politely to be released (Can I get down now?). Back to camp we drove with Jebali doing a credible impersonation of the old official mumbling in Yahya's (Abdullah's) ear before receiving his short sharp rocket.

In camp I found Medhi busy – a civilian lorry packed with people and driven far too fast had turned over when attempting a bend on the road to Ziki. One of our Landrovers arrived on the scene and had brought the injured to NFR Medical Centre. Medhi saved the life of a woman and patched up two men, but there was nothing that could be done for a child who sadly died. In reply to our signal a Skyvan landed on our camp strip and took the injured and the child to the hospital in Muttrah. Traffic accidents were all too common at that time, because there had only been traffic since the 1970 coup, and the drivers were inexperienced.

In early April I inspected the NFR recruits and took the salute at their passing-out parade at Ziki. They marched proudly by looking very smart and also very young indeed. Afterwards, I tackled Arthur and Raqaishi about the average age of our new soldiers. Since in those days birthdays were not recorded, nor remembered, it was impossible to judge accurately. When our recruiting teams visited the tribes they called for the boys who had reached puberty. It therefore transpired that some of our soldiers who would be fighting in Dhofar by the end of the month were no more than fourteen years old! The ages of this batch of forty or so varied between fourteen and eighteen as far as I could establish, but I didn't press the point further.

That day Raqaishi had invited Arthur, Saif Ali and myself to a *fuddle* in his bait in Ziki village, where he was a figure of some importance and the owner of a number of date palms. I was looking forward to this when a signal arrived from Bait al Falaj ordering me to send a half rifle company to Dhofar within forty-eight hours. Luckily a Beaver aircraft had just landed at Ziki strip to pick up a civilian traffic accident casualty. I managed to hitch a lift with this and it dropped me off at Bid Bid where I sent for Bob Hudson, the Royal Marine who commanded A Company. Bob had been to Dhofar before with the Coastal Patrol in 1966 and had already done his reconnaissance for our forthcoming tour. He had a very sound sergeant major who was much respected in the Battalion, Hamood, a Bedu from the country west of Bid Bid. Hamood had a fierce face with fine features and looked every inch a soldier. I saw Bob and two platoons off at Bait al Falaj Airport just after dawn on the morning of 8 April. The whole Battalion would be joining them in the south shortly.

A couple of days later the Recce Platoon and the Assault Pioneer Platoon left Ziki by vehicle to drive the 600 miles to Thamarit. The Assault Pioneers would remain initially at Thamarit Garrison, before becoming involved in Operation Simba, while Raqaishi's platoon was to be employed in patrolling the wastes to the north of the Dhofar *jebel* to prevent the *adoo* penetrating via the desert routes. Raqaishi was to operate out of Mudhai for the whole of NFR's tour of operations. They went off in grand style, the Arab soldiers beating the side of their Landrovers in time to their wild singing. My mind leapt back to my Danot platoon of Scouts as they left Awareh singing, on that morning a quarter of a century before.

On 16 April we had news that the Desert Regiment and the Firqa Tariq bin Zaid from Akoot had seized the *jebel* feature at Sarfait and were secure just 3 miles from the PDRY border. A successful diversionary operation, which included gunfire from the Sultan's yacht, *Al Said*, had resulted in no enemy opposition. Complete surprise had been achieved.

As the operation was launched a tremendous storm lashed Dhofar. Violent winds beat the *jebel* and the rain sheeted obliquely down. It was a helicopter nightmare made doubly bad by swirling mists, but despite this the operation went without a hitch. In the first two days over thirty civilian refugees came to the position, but nothing was seen of the enemy for forty-eight hours when a few *adoo* opened up ineffectively with small arms on the position at extreme range. The only casualty in establishing the position occurred when a corporal was killed by lightning and a staff sergeant injured during the violent storms.

Gradually the enemy opposition increased – a yardstick of the effectiveness of the position – and soon a regular daily supply of enemy mortar bombs and RCL shells fell on the Simba area. By this time, however, strong sangars had been built, and everyone took cover on the warning shout 'Incomer!' There were few casualties.

Before leaving for Dhofar NFR gave a party at Bid Bid and invited some seventy guests, civil and military, Omani and British. Deliciously spiced steaks were barbecued on palm sticks in the Mess garden and were thoroughly enjoyed, especially by the few English wives and Embassy girls who were there. Few realized the steaks were goat!

NFR officers entered into the spirit of things enthusiastcally and my heart sank when I saw David Nichols, one of our Marines, aiming Arthur's lethal crossbow at the two dachshunds belonging to the Defence Secretary's wife, who was sitting with me. 'Chipalata on a stick anyone?' called David, very clearly indeed. I blanched; Mrs Defence Secretary stiffened. An atmosphere built up. However, David was led quietly away and the dogs survived. Khalfan, one of our Mess staff, immaculate in white *dishdash*, NFR green cummerband and puggaree, silently topped up my important guests' drinks and all was well. Bill Kerr murmured in my ear, 'NFR isn't COUTH!' And we weren't.

Company by company, bit by bit, the remainder of NFR filtered down to Salalah by Viscount aircraft from Bait al Falaj. The move was spread over about a week and I travelled down on 27 April with a motley aircraft load consisting mainly of 'camp followers'. This was the official term in SAF for civilians attached to a military unit and included tailors, dhobies, cooks, mess boys, sweepers, donkey handlers and so on. Some of these last named were most venerable and dignified old men. I recall that one such greybeard carried a chicken in a bucket as his personal equipment! Enemies of the Sultan tremble! It was not too military a bunch and Jebali expressed disgust at our being included in such a group. He maintained an aloof silence in the seat behind me throughout the flight. Which suited me – there was a lot to think about.

74

Chapter 8

Operation Simba and a Trip to Tarqa

After one night in Umm al Ghawarif camp in Salalah, I flew by Skyvan to Sarfait, where B and C companies NFR had joined DR and Operation Simba a few days before. It is a distance of some 75 miles over the Jebel al Qamar 'moon country'. I sat in the co-pilot's seat and thus had an excellent view of the terrain below. Over Shirashitti it was easy to see how the *adoo* could escape detection and, even if spotted, remain safe from bombs and rockets; the wadis were deep and riddled with caves and the country covered in thick bush. Clear of the treeline to the north I could see Akoot, where I had stayed with Nigel Knocker during my recce. He'd told me then about Simba – now all his careful planning, the studying of air photographs, the meticulous working out of helicopter loads and lifts had paid off. DR was firm on its vantage point, and the *adoo* didn't like it one bit.

As we approached the PDRY border the Sarfait feature was easily discernible on the high escarpment and, beyond it and below, the little town of Hauf sitting by the sparkling sea. Sarfait overlooked the routes from Hauf into Dhofar, but the distance from the feature itself to the coast was considerable. Commanding as the position was, there was nothing to prevent enemy camel caravans passing at night through the broken country between the *jebel* and the sea.

A sudden crackle in the headsets, as the pilot switched to the battalion radio frequency, interrupted my thoughts and I heard the voice of the DR Operations Officer telling us to stand off for a while as the airstrip was under enemy mortar and RCL attack! We needed no urging and gained height rapidly to circle safely out of range. We tried to pinpoint the enemy weapons to the west, but the only spurts of dust we could see were those blossoming on Sarfait itself as the mortar bombs grouped nicely on the position.

After a short while we were told it was clear to land, but the pilot was advised not to linger after he had picked up the return load for Salalah. The aircraft seemed to be very vulnerable and so slow as to be almost hovering as we dropped onto the strip. This was beautifully sited in the centre of the battalion position and below the level of flanking ridges, on which I could see the sangars of company positions.

The aircraft made a very rapid turnaround indeed – perhaps spurred on by the sight of a burnt-out Augusta Bell 205 helicopter on the side of the runway, and by the holes left by the recent 'incomers'. When the dust had cleared I saw a battered Landrover rattling towards me. Several of these hardy veterans, stripped down to the basic shell, had been airlifted in as *jebel* runners and were invaluable on the widely dispersed Sarfait position.

In the side of a wadi which ran through the centre of the tactical headquarters was a shallow, wide-mouthed cave which enjoyed a superb view to the east and was also mortar proof! It was known as the 'Grotto'. Here I found Nigel and a number of his officers who welcomed me warmly and pressed a cold beer (from the paraffin-powered refrigerator) into my very ready hand. After a briefing on the operation to date and the plans for the future, including the occupation of a further position between Sarfait and the sea, I left with a guide to spend two days with Tresham Gregg and B Company NFR. As we picked our way over the rocks a familiar figure approached, hand outstretched. It was Pindook Murad, NFR Assault Pioneer Platoon Commander. His platoon, together with DR Assault Pioneers, had constructed the airstrip (nicknamed 'Mainbrace') at Sarfait. A Herculean task for forty or so men, they had shifted a huge quantity of rock, either manually or with explosive charges. Pindook was in good heart and reported all was well with his platoon. They would be returning to Salalah shortly.

B Company was holding the eastern flank of the Sarfait position, and its sangars were on a gentle forward slope overlooking a wide wadi which, like the slopes on its far side, was choked with bushes and stunted trees – country which provided plenty of well-covered approaches for *adoo* groups. There had been one or two bursts of Kalashnikov fire at B Company positions by over-optimistic marksmen who had fired from ranges far too great for accuracy with the AK47, a weapon primarily designed for close-quarter assault.

Tresham had constructed a screen of sangars forward of his main defensive area and close to the edge of the bushes. These were occupied by day, but after dusk his men withdrew to the main position, leaving the forward one booby trapped. A general-purpose machine gun (GPMG) was laid (aimed) on the vacated sangars to add to the reception arrangements. It was a well-known enemy tactic to attempt to 'take out' isolated positions by creeping up on them at night. They would have a nasty shock if they attempted it here.

I was suddenly confronted by a substantial figure dressed solely in microscopic frayed shorts, open sandals and a ginger-tinted beard, through which a broad smile was becoming visible. 'Hello, Colonel. Good to see you at the sharp end.' It was Graeme Smyth-Piggott, dressed for war! In response to my earnest request that he took care not to get his whiskers trapped in the working parts of his rifle, I received Graeme's stock reply. 'Don't give me a hard time, Squire – I mean Colonel!' Later that afternoon I heard his calm tones on the radio as he gave fire control orders to DR 81mm mortars to engage a group of *adoo* seen crossing to the front well out of small-arms range.

On the subject of British beards in Dhofar, some regiments in SAF discouraged them – on the familiar (and true) grounds that a 'smart soldier is a good soldier'. In NFR I allowed them. I had already seen how the majority of British officers were easily discernible amongst a group of Arab and Baluchi soldiers. No matter how tanned they happened to be their faces somehow always gleamed whitely, and in build they were normally taller and bulkier than their men. Beards were traditionally worn by the Omani soldiers, unlike, of course, the British Army where they were forbidden, except for infantry assault pioneer sergeants.

It seemed to me that, in a situation where the officers were required to dress exactly as their men, with no badges of rank, the more the British could conform in appearance and, incidentally, the more they could cover their faces, the better. We all took pains to cover our watches with khaki wrist bands and to bind the shiny parts of our rifles with black masking tape; our shirts and trousers were dyed with green and brown spots and our hair was covered in an issue green *shemagh* (headcloth). To top all this careful camouflage with a pale moon of a face – or a red rising sun as the case or complexion might be – seemed, to my way of thinking, spoiling the ship for a haporth of hair. In short, I allowed beards on the *jebel*. But not in barracks. There were some corkers grown as a result. Some officers were soon engulfed in hair of amazing hue. As my own effort would turn out to be a nasty mix of ginger, brown and white, I remained clean shaven. Tresham Gregg was unbearded too. Although his attempts to grow one failed, despite extreme effort, he did very well without one.

I met and chatted to all of B Company soldiers the next day. In each sangar I was presented with a cup of very sweet cardamom tea, specially brewed. By the time I had finished my rounds I was awash.

Everyone was in excellent spirits and assured me that the food was good, and, *Al Hamdu Lillah* (Praise be to God), the water plentiful.*

Thanks to the regular air resupply the soldiers at Sarfait ate fresh rations daily. Live goats were prepared for their flight by wrapping their bound hindquarters in polythene bags. This ensured a reasonably comfortable ride for those travelling with them and reduced the burden of cleaning the aircraft afterwards. A lesson that had, of course, been learnt the hard way.

On the north-western side of the feature where I went next, Peter Tawell had sited C Company NFR with good fields of fire across the bare rocky plateau which faced him, with not a tree or shrub in sight – a totally different panorama to that confronting B Company. Peter was also aware of the vulnerability of some of the forward sangars and had sited Claymore mines to protect them. I also noted a burmail lying on the ground in front of his own sangar. 'That,' said Peter, 'is my very special brew – a nice blend of petrol and sugar plus a little device which ignites the lot if I fire a round at it.' He had already tried the plan for effect and said that not only did it explode in a satisfactory way – spewing burning streams of liquid – but it also lit up a wide area very nicely to enable small arms to engage any targets accurately. A simple but effective improvization.

While I was with C Company there were a number of 'incomers' – largely recoiless gun (RCL) rounds. Christopher Kemball, the Company Second in Command, estimated as accurately as he could where the enemy gun positions were and engaged those areas with his two mortars.

I spent my last day on Sarfait with Nigel at Battalion Headquarters. His own quarters consisted of a tent pitched under the lee of a wadi side and surrounded by stout stone walls. The previous day the canvas roof had been torn in a number of places by *adoo* shell fragments. But, as Nigel pointed out, the holes provided good ventilation during the hot nights. I slept very soundly that night – perhaps due to this thoughtful ventilation, but more likely I found the camp bed uncommonly luxurious after a sangar rocky floor.

Well satisfied with B and C Companies' performance and morale, I flew back to Salalah via a night at the resupply base (airhead) at Akoot, where the half of A Company under David Nichols were installed. A couple of days later an attempt was made to move the airhead closer to Sarfait and to a place called Janook. Arthur and other old hands sucked

---

*Thanks to the regular air resupply water was delivered in burmails by helicopter. The ration was one gallon per man per day for all purposes – drinking, cooking, washing and shaving.

their teeth and said Janook was too near the treeline – the *adoo* would be able to harrass the airstrip with mortars and machine guns, while remaining hidden themselves. And, on this occasion, the old hands were proved correct. David and his small force, boosted by the Saladins of the Armoured Car Squadron, were engaged almost immediately when they reached the Janook area. They fought a brisk action inflicting a number of casualties on the *adoo*, but also receiving some themselves. Clearly it was not the best place for the airhead which David then resited at a more suitable spot further north, nicknamed 'Manston'. The armoured cars were commanded by Major Patrick Brook of the Blues and Royals, an extremely brave officer who fought throughout the Dhofar War.

Back in Salalah I was kept very busy between 5 and 12 May taking over responsibility for the defence and security of the Salalah area from Peter Worthy, the Commanding Officer of the outgoing Jebel Regiment (JR).

One of the many and varied jobs of the Salalah garrison was to provision the coastal towns of Tarqa, Marbat and Sudh with food, and also ammunition and supplies for the *askars*,* BATT and Dhofar Gendarmerie. This was done by a vehicle convoy which, because of the numerous attempts to ambush it, was heavily escorted and its movements kept secret. The operation was referred to as the 'Tarqa Road Opening' and it took place every fortnight or so. During my takeover such a road opening was due and Peter suggested we both went in order that I could see how it was done.

The vehicles formed up outside the fort which housed NFR Battalion Headquarters in Umm al Ghawarif camp. Ready to move in front of the supply 3-tonners was a screen of Landrovers containing a platoon of NFR and some of Z Company, a force permanently stationed in Salalah under the leadership of one Spike Powell – about whom, more later. This small force would act as vanguard and clear likely ambush spots on the way. Travelling just behind this screen was a section of assault pioneers to deal with any mines. The *adoo* used two types: the Russian TM46 anti-tank mine, which would blow a Landrover to bits and write off a 3-ton truck; and the Chinese PMN anti-personnel mine which often maimed without killing. A number of NFR soldiers were wounded by these during this tour of operations, losing one or two legs.

Close escort to the convoy was provided by soldiers of Headquarter Company – drawn from the clerks, drivers and cooks. Peter and I were 'free runners' in our own Landrovers and both Battalion Intelligence

* Armed tribesmen employed by the Wali.

Officers accompanied the little force – Dick Simmons of NFR and Hugh Jones of JR. Hugh travelled in the leading stores 3-tonner and was in charge of the supply vehicles.

Our route lay along the coastal strip to Sudh and it would be necessary to negotiate one or two *khors* along the way. These were wadi mouths where the wadi reached the sea. Of these the largest was the Khor Sawli which was flanked by low hills. This was a well-known enemy ambush spot, and would be piquetted before our arrival by a platoon of Dhofar Gendarmerie (DG) from their camp at Ma'Murah. The DG would also sweep the graded road between their camp and Umm al Ghawarif for possible mines before we started, thus giving us a good fast start along that route.

We 'netted in' our Racal radio sets so that we could talk to each part of the road-opening force as well as to Battalion HQ, to the detachment of 25-pdr guns on the airfield, and to SOAF – the Sultan's Air Force. And off we went, bowling merrily down the road to Ma'Murah, which we reached without incident.

After leaving Ma'Murah the vehicles were ordered to fan out and pick their own route, avoiding previously made vehicle tracks in the sandy plain as being likely spots for mines. It was pleasant motoring along in the open Landrover, the rush of air relieving the heat of the late morning. I chatted to Mohamed and Jebali while Abdullah sat silently as always, the headset of the vehicle radio clamped firmly over his ears. I was travelling behind the forward screen, well in front of the supplies vehicles, and I could see the low hills of the Khor Sawli beginning to emerge through the heat haze to our front. Suddenly there was a loud cracking explosion from behind and I heard the whine of fragments through the air. A column of smoke rose in the centre of the leading fan of supply 3-tonners. Mohamed was already turning the Landrover and we raced back to see what had happened.

I feared a mine and unfortunately I was right. Hugh Jones's 3-tonner had struck a TM46 anti-tank mine as it crossed a narrow wadi. The front of the vehicle was badly damaged with a plume of black smoke hanging over it. Miraculously the driver, although shocked and badly shaken, was without serious injury. Hugh, however, had been blown through the cab cupola and was lying on the rocky ground some yards away. He was unconscious and had a wound in the back of his head, which we bound with a field dressing. Peter called for a helicopter from Salalah on his radio and in a very short time indeed one arrived. The Medical Orderly carefully placed Hugh on a stretcher and he was whisked away to the Field Surgical Team at the Airport. The Assault Pioneer section remained to ensure there were no further mines in the area, and the rest of us climbed back into our vehicles. We believed the mine had been washed down the valley in the rains.

It was a sadder and more thoughtful force which drove on to the Khor Sawli – we were worried for Hugh. The DG were well positioned on the low hills and waved to us as we drove through. There were no incidents and we off-loaded our stores safely at Tarqa.

A short time after starting our return trip, Peter returned to Salalah as the news on the radio about his Intelligence Officer, Hugh, was not good. The empty supply vehicles together with their escort headed back to Umm al Ghawarif camp, their job completed. This left me with the 'teeth' of the small force, mounted in Landrovers. Besides my own vehicle there were two with elements from the NFR rifle platoon, a couple of 'Z' Company 'gunships' bristling with weapons, including .50 Browning machine guns mounted on traversing brackets, and finally Dick Simmons, my Intelligence Officer, with his driver, radio operator and an escort.

While the stores 3-tonners travelled back along the coastal route, my group planned to sweep round in a wide arc to the north, keeping out of small-arms range from the *jebel*, but perhaps able to intercept any enemy who might have ambush plans for our 3-tonners. Leaving plumes of sand which marked our progress, we roared off in a well-spaced 'box' formation – three vehicles in front and three behind. As we reached each of the shallow wadis, which scored the plain between the *jebel* and the sea, we dismounted and crossed them on foot to make sure no enemy parties were lying up in them. The drivers of the Landrovers remained with their vehicles until the wadis were cleared and then moved forward to pick us up again.

Keeping parallel to the escarpment and several hundred yards from it we made very good progress until we came to the Wadi Arzat. We halted the landrovers short of the wadi as usual and moved forward on foot. Suddenly I heard the sound which I had become so familiar with on our 'crack and thump' training in the Wadi Mansah near Bid Bid: the flat snap of bullets over our heads. As one man we dived into the ground and, I'm happy to say, our training paid off as we rolled to one side and strove to locate the *adoo*, but they were well out of effective small-arms range. The reason why the enemy rounds were reaching us, despite the range, soon became obvious when we noticed (uneasily) that those rounds striking the ground and rocks around us were detonating with angry cracks and vicious little clouds of whining fragments of metal and rock! We were under fire from a Russian Shpagin heavy machine gun firing bullets with explosive heads; it was nasty to be on the receiving end of and it was particularly frustrating not being able to fire back with our own small arms. However, with a sudden clatter, the Z Company Brownings opened up, its gunners having estimated the approximate position of the Shpagin. The Browning had sufficient range, but it was very difficult to pinpoint the enemy over such a distance. I dashed across to my Landrover and contacted SOAF on the radio. A Strikemaster was scrambled and, within minutes, we were talking to the pilot as he circled overhead. It was a marvellous opportunity to put into practice our recent training with jets in the fighter ground attack (FGA) role. We did so with enthusiasm which the pilot shared as he strafed the area from which our Shpagin was firing with Sura rockets and machine guns. The enemy firing ceased and did not reopen. Perhaps they had suffered casualties, perhaps not. One thing was certain – the Strikemaster had been close, if not on target, and the contact was over. The pilot circled over the area for some time, hoping to detect movement in the thick country below. He then swooped low over us before heading back to the airstrip.

We continued with our patrol until we were north of Salalah and had received a message that the supply convoy was safely back in camp. We headed back for Umm al Ghawarif, passing alongside one of the 'hedgehogs' before entering the perimeter fence. As we did so Abdullah handed me a headset – I was wanted on the radio. The news was sad: Hugh had died of his wound. He was a highly popular and effective officer; not only the Jebel Regiment but SAF as a whole would miss this warm, intelligent and cheerful personality greatly.

By 12 May the handover was completed and Peter Worthy left to join his regiment in Nizwa. NFR Battalion Headquarters and Headquarter Company were installed in Umm al Ghawarif Camp in Salalah. The operations room in the fort was constantly manned by one of my officers who knew to call me should a significant contact be developing on Salalah plain or in the coastal towns. Each evening I held a briefing in the operations room in which everyone was brought up to date on the situation in Dhofar. This briefing was attended by the officers commanding all the units in the area. SOAF, Oman Artillery, Dhofar Gendarmerie, SAS and the Baluch Guard were all represented amongst others, and it was a good opportunity to co-ordinate future operations and administrative matters. If I wasn't in Salalah then Arthur would stand in for me. He had to do rather a lot of that for the last half of May, as I spent most of the time on the *jebel* – either at Sarfait or Habarut.

Sarfait was of particular interest to me at this time for two reasons. The first concerned the occupation of a subsidiary position, nicknamed 'Capstan', between Sarfait scarp and the sea. The second was connected with the planning of an operation, which I was to command, on the PDRY border west of Sarfait.

'Capstan' was the feature on the map which Brigadier John Graham had pointed out during my briefing in Bait al Falaj. If we could establish a force on that prominent feature and link it to Sarfait on one flank, and with the sea on the other, by mines and wire, we would deny easy access to Dhofar from the PFLOAG base at Hauf. It would cause severe problems for the *adoo* – their only alternative routes would be either across the 'moon' country north of Sarfait, or through the open desert even further north. Either way they would be unable to move by day, as they would be quickly spotted by SOAF aircraft.

It was thus recognized that the enemy would fiercely contest any attempt to extend the Simba operation towards the sea. I was interested because the Capstan force was to include one company from DR, Red Company, and, from NFR, B Company under Tresham Gregg. Several reconnaissances had been made by night to examine the best routes to Capstan and these had highlighted two difficulties. The first was immediately apparent: how to get off the Sarfait scarp and into the country below; the cliff in places was sheer; even the best route required the use of ropes in places. It was to be no easy task for heavily equipped soldiers. The second problem showed itself as the recce parties started to move from the bottom of the scarp. The ground was extremely broken and covered in thick bush. From the height of the Sarfait position it had appeared reasonable going – for those down amongst it, it was a different matter. The rate of progress was, at the most, about 2 miles an hour.

These two problems – the steep descent followed by difficult country – presented a third: how to carry sufficient supplies of food, and, vitally, water, to be able to sustain a force on Capstan for the first twenty-four hours or so. Air resupply might well be impractical on the first day. There was no doubt that donkeys could provide the answer to carrying supplies, but how to get them down the cliff? As the move would need to be done at night and silently, in order to achieve surprise, getting the animals to the foot of the scarp was no easy matter. A roping system was eventually devised by Nigel and DR, and was rehearsed after dark, to the accompaniment of much cursing and a more limited amount of muffled laughter. In the event it proved impossible to get the animals down that steep cliff and so that idea was abandoned. The companies had to lift the heavy gear themselves.

The Firqa Tariq bin Zaid under Johnny Braddell-Smith had a close look at Capstan by night. In everyone's minds was the thought that the *adoo* might be on the feature first, waiting eagerly for the SAF force as it clambered along the nightmare route in the dark.

As dusk fell on 23 May, Red Company DR commanded by Major Ben Hodgson of the Parachute Regiment, and Tresham Gregg's B Company of NFR silently roped themselves, their weapons, their ammunition, rations and water down the escarpment. Each man carried a very heavy load. It was the start of a hellish and difficult night. No enemy was seen, but the country proved enemy enough. The descent of the cliff took much longer than the worst pessimist had estimated, which left little time to cover the miles to Capstan before day break. It was a very tired force indeed that eventually arrived, with most of the night gone, at the foot of their objective. The forward scouts reported the feature clear of enemy and the sun rose as the exhausted soldiers were building their sangars. They were on Capstan. As the radio message crackled through the tension eased in the Sarfait operations room. The all-too-possible situation of the force being caught on low ground in daylight had been averted.

It didn't take the *adoo* long to react. They swiftly built up a force of some seventy-five men and made a number of determined attacks on the Capstan position, supported by heavy firing from mortars, machine guns and recoilless guns. In the fierce firefight that ensued, and which continued spasmodically throughout the hours of daylight, SAF gradually achieved the upper hand. It speaks well for the bravery and determination of the *adoo* that they continually pressed forward with a force inferior in numbers to that of the defenders.

Red Company and B Company GPMGs and mortars took their toll, and the enemy casualties mounted. As was their custom they soon split into smaller groups and, although these proved more difficult to locate and hit, they lost the possibility of properly co-ordinating their attacks. SAF casualties in comparison were light, which was just as well, as there were severe difficulties in evacuating the wounded by helicopters which were an easy target for enemy weapons.

At the end of the first day Ben Hodgson was wounded in the arm and was evacuated by helicopter together with two other casualties. Tresham Gregg then took command of the operation and sent out fighting patrols to get the enemy off balance. He also organized ambushes to ensure the *adoo* were not able to surprise the SAF position by night.

Red Company of DR and B Company of NFR had done very well and this was recognized by a number of awards. Ben Hodgson, who initially had commanded the operation received a Bravery Medal, as did Corporal Salim of B Company NFR. Salim had beaten off a number of enemy attacks with his GPMG, coolly engaging his targets effectively, even though his sangar was being slowly destroyed around him by the impact of enemy machine-gun bullets. B Company morale on Capstan could not have been higher, and I attribute this to the leadership displayed by its commander, Tresham Gregg, who was later awarded a Sultan's Commendation. The experience was valuable in shaking down the Company into a well co-ordinated body which had proved itself under fire. The soldiers gained confidence in their officers and NCOs; the commanders, for their part, knew that they could rely on their soldiers; they had passed the test.

Due to the approaching monsoon season, the imminent departure of DR to the north, and the difficulties in resupply and evacuation of casualties from Capstan, it was decided to withdraw the two companies after the initial contact with the large *adoo* force had been successfully concluded. Resupply in particular had proved a major problem. By the end of Day 3 the enemy mortars had zeroed in on the helicopter landing zones which meant that battle-weary soldiers had to collect ammunition, water and rations from the base of the cliff by night.

With the benefit of hindsight it could be argued that to attempt to start the long process of developing the barrier from Sarfait to the sea just before the monsoon closed in was unwise; equally it might be considered that once firm on Capstan the force should have remained as a necessary link in the eventual chain, and from which ambush parties could possibly operate throughout the monsoon. Against this was the stark fact that SAF casualties, with limited forces available, would have been unacceptably high. The main reasons for withdrawal, however, were the enormous problems evacuating casualties, and resupplying water and food.

Anyhow, the decision was made and the two companies were withdrawn to the main feature. Again the move was done by night, but this time the objective was definitely in friendly hands, which reduced the tension felt at the end of the weary march between the two features and as the heavily laden soldiers clambered slowly up the precipitious scarp.

PFLOAG made much of their 'victory' on Radio Aden and their broadcasts were full of the withdrawal of a beaten SAF force. In truth, the *adoo* had suffered heavily in the contact and the propaganda broadcasts from the Yemen Republic rang falsely in the ears of those rebels who had bravely strived, but failed to press home their attacks on Capstan. Ben Hodgson and Tresham Gregg were interested to learn that Radio Aden had reported them both as having been killed during the operation.

The main reason why I was spending time in Sarfait, however, was to plan the operation to the PDRY border to the west and overlooking Hauf. This town, besides housing the notorious school for boys taken from the Dhofar *jebel*, had been a sanctuary, training area and supply base for PFLOAG since 1967. It was a brazen and highly irritating thorn in the Sultanate's side throughout the Dhofar conflict. Things had come to a head on 5 May, when South Yemen forces had opened fire across the border on the Sultanate fort at Habarut. Qaboos complained to the Arab League and subsequently to the United Nations but, rightly considering that such a provocative move by PDRY needed a swifter and firmer answer than would eventually be produced by either organization, he decided to act.

Colonel Mike Harvey, the Commander of Dhofar Area, was called to Bait al Falaj for urgent talks with Brigadier John Graham. On his return he briefed me at Salalah. I was told to plan a three-company operation to secure a position west of Sarfait and on the Dhofar/PDRY border overlooking Hauf. From there we were to control the attacks of SOAF Strikemasters and the shells of the Oman Artillery onto selected targets in the town. These were to include PFLOAG Headquarters, of which we had an adequate description from our intelligence sources. There was no doubt that such an operation would stir up a hornet's nest of *adoo*. A strength of three companies would enable me to piquet the route out and back, and protect my observation post perched on the scarp above Hauf.

I was to take two DR Companies and C Company of NFR, plus elements of the *firqa* Tariq bin Zaid under Johnny Braddell-Smith. After my briefing I flew to Sarfait and spent several days planning. I examined countless air photographs of Hauf and the approaches to the border, and made several helicopter flights, flying well clear of my objective, which I studied through binoculars. Finally I briefed the company commanders, SOAF pilots, the Oman Artillery officer who was to support us and the *firqa* leader. I went into every aspect of the operation in fine detail including the timings and targets of every aircraft sortie. We felt confident and ready to go. All that was required was final political approval to proceed. We expected this approval the night of the briefing and aimed at leaving Sarfait under cover of darkness. Dawn came – but no approval. Dawn broke the next day without approval ... and the next ... and the next. Nerves were beginning to get rather frayed and I had several heated radio conversations with Headquarters Dhofar. At last, after four nights being poised to go, we were told that the ground operation was off – for political reasons. The Strikemasters would still go in as planned – the pilots had sufficient details of all the targets to enable them to attack without a ground controller. The Oman Artillery guns in Sarfait would fire their planned programme too, albeit without the benefit of a forward observation officer correcting the fall of shots.

On 25 May the Strikemaster and artillery attacks went in and continued intermittently until the 27th. All the military targets were accurately struck as planned; some secondary explosions and fires were seen afterwards. It was a stern lesson to PFLOAG for their cross-border excursions.

The Strikemasters did not have it all their own way and there was a good deal of return fire. Squadron Leader Peter Hulme's aircraft was hit by a Shpagin heavy machine gun as he participated in the final air strike. As he was attacking an enemy storage area with rockets a round severed his aircraft's main electrical cable and ruptured the fuel pipe. The radio would not work, and fuel and vapour poured into the cockpit. Although Peter's first thought was to eject over Sarfait, which would have been the safest option, he decided to try and get his aircraft back to Salalah. Despite running out of fuel short of the airstrip he glided in and made a perfect flame-out landing. He was awarded the Sultan's Gallantry Medal for saving his aircraft in this courageous way – we needed all the Strikemasters we could hang on to!

On 28 May Sultan Qaboos spoke to his people via Radio Oman in Muscat.* In this he explained why the cross-border attack was made and he took the opportunity to strongly re-emphasize two points. The first concerned the absence of Islam in PFLOAG ideology, compared with the Omani way of life, where the cornerstone was the Koran. The second was a reminder of the development programme for the country already in train.

It later transpired that a total of seventeen PFLOAG members were killed during the aircraft attacks and shelling of Hauf, one of whom was the leader of the 'Political House'. Perhaps the most significant aspect of the whole affair, however, was that although a protest was made to the UN by the PDRY Government over the bombing at Habarut (see following chapter), no such representation was made with regard to the strike against Hauf. Certainly the activities in that little town would not stand up to close scrutiny by an independent observer.

Having drawn up the plans for the Hauf operation, my task at Sarfait was over and I flew back to Salalah. B and C Companies would move shortly afterwards, once the Desert Regiment at Sarfait had been relieved by Bill Kerr and the Muscat Regiment from Nizwa in the north.

---

* An English translation of this speech is at Appendix 1.

Chapter 9

The Fight at Habarut and the Battle for Marbat

Habarut lies precisely on the border between Dhofar and South Yemen, some 50-odd miles north-west of Sarfait. It consists – or used to consist – of two forts, one on either side of the frontier; there were no other buildings. The importance of the area for the tribes lay in the shallow wells in the bed of the Wadi Habarut, a tributary of the great Wadi Atina, which wound down from the sands to the north.

The Sultanate fort was garrisoned by a platoon – some twenty-odd soldiers – of the Dhofar Gendarmerie (DG) and, early in May, Second Lieutenant Hassan Ehsan was the officer in charge. Life was pleasant for the Habarut garrison: there was plenty of water and news to be exchanged with the tribesmen who watered their camels amongst the date palms fringing the wells. Relations were cordial between the SAF soldiers and those of the PDRY who manned the opposite fort – after all we were fighting PFLOAG not the Yemeni Army! Live and let live was the order of the day. Hassan Ehsan felt confident that the Mahra and Bait Kathir herdsmen at the wells would tip him off about any PFLOAG parties attempting to cross into Dhofar from South Yemen, he was in daily radio communication with Salalah and could swiftly pass on any useful news which he might glean.

Early on the morning of 5 May, before the blood-red sun had lifted over the Jebel al Qamar, the peaceful routine at Habarut was rudely and suddenly shattered for Hassan and his men by the ugly thump of mortars and the stammer of heavy machine guns firing from the PDRY fort. The Dhofar Gendarmerie were taken completely by surprise and the Garrison lost five killed, which included a member of the local *firqa*, almost immediately. After the initial shock Hassan Ehsan collected and controlled his force, and supervised the defence of the Sultanate fort with the platoon's small arms. He opened his radio link with Salalah and kept a startled duty officer at Headquarters Dhofar informed of the situation.

It was impossible for SAF to fly in reinforcements that day due to the heavy fire from the PDRY infantry, and an attempt by a helicopter to fly in to lift casualties was warned off by Hassan. The attack continued throughout the day; that night Hassan lost another man killed and two soldiers were wounded when a mortar bomb plunged through the roof.

The next day a relieving force consisting of half of Red Company of the Desert Regiment was flown in from Sarfait by helicopter. Having occupied suitable ground on the Sultanate side of the besieged fort they opened up on the enemy with mortars and machine guns. That same day SOAF dropped warning leaflets onto the PDRY which stated that severe retaliatory action would follow in the absence of a ceasefire. The Yemeni guns and mortars continued, however, and SOAF Strike-masters strafed the aggressors with machine guns and rockets before depositing a 500lb bomb squarely on the PDRY fort itself.

That night Hassan withdrew his force under cover of darkness and the area was evacuated (Red Company was shortly to be required for Capstan). Hassan Ehsan's courageous performance at Habarut was recognized by a bravery award from the Sultan. It was later learnt that the former leader of the 'Ho Chi Minh Unit' (which was tasked to guard the *jebel* supply trails) was relieved of his command early in 1972 in order to plan and carry out the attack on the Sultanate fort at Habarut. He was killed by the SOAF strike on 6 May.

As already mentioned in the previous chapter, it is interesting to note that immediately after the SOAF retaliation attack at Habarut the PDRY Government lodged a protest with the United Nations. After the far more destructive attack on Hauf, however, no protest was made. Perhaps Aden was disenchanted with the PFLOAG rebels. Whatever the reasons Oman gained political credence as a result of the two incidents, at the expense of the PDRY's good name.

Habarut could not be left unoccupied, however, for a number of reasons. 'Face' must rank as an important factor, and the area with its water and confluence of camel trails was one which SAF needed to keep under observation. C Company NFR was therefore ordered on 22 May to re-establish a *jaysh* (army) presence at Habarut. The Company flew smoothly in by helicopter from Sarfait, and Peter Tawell established his platoon positions on the high ground on either side of the wadi and overlooking the two forts. There was no opposition. Peter sited his company headquarters in the wadi itself and then took a patrol to the Sultanate fort, where he discovered a shambles. South Yemeni soldiers had placed explosive charges within the building and had reduced it to a shell. Peter quite correctly left the shattered fort unoccupied and his company remained on its commanding piquet positions.

The next morning mortar fire was opened on C Company's position from across the border. Peter replied effectively with a pack howitzer, which had been flown in by the Oman Artillery, and with his own 81mm mortars. One or two of the enemy rounds fell on to the Company Headquarters area which was well located under the steep wadi side. It looked, and was, as safe a position as was possible, which made it all the more tragic when Abdul Majid, C Company Sergeant Major, was killed by a mortar fragment. A tiny splinter struck Abdul in the head, hardly leaving a mark and, unbelievably, he pitched forward onto his face close to his Company Commander. Abdul was a delightful and brave personality. Easily recognizable by the pork-pie hat he sported on operations instead of the customary *shemagh,* he was a close friend of Peter's.

I heard the news about the renewed fighting at Habarut and of Abdul's death on the radio and, taking Medhi, our Medical Officer, flew immediately to the area by helicopter. The pilot approached at high altitude before swooping suddenly and sickeningly down in close circles to within feet of the wadi bed. As soon as Medhi and I had leapt clear, the helicopter swerved off and disappeared at very low level indeed, travelling along the course of the wadi. It would return to pick us up later that day – *In sha'allah* (God willing!)

Medhi had accompanied me in case there were any wounded and we stood in the wadi feeling rather exposed – it was my first visit to Habarut and I had no idea of Peter's dispositions. One thing was certain – they were brilliantly concealed! 'Hello, Colonel. Nice to see you, Medhi,' and we spied Peter and Christopher Kemball, the Company Second in Command, approaching through the tangled palms at the wadi edge.

Peter showed me round his platoon positions in detail, while Medhi made his own tour, treating cuts, bruises, gashes and disorders; and dispensing a great deal of laughter and warmth as he did so. I was happy that it would take a much larger force than ever could be mustered by the enemy to dislodge C Company soldiers from their well-chosen positions. Peter had sited his weapons to provide mutual support for his platoons, and also to cover the PDRY fort and area. His pack howitzer had a wonderful field of fire and its grinning Omani gunners had obviously enjoyed their recent action. One of them was polishing the breech as I approached and tapped the elderly muzzle affectionately with his hand as he extolled the gun's virtues to me.

That afternoon, with a small patrol, Medhi and I walked down the wadi for about half a mile or so until we reached the main well. Up to that time the Company had lived on the water it flew in with, and an air resupply of two gallons per man per day had been arranged. For the longer term, however, it would obviously be better if water could be obtained locally, and much more economical too. Two gallons per man was twice the normal ration, but Habarut was blisteringly hot – the impact of the noon sun was like a physical blow from a scalding hand. Within the wadi bed itself, and in Peter's Headquarters, the shade temperature was well over 120F, and there was not a breath of cooling breeze. The night brought little relief, the rocks seeming to store up the heat from the sun and the temperature in the wadi remaining at about 95 throughout the hours of darkness.

On arrival at the well we saw three dead frogs floating in the water – not a promising sight. I took a sample of the water for Medhi to have analysed at Salalah in case it had been poisoned by the PDRY force – although this was an act that by ancient and unwritten law was considered unthinkable. There had been no cases as far as I knew in the Dhofar War up to then. In the event the water was pronounced unfit for human consumption, although whether this was due to poison or not I have never been able to discover.

Late in the afternoon we heard the clatter of the returning helicopter's rotors and the pilot's voice came through on the radio asking for clearance to land. Medhi and I moved out to the landing pad having said goodbye to Peter and Christopher, and their men. I was happy and confident after seeing what I had of C Company, but they had suffered a cruel blow in the loss of Abdul Majid. *'Allah Kareem,'* said the soldiers (God is Generous) – like my Somali who had lost his wife under the wheels of my truck so many years ago. (He giveth and He taketh away.)

In came the helicopter and the dust leapt from the wadi under the whirling blades. Medhi and I got in quickly, and some empty water jerricans and a mail bag were thrown in beside us. No SOAF chopper pilot lingered on the ground a moment longer than was absolutely necessary and we dived away down the wadi, twisting and turning before climbing steeply until we were beyond small-arms range.

On the western edge of the Salalah Plain, close to the *jebel* is a place called Adonib. A waterhole in the wadi of the same name gave it its importance, and the Bait Kathir and Bait Said tribes watered their stock there. The Firqa Bait Said was based at Adonib with half of A Company NFR under Bob Hudson (David Nichols still had the other half at Manston). Bob was carrying out a patrolling and ambushing programme on the tracks frequented by the *adoo* which ran east to west along the seaward edge of the *jebel*. I wanted to see something of

91

A Company and find out how their operations were developing, so, as our route from Habarut back to Salalah passed close to Adonib, I asked our pilot to drop me off.

I remained with Bob and Simon Hill of the Parachute Regiment overnight and was impressed with the imaginative and daring ambushes which they were carrying out. Simon, a small dark man, tough as old leather and burnt about the same colour, told me enthusiastically about an ambush he was about to lay. High on the scarp he had discovered a cave with evidence of enemy occupation. He planned to occupy it by night with one or two of his men and remain there for a couple of days – the evidence pointed to the fact that it was visited by an *adoo* group regularly. This was the sort of work which required courage of a very cool and disciplined order. I questioned Simon closely to make sure all unnecessary risks had been eliminated and that there were arrangements for a relief force to go to his aid if necessary. The plan had been worked out meticulously, but despite all precautions was still of a high-risk nature. Simon's point – and it was valid – was that anyone sitting waiting in a cave, or even (and he later tried this too) at the bottom of a wadi, had such an advantage of initial surprise that they should win the firefight even against a larger superior number of enemy. Easy in theory, but not all possessed the iron nerve to see them through the long waiting hours. The bushes all seem to crawl at night as I had noticed many times myself!

A Company soldiers were cheerful and confident, obviously impressed and proud of their officers' aggressive patrolling pattern. It was a hard and fit company taking on the style of its leaders as often happens in infantry units and sub-units. I was surprised and disappointed to hear, however, that their impressive Bedu Sergeant Major – Hamood – had pleaded compassionate problems and was anxious to go on leave to northern Oman. Although genuine enough, his difficulties at home did not seem to be of such importance to necessitate a key man being away from the Company at a time of such significant operations on the *jebel*. I could tell that Bob and Simon were disappointed too. Eventually we sent Hamood back to sort out his affairs – but his real reasons for wishing to go on leave at that time were to become only too apparent several months later.

On my return to Salalah I soon became heavily involved in the day-to-day business of organizing and running the defence of Salalah, in addition to the patrol and ambush operations on the plains and in the foothills. I was busy, too, visiting and getting to know the units I was responsible for as Plains Commander.

At the end of May, NFR Companies adjusted to a new pattern of locations and tasks. A Company was complete in Adonib, David

Nichols having brought in his two platoons from Manston. Simon Hill was now the Company Commander and Bob Hudson had become my Adjutant. The Company's task in Adonib remained to patrol and ambush the *adoo* resupply routes, and prevent enemy movement onto the plain from the west.

C Company handed over Habarut, which was now all quiet, to the Oman Gendarmerie who were flown in from the north and were to look after the area in the long term, on a company rotation basis. C Company, free of Habarut, then relieved David Nichols at Manston. The task for Christopher Kemball (Peter Tawell being on leave) was to protect the Simba airhead and, in addition, to patrol and ambush vigorously with the aim of destroying any enemy groups in the area. This he proceeded to do effectively.

B Company moved in to Salalah, the Capstan task over, the Muscat Regiment relieved the Desert Regiment at Sarfait and would sit tight on the *jebel* during the monsoon. (MR received almost daily heavy mortar and RCL fire from all directions during the next few months. An average number of 'incomers' was about forty, although on 20 August a total of sixty-one rounds fell accurately on the position. Luckily – thanks to the excellent sangars – casualties were light.) In Salalah, B Company was responsible for patrolling and ambushes on the plains, and was available for any additional operations ordered by me or by the Dhofar Commander, Colonel Mike Harvey. Later (see Chapter 11), when the Company was tasked with helping to train the Iranian Special Forces, they carried out an ambush operation, but this was aborted when an Iranian officer was wounded in the back by one of his own soldiers. Tresham was not impressed.

On 8 June 1972, the eve of the fourth anniversary of PFLOAG's revolution in Dhofar, an *adoo* group, which had evaded our ambushes and patrols, fired two 75mm RCL rounds at RAF Salalah. The first shell was wide of the mark and exploded harmlessly, but the second was on target and struck an earth-filled plant box on the Officers' Mess verandah. Unfortunately, a group of officers were sitting only a few feet away enjoying an evening drink. Although the earth absorbed a proportion of the force of the explosion, several officers were injured. Two were seriously hurt, one of whom was Peter Hulme who had so recently been awarded the Sultan's Gallantry Medal for the Hauf operation. Peter was evacuated to a hospital in the United Kingdom, but happily returned to Oman in due course, limping but operational.

It was another occasion when we blessed the presence of the Field Surgical Team in Salalah. The FST was staffed by Royal Army Medical Corps doctors from the UK who performed amazing operations in their canvas theatre at the airport. Immediately outside their post was a helicopter pad which delivered the wounded from the *jebel* so that soldiers were being operated on in some cases literally minutes after being hit. Many lives were saved by this excellent team, and its presence was a major boost to the morale of those involved in the fighting.

The shelling of the airfield showed how the *adoo* liked to mark appropriate anniversaries with attacks on the Salalah Plain, and we thought that this habit could perhaps be turned to SAF's advantage. The anniversary of the accession of Qaboos as Sultan was due later in June. The previous year this event had been acknowledged by PFLOAG with mortar and RCL attacks against three hedgehog positions and the airport, where two helicopters and an aircraft hangar were damaged. Subsequently SAF had discovered the enemy mortar base plate position and had recorded the grid reference. This year we would be ready for them and I mounted Operation Narr (fire) to lay ambushes in a number of likely enemy approaches. After dark we established ourselves quietly in position in the foothills, having walked for several miles, as the noise of vehicles would obviously have given the game away.

On the left was Simon Hill with A Company from Adonib; his task was to ambush the Wadi Thimrin where it entered the *jebel* and the surrounding area. In the centre was B Company with Tresham Gregg, watching the Wadi Jarsis. My own tactical headquarters consisting of myself, Jebali and Abdullah the Silent (plus radio) was located with B Company. Alongside me was Hugh Colley, the Commander of the Oman Artillery, who would come into his own in the second phase of the operation. On the right flank was the colourful character Raye Barker-Schofield with a combat group from the Dhofar Gendarmerie. Working with him was the Firqa Qaboos,* their joint task being to lie in wait in the Wadi Arzat at the bottom of the escarpment. Finally, the *Firqa* Sahaladin (named after that famous and feared Muslim warrior) covered the immediate approaches to the airfield and gave depth to our ambush positions. In reserve in one of the hedgehogs were Spike Powell's Z Company Landrovers, ready to reinforce any area or to cut off enemy groups trying to escape the net. Standing silently but ready were the guns of the Oman Artillery, having been moved to a position within range of the *jebel*, and the aircraft of SOAF.

I have gone into some detail on the organization of Operation Narr as it was typical of a number we carried out and I believe that they prevented a number of *adoo* attacks during the *khareef* (monsoon).

---

* Previously named Firqa Jaboob, it was formed from the Bait Jaboob tribesmen living in the Wadi Arzat area.

Throughout the hours of darkness we lay, eyes sore from peering, or trying to peer, through the gloom. On this occasion the ambushes were not sprung. We saw no *adoo*, but there were no attacks on the plain. As daylight came I told Hugh Colley to engage areas which intelligence sources had indicated were occupied by the enemy. We could pinpoint these exactly from our positions at the foot of the escarpment. Clearly it was vital that no *jebali* civilian was endangered by this bombardment and we had taken extensive and careful precautions to ensure this could not happen. Hugh gave the orders to his guns and quickly and precisely the fall of shots were corrected by the forward observation officers with A and B Companies.

It was a lesson in accurate gunnery and afterwards, through those same intelligence sources, we learnt that the enemy had suffered casualties; but perhaps more importantly, the gunfire had been so un-expected and effective that the wavering morale of the less-committed *adoo* had been lowered. The number of SEPs steadily increased, with a corresponding swelling in the size of the *firqas* loyal to the Sultan.

Immediately following Operation Narr *we* mounted another – Operation Moyya (water). This was primarily aimed at trying out the newly raised Firqa al Mutaharika under its ex-*adoo* leader Hilal Fadhallah.* I had talked to Hilal at length in my office in Umm al Ghawarif fort immediately following his defection from PFLOAG and I had been impressed with him. He had a fine strong face, a steady piercing gaze and a sense of humour. Thin and hard, he looked every inch a tribal warrior. It is not always that a man's personality is reflected in his face, but it often is – I had found this particularly so with the Somalis and found the same again now with the Dhofaris. I had, of course, been wrong a number of times, but I would put my money on Hilal as a brave, honest man and a good leader.

During our talk Hilal had told me that he had knowledge of a small enemy group occupying a piquet position in the Wadi Jarsis. This was the tribal area of the Firqa al Mutaharika and I listened attentively. Hilal wanted to attack the enemy piquet with support from SAF and I agreed immediately. Operation Moyya was launched – water to follow the fire!

Moving after dusk, Tresham Gregg and B Company NFR established a firm base in the *jebel* foothills, within the Wadi Jarsis. From this position Hilal and his men moved swiftly forward on bare feet over the sharp rocks of the wadi bed, climbing silently upwards into the mountains. The men of the Mutaharika knew every inch of the way. As

* After I had left I learnt that Hilal had achieved a reputation as one of the outstanding and most successful *firqa* commanders.

boys they had herded their goats along these same precipitious paths, courted their women on the bush-clad slopes and had fought against raiding tribes over these rugged gorges. It did not take them long over such familiar terrain to reach the enemy hill which stood in the wadi. A small bump in the valley; a boil to be lanced. The whispered word received from their brothers and cousins was proved true – a group of three or four *adoo* were resting at the spot and saw Hilal's men approach. There was a fierce exchange of fire and the enemy fled, carrying a wounded man with them. Hilal followed up for a short distance, but conscious of the need to return to the firm base before daybreak, broke off the chase. The *firqa* slipped back through B Company who remained in position to ambush any *adoo* follow-up groups; there were none.

I was pleased with the way that this new and untried *firqa* had pressed through to its objective, and I formally paraded the Mutaharika and warmly congratulated Hilal in front of his men. I felt encouraged by this small operation and it enhanced my optimism for the future of the province.

The 19th of July 1972 was to prove a significant date in the Dhofar War. In retrospect, the battle that was fought that day was recognized as being the turning point of the conflict and became known as the Battle of Marbat. More correctly, perhaps, it was the battle *for* Marbat.*

Marbat drew its livelihood from the sea – a row of fishing boats were drawn up on the pale beach and nets were strung out to dry along the baking strand. Many of its small white houses had wooden doors and shutters beautifully carved with Islamic designs. It was, and still is, a picturesque and beautiful spot. In 1972 only a tortuous track connected it to Salalah, some 70 or so miles to the west. This track was subject to ambush by the *adoo* who would clamber down the precipitous cliffs of the Jebel Samhan by night and lie up during the day.

Being such an isolated and vulnerable spot, pinched between the sea and the frowning *jebel*, it had its own small garrison of regular and irregular troops. These included a detachment of Dhofar Gendarmerie (DG), a 25pdr gun manned by a couple of Oman Artillery gunners, a group of *Wali's askars*, the Firqa Gamal Abdul Nasser[†] and a detachment

* Also spelt Mirbat. Vowels are not always written in Arabic script which results in alterations in transliteration.

The battle is recorded in detail in *Who Dares Wins* by Tony Geraghty and also in *SAS Operation Oman* by Tony Jeapes.

[†] In the event this *firqa* was away on the day of the battle. It had responded to enemy diversionary tactics and disappeared deep into the mountains.

of B Squadron SAS – nine men under the command of Captain Michael Kealy. Resupply of this small force was done by helicopter.

North of the town, and separated from it by a shallow wadi, was a huddle of buildings which included the market, the *Wali's* fort manned by *askars* and the 'Batt House' containing the SAS group. Some 500 yards to the north-west was the fort containing the DG with, alongside it, an emplacement containing the 25pdr gun. The entire town, including both forts, was embraced by a barbed-wire perimeter fence.

About a mile north-east of the town was an isolated – and therefore dominating – hill known as Jebel Ali. It was a significant feature as far as the defence arrangements for Marbat were concerned, and had not been ignored by those responsible for the safety of the town. On top of the *jebel* was a sangar occupied by a section of the Dhofar Gendarmerie. By day this lookout position commanded a fine view of the approaches to the town from the north and the east; by night it was a valuable listening post.

As the pale fingers of dawn touched the sky on the start of what was to be a long and bloody day, the sentry on duty in the Jebel Ali sangar saw a shadow move ... move, take shape, and become a man; then divide and become two men, before splitting again to form a stealthily advancing group. Frantically the sentry seized his rifle and shouted wildly to his comrades, aimed his weapon, fired a single shot, and died in a flashing explosion of grenades and a ripple of AK47 automatic fire. In the firefight that followed four of his fellow gendarmes died too, their bodies leaping under the impact of flying fragments and bullets. The remaining four men of the section escaped.

The taking out of the Jebel Ali piquet served as a signal for over 250 hard-core *adoo* of the Ho Chi Minh and the Central and Eastern Units who were lying waiting in the cold dawn. They had assembled on top of Jebel Samhan having travelled many miles from all areas of the mountains. Never before had the enemy assembled such a large force to oppose the SAF. It was an impressive achievement over such difficult terrain. Just before dawn the *adoo* scrambled down the 500-foot escarpment and lay in wait.

On the signal a heavy mortar bombardment was directed at the town, and particularly at the forts and buildings to the north. The *adoo* rose to their feet and moved from their positions north and east of Marbat, heading determinedly for the perimeter wire. Their aim was to kill the defenders and to capture the town; they were confident of success and fanatically prepared to die in order to achieve it.

Kealy and his men were alerted by the thump of mortars and the crashing reports of the bombs falling within the perimeter fence. They ran to their stand-to positions and were amazed to see scores of enemy in the half-light, loping towards them in knots of a dozen or so men. Quickly the SAS brought their .50-inch Browning machine gun, a single 81mm mortar and their rifles into action. The sudden roar of the 25pdr gun proved that Gunner Walid Khamis was also alert. The *Wali's askars*, excitedly shouting from their fort, swelled the noise with their ancient rifles. They were to fight well that day.

For five hours the battle raged. In terms of warfare it was small in scale, involving comparatively few men, but for those participating the size of the affray was of no significance – it was a fierce conflict, with bravery shown on both sides. The most bitterly contested area was that of the 25pdr gun position, and it was here that the enemy pressed home their most determined attacks. The gun itself fell silent and Mike Kealy took Trooper Tobin, the detachment medic, and dashed the several hundred yards from the Batt House, under heavy fire the whole way. In the gun position Kealy found a dead soldier of the DG and three badly wounded men: Corporal Labalaba and Trooper 'T', both Fijian SAS men, and Walid Khamis of the Oman Artillery. A further soldier of the DG was also lying, unwounded but shocked, in the bottom of the sangar.

Kealy was immediately involved in close-quarter fighting with the *adoo*, who were attempting to get through the wire, while Tobin did what he could for the wounded. Labalaba, despite an appalling face wound, was loading the 25pdr gun and firing it over open sights at point-blank range at the shrieking enemy. Trooper 'T', bleeding freely from head and shoulder wounds, sat with his back propped against the bunker wall while he accurately picked off the *adoo* on his side with his rifle. Suddenly Corporal Labalaba fell soundlessly to the ground. The big Fijian was dead. Not long afterwards Tobin fell too, mortally wounded. It was left to Kealy and Trooper 'T', one on either side of that nightmare sangar, to hold off the fanatical *adoo* horde. It was a scene made even more hideous by the shattering din of exploding grenades, and the screams of the wounded. Kealy ordered the unwounded DG soldier to fill the spare rifle magazines and this the man did, working feverishly and passing them up to the two brave defenders.

Kealy recalled afterwards:

I fired at the one who was threatening 'T' and he disappeared. His body was later found. I then engaged the enemy on the right of the fort and managed to hit one of them. While this engagement was taking place the enemy on left and right threw grenades. Several exploded near us and one landed by the wounded but failed to explode. I heard a light machine gun and thought I had been hit as something passed through my hair. Then the enemy breached the wire and were twenty metres inside when the first jet strike came in. They then turned back and retreated. I placed an air panel on the body in the bunker so that our position would be known.

Without the timely and then continuing intervention by the SOAF Strikemasters, which had been called in by Kealy, the gun position must have fallen, and perhaps the town of Marbat too. But intervene they certainly did, with shattering effect on the surprised enemy. They had taken off in misty monsoon conditions which would normally have prevented any flying at all – let alone attempt such abnormally close support to our own troops, in some cases down to a few yards. Despite a hail of bullets from a variety of weapons, the pilots strafed the *adoo* on the perimeter wire with cannon fire and hit those further away with bombs. They kept up their attacks until out of fuel and, having filled up at Salalah, returned to their task once more. Two aircraft were severely damaged; it is a miracle that none were lost. The Strikemasters formed one of the two decisive cards played that day. The second resulted from sheer chance – a happy and remarkable coincidence.

B Squadron SAS, of which the Marbat detachment was a part, was due to be relieved by G Squadron the following day. On the morning of the attack the newly arrived G Squadron was getting ready in Umm al Gharawif camp to check its weapons on the ranges at Ma'Murah. Each man, therefore, was dressed in fighting order and ammunition was ready for issue. Vehicles were standing by. It was the only day in its Dhofar tour of duty that the Squadron was going to operate as a whole; thereafter it would split into small teams and disperse widely in the province in order to take over a variety of operational tasks. When news of the assault came through on the radio, the Squadron was rushed in the waiting vehicles to Salalah Airport and ferried by helicopters to the beach about 3,500 yards south-east of the beseiged town.

Operating in groups of ten men, G Squadron skirmished forward to Marbat, taking on a number of enemy parties en route and defeating them by skillful use of fire and movement – in army parlance, 'pepper-potting', one group supporting another. A total of nine *adoo* were killed and four wounded in this way, without loss to the SAS. Eventually the advancing SAS reached the perimeter wire; Marbat was relieved!

Making use of the relieving force helicopters, a platoon of B Company NFR under Graeme Smyth-Piggott reoccupied the Jebel Ali piquet to the north of the town. The enemy force withdrew to the north and took most of their dead and wounded with them, but not all. Twenty-nine enemy bodies lay within the perimeter fence in Marbat, and nine badly wounded fighters were also left behind; three enemy had been captured by the SAS relieving force. A *firqa* follow-up group later made contact with the withdrawing *adoo* 10 miles north of Marbat and claimed killing a further nine. The most reliable estimate of the total final figure of enemy dead was later given as eighty-six with an unspecified number wounded. A total of seven of the Marbat Garrison were killed and a further twelve wounded.

On 23 and 24 July, while the memories of those who took part in the battle were still fresh, I took statements from Captain Mike Kealy and some of his men, and from the Officer Commanding G Squadron. I passed my report to the Commanding Officer of 22 SAS. No publicity could be given to the event at the time in the interests of security, but four years later a number of gallantry awards were made. Mike Kealy was decorated with the DSO. The SAS Corporal who directed the supporting fire and in particular controlled the aircraft strikes received the Military Medal. Trooper Tobin was awarded the DCM and Corporal Labalaba was also decorated – both, alas, posthumuously.

Gunner Walid Khamis, of the Oman Artillery, was decorated by Sultan Qaboos to mark his gallantry and two SOAF pilots received bravery awards: Squadron Leader Neville Baker, who flew a casualty-evacuating helicopter, and Squadron Leader Stoker, who led the Strikemasters, and whose aircraft was one of the two badly damaged by *adoo* fire.

When I took his statement, G Squadron Commander, a modest Guardsman, summed up the scene at the DG Fort and the 25pdr gun position at the end of the battle. Speaking quietly he played down his own vital part in the day's action (for which he too was later decorated) but spoke with feeling as he described his arrival at the Marbat perimeter wire.

When I reached the Fort I was speechless at the sight of that area. There were pools of blood from the wounded, 84 millimetre blinds [unexploded projectiles], many rings from grenades, and the 25 pounder gun was holed many times through the shield. The ground was scarred by the many grenades which had exploded. It was obvious that an extremely fierce close-quarter battle had been fought there. Each member of Captain Kealy's men made a point of coming up to tell me of that Officer's action and all that he had done. They told me that he was the bravest man they had ever seen. From my own observation it was obvious that Captain Kealy's action had saved the gun and the Fort. Also, I sincerely believe that his inspired leadership and bravery had saved the lives of his men, and the town of Marbat from being captured.

In 1979, Mike Kealy, then a Major, died of exposure while taking part in an exercise in the Brecon Beacons in Wales. I had known him since 1965 when he was commissioned into the Queen's Royal Surrey Regiment and posted to my Company in the First Battalion in Munster. He was a delightful personality with a broad, unique sense of humour. He was the Hero of Marbat – a brave man among brave men.

Chapter 10

Change of Commanders and More *Jebel* Operations

The Sultan's Armed Forces, together with the irregular *Firqa* Forces, were steadily increasing in numbers in the early 1970s. Also growing slowly was a realization in the British Government of the seriousness of the PFLOAG threat to Dhofar, to Oman, to the Gulf, and thus, a frightening thought, to Western oil supplies.

These two growths – in Oman's forces and in UK concern – prompted two decisions. The first was to elevate the ranks of the officers due to replace Brigadier John Graham as Commander SAF (CSAF) and Colonel Mike Harvey as Commander Dhofar, when these two completed their highly successful second tours of duty in Oman. The second was to establish a subsidiary Headquarters in the north and to post in a full colonel from the British Army to command it.

Thus when the dust cleared, the command structure showed Major General T.M. (Tim) Creasey OBE as CSAF, with his Headquarters in Bait al Falaj. Two autonomous subordinate commands were formed: Dhofar Brigade, based in Salalah and headed by Brigadier J.S. (Jack) Fletcher OBE (of my Regiment), and Headquarters Northern Oman with Colonel J.G.F. (John) Head MBE, an Irish Guardsman, at the helm.

The first of these newcomers to arrive was Brigadier Jack Fletcher, in August 1972, and I was very pleased indeed to see him. I respected him as a dynamic, imaginative and thoughtful commander, and as a brave soldier. He was also an admirable friend and a man with a strong sense of humour, reflected in an eye that twinkled more than most. Jack had commanded the Battalion in which I was a company commander in Northern Ireland. His were the first soldiers to walk down the sad shambles of the Shankill and the Falls Road on 14 August 1969. The Battalion remained in the city for over a year after that and Jack had proved his outstanding merit as Commanding Officer over and over again, and had been decorated with an OBE (Gallantry) as a result. It was some measure of HMG's enhanced awareness of the Dhofar situation that a man of Jack's calibre and potential had been sent to Oman. His arrival was followed by another 'proper soldier' and giant personality – the new CSAF General Creasey, a brilliant commander and the perfect man for the job.

Until Jack's bungalow, which was being built outside Salalah and by the sea, was ready for occupation, he stayed with me in my quarters in Umm al Ghawarif Camp. He addressed himself to the task of learning all he could about the Dhofar War, and then personally conducted operations with an enthusiasm and energy which quickly earned him the nickname of 'Dynamite Jack'!

Just before this change of command in Dhofar, I had switched NFR rifle companies in their tasks. A Company relieved C in Manston, and C Company came in to Salalah to take over from B. Thus released, B Company moved to Adonib to carry out patrols and ambushes on the same lines as their predecessors in A Company.

Later Jack nicknamed the Adonib activity 'Operation Hornbeam' and allotted me three Augusta Bell 205 helicopters for use by the company there. Tresham Gregg and B Company employed these to good effect. The task at Adonib was unchanged: to prevent enemy movement and resupply from the west. To achieve this B Company operated in two halves, each of two platoons. At any time half the company was on the *jebel* patrolling and ambushing by day and night, while the other half remained at Adonib. The length of a patrol varied between three to five days, and was normally lifted in to its area by helicopter relays and resupplied with water daily by air wherever the patrol happened to be. It might be thought that the clattering choppers, their blade-wash producing miniature sandstorms, would utterly jeopardize the patrol position and ruin its effectiveness. Not a bit of it. We turned what might be a severe limitation to our advantage. For instance, two platoons (normally about two lifts of three 205s, or three lifts of two aircraft each) would leave Adonib and their aircraft would touch down at point 'A' on the *jebel* for a couple of minutes. They would then fly off to point 'B' and repeat the procedure, and point 'C' too, perhaps, before returning to Adonib. The platoons might have got out at any one, or two, or perhaps three of these points as far as the enemy were concerned. Yes, SAF were on the *jebel*; yes they would be patrolling and ambushing – but where? When? There were many permutations on this theme (including empty helicopters and no patrol at all) and tricks could be played with resupply aircraft and the recovery of the patrol on the same lines.

Operation Hornbeam was proving extremely effective and we were making it very difficult for the *adoo* to get through the area. It was a strain on the Adonib Company, both physically on all and mentally on the commanders. The patrolling rate was intense and the soldiers became very hard, fit and lean. ('Fined down like race horses,' Penelope Tremayne, a rare visiting journalist put it.)

At Manston, A Company, hardened by many weeks in Adonib, commenced patrols to try and contact enemy parties and bring them to battle. I accompanied Simon Hill, David Nichols and their men on one of these. We walked through the night along a fearsomely rocky wadi bed to ambush a waterhole at dawn. We didn't see any enemy, but we certainly covered some miles, and I was impressed by the expertise shown by the soldiers. Their movement was silent, with no clattering of boots or weapons, and at halts they sank quietly into an outward-facing circle, each man with his rifle at the ready. There was a furnace-like heat in the wadi, retained even at night, and this, together with the physical effort in clambering over boulders and stones for hour after hour, was cruelly debilitating to any but the fittest. I can recall the night well because of the 'Khamikaze moths', as we called them. These large and meaty insects, for some reason unknown to me, constantly flew noisily into our faces with a fearful whack and a whirring of wings. Perhaps they were attracted by our eyes showing whitely in the dark – whatever the reason they were highly annoying to sweating and heavily laden men picking their way carefully over rough ground whilst denied the luxury of a muttered curse or two.

For some time the problem of the RCL and mortar attacks on Salalah during the monsoon had exercised the minds of those concerned with the security of the Plain, the last of these having resulted in the wounding of Peter Hulme and others at RAF Salalah. Since then, thanks to the Operation Hornbeam patrols, there had been fewer stand-off attacks, but the possibility remained. Brigadier Jack came up with the idea of a new hedgehog sited to the north-west of the airfield, but nearer to the *jebel* than the other four. Near enough, in fact, for a .50 calibre Browning machine gun and a 81mm mortar placed there to be able to engage the enemy gun or base-plate position in the foothills. If the hedgehog was located near enough to the escarpment the chances of detecting an enemy weapon from its muzzle flash or dust disturbance would be enhanced.

Jack asked me to look into the possibilities of constructing such a position and, if we went ahead, arrange the manning of it. I spent some time out on the plain in my Landrover with Mohamed, Abdullah and Jebali. We stuck to the recognized procedure of avoiding other vehicle tracks in case of mines and, where we were forced to cross a suspicious patch I made Jebali jump out and probe our proposed path with his bayonet. He did this with an enthusiasm and panache which made me blanch but, luckily, we found no mines.

We found the ideal spot for our hedgehog in an area locally known as T'Shok. Not only was it close enough to the *jebel*, but it covered a popular approach route for the *adoo* along the shallow (at that point) Wadi Thimrin. However, because its own weapons needed to reach the *jebel* the hedgehog itself would be within range of the enemy, and would need to be well protected with shell-proof shelters. Additionally, it would need to be constructed with as low a silhouette as possible.

The next day I showed Peter Tawell the proposed position and handed over the task to C Company. We managed to get hold of a JCB and work went on apace. T'Shok Hedgehog was soon established and undoubtedly denied the enemy a favourite approach for their monsoon raiding parties. Later it successfully engaged an enemy RCL which opened fire on the airstrip. Once the new position was established everyone wondered why it hadn't been thought of before!

My United Kingdom leave was due in the middle of August 1972 and I flew back to Muscat and thence to England via Bahrein and a night in the Gulf Hotel. The day of my arrival in London coincided with the return of my wife Paula and our two children from a holiday spent in a barge on the Canal du Midi. We returned together to Canterbury where we were living. Suddenly the dusty plain and rocky mountains of Dhofar had given way to Canterbury's cool and ancient streets. The teeming, noisy and colourful *suk* was replaced by the ordered shops of a cathedral city. The change was abrupt and it took me a while to adjust – indeed, it seemed that by the time I had, it was time to return to my other utterly different world. A world in which I was now so deeply involved that it was Canterbury that appeared alien, not Dhofar.

Arthur met me at Salalah Airport. He smiled rather lethally, and – all in one breath – said, 'Welcome back, Colonel – hope you had a good leave. The whole Battalion is doing an operation out of Thamarit tomorrow.' When we got back to Umm al Ghawarif camp he briefed me in detail.

The Dhofar Brigade Commander intended to commence post-monsoon operations on the eastern *jebel* while the Operation Hornbeam patrols were to continue to try and prevent enemy resupply. With this in mind A and C Companies NFR were to work in independent areas, each with its own SAS groups and associated *firqas*. They would move by foot from Salalah by night and climb the southern escarpment to achieve surprise. Immediately preceding this operation, which was to be known as 'Sycamore', a battalion-sized diversion would be mounted by NFR. This diversion would be launched from Thamarit on the northern side of the *jebel*, and it was hoped the enemy would believe that SAF were attempting to open the Midway Road. Thus, with luck, enemy attention would be focussed on the north at the crucial time of the SAF move onto the *jebel* from the south for Operation Sycamore. As all three companies were involved in both the diversionary operation and in either Sycamore or Hornbeam, there was a busy time ahead for NFR.

Arthur had drawn up all the plans for the Battalion's air move to Thamarit. For the walk from there to the *jebel* our heavy weapons and spare water would be carried on donkeys and we would move in by night in order to be firmly established on commanding ground by dawn.

So the next day the Battalion was shuttled by air 'over the hill' from Salalah to Thamarit, or 'Midway' as the Garrison was known. This dusty outpost squats in the desert some 60 miles north of Salalah. The permanent garrison dates from 1971 when it was decided to provide a logistic base in northern Dhofar. At Midway Garrison was a supplies centre (Ordnance Maintenance Park in military parlance), reserve transport and a workshops for the repair of vehicles, weapons and equipment. The airstrip, originally made by the oil exploration company for use by its own small aircraft, had been lengthened and compacted so that it could accept any aircraft likely to operate in the country.

Huge Kenworth diesel trucks and trailers, working under a contractor, plied to and from Bait al Falaj along the unmetalled road. They carried 35 tons of warlike or administrative stores, or 8,000 gallons of petrol each which, from Midway, were distributed to SAF and SOAF units either by air or road, depending on the location.

In 1972 the Garrison maintained a radio link with all the civilian oil-drilling and exploration camps run by the oil company known as 'PDO' (Petroleum Development Oman). This ensured military support would be provided if the security of these camps was threatened, as was the case from time to time. At that time too, Midway was fast becoming the civil development centre in northern Dhofar. Medical centres, schools and government shops were being built in the area, and at Mudhai, some 50 miles east-south-east, a small dam had been made round the springs to improve the water facilities.

Also in 1972, it rained – the locals said for the first time in seven years – but only on one day.

Looking south from Midway Garrison the road ran straight to the *jebel* which showed as a grey smudge rising gently from the gravelly plain. This was the reverse slope where the plain gave way gradually to the hills – unlike the rude abruptness of the escarpment on the Salalah side. Once the road entered the hills it buckled and twisted, seeking out the slopes a vehicle could negotiate, although these proved increasingly more difficult to find as the mountains steepened and the wadis deepened. Soon the road, in its desperate search for a feasible incline, was making huge coiling detours, looping round impossible crags and meandering up and down steep rocky slopes, but always nudging south, to Salalah.

In the late afternoon I stood with Arthur, Abdullah and Jebali by the side of the Midway Road as the leading company walked past heading for the *jebel*. The men moved easily and they had a professional air; NCOs muttered quiet orders otherwise the ranks were silent. My little group – Battalion Tactical Headquarters was rather too grand a name for it – would slot in after the vanguard company, and in front of the other two rifle companies which would deploy one on either side of the road. Sandwiched between my party and the rear companies were the donkeys with their venerable handlers – it seemed to be my fate to travel alongside these *shabers* (old men) both in aircraft and on foot! The animals were heavily laden with mortar barrels or bipods, ammunition or water. They had all undergone minor operations to ensure there would be no hee-haws to mark our progress!

It was the first time all NFR companies had been together since Bid Bid and morale was high. For me it was a night I remember clearly. Not because there were any exciting incidents or mishaps – it was simply a long and tiring slog – but because of that very special and unique feeling which every infantry battalion commander who has marched out on an operation with seven hundred or so of his own fighting men has experienced. There was a pride in the fitness and efficiency of the soldiers and a primitive pleasure in the feel of a heavy pack on one's back and a weapon on one's shoulder – an elemental feeling, unsophisticated and perhaps naïve, but I make no apologies for admitting to it. It felt good that night, walking down the Midway Road.

When we reached the low foothills we moved off to a flank, but kept roughly parallel to the road as we climbed to the higher ground. The sure-footed donkeys (this particular bunch had been imported from Somalia) made light work of the steep slopes and I was impressed with their performance and that of the old veterans who capered alongside their charges, pushing and cajoling, clucking and complaining. It was properly dark by the time we had ascended to the main plateau and clambered on steadily towards our objectives.

When dawn came it found NFR deployed with two rifle companies forward, each on a significant hill overlooking the road. The third company was covering the rear, but was also on a dominating piquet. I was with one of the forward companies which gave me a fine view of the road to the south. Everyone was tired after the night march followed by the building of sangars before dawn, and I ordered 50 per cent stand-to – half the soldiers could sleep at a time in each position.

The northern part of the Jebel Qara was clear of the monsoon cloud, and as the sun's heat steadily increased, soldiers stretched their *shemaghs* over twigs to provide shade. We lay silently hoping for a contact with the enemy, confident that we were in the best possible position to develop any engagement to our advantage. Probably the *adoo* agreed because, although there can be no doubt that we were under observation from unseen eyes throughout, there was no attempt to take us on.

I decided we must penetrate deeper into the mountains to try and draw the enemy out, but was severely limited with regard to time and space. Companies would be involved in Operations Sycamore and Hornbeam immediately following our diversion and I must therefore be able to march the Battalion back to Thamarit in one night.

My thoughts were interrupted by the clatter of a helicopter and a 206 Jet Ranger appeared over the mountains at very high altitude. As was the normal routine we immediately contacted the pilot on our radio; he said he was flying in the Brigadier who wished to visit the operation. We cleared the chopper to land and it lost height rapidly to deposit a buoyant Jack Fletcher before darting away down a convenient wadi to Midway in order to refuel.

The arrival of Commander Dhofar Brigade's helicopter was to be an increasingly familiar sight on all future operations. Jack always had words of encouragement and advice – he never got in the way of the commander on the ground, but was always ready to provide extra support to reinforce success, or to assist operations generally. He was, briefly, in touch.

On this occasion Jack encouraged the idea of moving on and this we did – leap-frogging the companies forward to secure high ground, always keeping at least one of them firm on the ground to cover the movement of the others. Jack's helicopter proved useful on its return in enabling me to take a look at the ground over which I planned to move. But throughout the day the only sign of the enemy were a couple of flares fired on hills in front of our position – some sort of warning no doubt. We engaged those positions with our mortars for good measure, but there was no response. Arthur said, 'They're here somewhere – and we'll know where if we occupy a position overlooked by one of theirs, or if we fail to piquet our route properly.' If he was right then at least our tactics that day were sound.

That night we commenced the long march back to Thamarit. It was essential to ensure that there was no relaxing of vigilance during this move as at this stage we were at our most vulnerable should the enemy try to ambush the return route. With this in mind we had varied it as much as possible from the outward one.

Curiously, the diversion, although we saw no enemy, achieved its aim. I believe there was always a tendency in SAF at that time to think that the *adoo* reacted to the broader tactical situation more rapidly than was the case. In 'contact' situations their reflexes were incredibly fast – small groups of men scampering over the rocks to outflank or cut off a SAF force – or to escape ambush, and so on. But in the broader situation – the mounting of Operation Simba, or the blocking of routes by Hornbeam and similar operations – PFLOAG took time to meditate and discuss the counter moves. Thus, when a battalion force appeared on the Midway road and, by chance, encountered no enemy en route, there was no immediate reaction. The enemy waited to consider the move – what was SAF about to do in such numbers? How could they counter it, and where? Thus, although we did not achieve the contact we would have liked, PFLOAG's attention was drawn to the north and a possible SAF development of this operation from Thamarit. They gave thought to the redeployment of their heavy weapons to cover this new threat. We will never know the total degree of success of the diversion, but it is a fact that when A and C Companies, working in independent company groups with the SAS and *firqa*, walked up to the jebel from Salalah they were totally unopposed, and secured excellent positions from which to launch their future operations. Subsequent SEPs confirmed that at the time of the launching of Sycamore they were expecting SAF operations on the Midway Road.

Sycamore continued for four months until the end of the year, patrolling and ambushing to mop up the enemy Eastern Unit groups. We worked in areas which the *adoo* had considered safe up to that time: the Jebel Arran and on the hills commanding the Wadi Arzat and the Wadi Sahalnaut. There were many hard contacts and heavy casualties were inflicted on the enemy with comparative light loss to ourselves. During the period, I changed over B and A Companies to give the former a chance to operate in fresh country, and the latter, who had suffered eleven casualties, seven of whom were killed, a chance to draw breath. (They didn't take it, but instead, through intensive patrolling out of Adonib, captured an enemy camel caravan of resupplies, but that is another story which I shall tell later.)

I spent some time with each of the Sycamore and Hornbeam companies – as much as I could spare from my commitments on Salalah Plain. I often took Mehdi with me on my visits, not only for the obvious medical advantage in this, but for morale purposes too – wherever he went soldiers seemed to be the brighter and better as a result. I recall two visits with Medhi in particular. We were sitting on the edge of Viv Rowe's sangar – Viv was the new Royal Marine Second in Command of C Company. The sangar overlooked a scrubby valley and we were talking about philosophy, of all things. 'Yes,' said Medhi expansively, 'you cannot avoid your fate; if it is written, then it is written. If I am to die, then I am to die, whatever I do to prevent it. You see ...' suddenly he was interrupted by the rattle of an automatic rifle and bullets whistled over our heads and howled from the surrounding rocks. Medhi and I cleared the sangar wall in a flat dive and landed in a heap on Viv who – good soldier that he was – was already in the bottom, cleaning his nails with a knife. 'Go on, Medhi,' he said in his slow Welsh voice, 'go on about fate and how you can't avoid it ... just getting interesting, that was.' Medhi laughed as much as us and, in the meantime C Company weapons gave the single brave *adoo*, who had crawled through the bushes to within reasonable rifle range, a hard time.

The other vivid memory of Medhi concerns a visit to B Company soon after it joined Operation Sycamore. Hardly had we stepped out of the helicopter – indeed perhaps because of the helicopter's presence – than the position came under fire from a RCL and a heavy mortar. One or two Kalashnikovs joined in for good measure. Unfortunately one of the mortar bombs landed on the edge of the mortar sangar killing a corporal and wounding two soldiers. While the bombs were still falling Medhi darted across to the injured men and fixed a saline drip for one and placed him on a stretcher. The other, being slightly wounded, could walk. When the attack was over I helped Medhi carry the man to the helicopter which whisked them off to the Field Surgical Team in Salalah. Medhi was a grand man.

Simon Baisley, the excellent Oman Artillery FOO with B Company, strolled over to me when the chopper had gone. A very hairy man, Simon, without his shirt but complete with beard, was the same colour as a coir mat and quite as rough in texture.

'What do you make of that?' he asked, pointing to the Sultan's red, white and green flag fluttering starkly from a stick protruding from the top of a thorn tree. While I was searching for a suitable reply (the School of Infantry gave no solution to problems involving sticking large flags in camouflaged defensive positions), Simon went on, 'We took over this bloody position from Simon Hill and A Company. He put the flag there to provoke the *adoo* and it does! They hate it. The point is,' he continued bitterly, 'it's over my ****ing sangar.'

I asked why he didn't take it down then. 'I can't do that,' he replied, 'the soldiers think it's funny.'

'I see,' said I – but didn't.

We all had the greatest respect for the *adoo* mortarmen. Anyone who has fired these weapons knows that it normally takes a number of ranging rounds before one is properly on target. 'Proving the belt' and other such cries ring out as the first bombs fall well out of the field of view of the binoculars trained eagerly on the target. The *adoo* had the uncanny knack of putting the first bomb smack in the centre – most disconcerting if one was caught in the open. This happened to me during a visit to C Company, commanded now by Christopher Kemball as Peter Tawell had completed his secondment and returned to his Regiment in England. I was walking between two sangars when we heard a few muted pops in the distance. Someone screamed 'Incomers!' and once more I had the chance to practise my flat trajectory dive over the sangar wall. The soldiers just had time to show their appreciation of my agility with a few rude guffaws when the bombs fell – right between the two sangars! I heard Arthur's sardonic laugh from a neighbouring hole. 'Enjoying your visit, Colonel?' he called in what I described as very mercenary fashion indeed. But they were good mortarmen and treated us to about a dozen remarkably close rounds before calling it a day. No one was hurt.

Christopher was to prove an excellent Company Commander and was very successful in his imaginative ambushes. He was thoughtful for his soldiers too, and possessed an alert and keen brain. He had been decorated for gallantry in Northern Ireland with the Greenjackets and was to earn a similar award from the Sultan for his admirable performance on the *jebel*. C Company casualties were light and yet their operations were aggressive, which I attributed to the methodical care Christopher spent in planning, and his ability to achieve surprise by his original ideas.

During one of C Company's ambush operations a newly commissioned Omani officer of Christopher's, Hamed Hamdan al Hawseneh, was awarded a Bravery Medal. An extract from an article that Christopher wrote about this operation reads:

Shortly after 7 a.m. two *adoo* lead scouts appeared over the top of this knoll, heading directly for Hamed Hamdan's position. He waited until they were about 25 metres away before opening fire and killing the right-hand man with his first burst. However, the other *adoo* (a woman) was only wounded and fired a complete magazine on automatic at him; afterwards Hamed discovered three bullet-holes in his *shemaagh*! It was extremely difficult to locate her as she was almost hidden by trees and by this time heavy return fire was coming from the remainder of the enemy patrol who were in fire positions behind the bare knoll. However, eventually the

GPMG gunner saw her doing a snake crawl back down the wadi and a burst from him stopped all further movement.

Later this *adoo* group called up reinforcements and Christopher's men engaged them successfully with mortars, artillery and, eventually, Strikemasters. This illustrates the kind of small actions which were being fought over the last four months in 1972 in the eastern *jebel*.

Those less than fully committed of the enemy surrendered to the government forces in increasing numbers. Unfortunately the hard-core terrorists continued to fight bitterly, the few women with them perhaps even more fanatical than the men.

Meanwhile, back at Adonib, B Company, before changing over with A on Sycamore, had located an enemy base at Killi waterhole, some 8 miles to the north-west, as the (hooded) crow flies. We later discovered that this base was used by the *adoo* Firqa al Shaheed Amer Salim of the Ho Chi Minh Unit and was about forty hard-core strong, plus attached militia. Its tasks included camel train protection and stand-off heavy weapon attacks on Adonib. (I had experienced one of these when there were no SAF casualties, but a tiny bedu girl, camped in the Wadi Adonib with her family, received fatal injuries from a mortar splinter; she was a beautiful little thing and we flew her back to the Field Surgical Team who did all they could.) The enemy *firqa* normally operated in patrols of between ten and fifteen men out of Killi, but had a rapid reinforcement capability from both the Ho Chi Minh and the Western Units against a SAF threat. I decided I would like to try and bring the Firqa al Shaheed to battle and asked Headquarters Dhofar Brigade for some extra soldiers in order that I could release all of B Company NFR from Adonib. Jack Fletcher came up trumps immediately with two platoons of the Frontier Force,* two platoons from the Muscat Regiment commanded by Major Martin Robb and two *firqas*: the Firqa al Nasser (Bait Kathir tribe) and the Firqa Socotri. I was also given helicopters, Oman Artillery support and Strikemasters on call.

I drew up an outline operation order, largely to clear my own mind as traditionally, and for obvious common-sense reasons, orders in a SAF battalion were verbal in Arabic at all levels. To this order I appended a note on *adoo* tactics, mainly for the benefit of the more recently joined British officers amongst us.†

I planned to hold Adonib with a Frontier Force platoon and the Firqa Socotri. Just to the west my own Assault Pioneer Platoon would secure

---

* The Frontier Force at this time was still known as the Baluch Guard but I have kept to the one title in this narrative in the interests of clarity.
† It is reproduced in full at Appendix 2.

a mine-free area and provide close protection for the two 5.5-inch and three 25pdr guns – their shells could just reach the area of Killi from that spot. The rest of the force would fly in by helicopters. In the first phase a firm base would be established by the second Frontier Force platoon at Kumasi, a dominating feature about 4 miles due north of our objective. B Company's two 81mm mortars would also be positioned there to cover our eventual withdrawal, which would be on foot through this firm base.

At the same time as the Frontier Force platoon secured Kumasi the two Muscat Regiment platoons would fly in to seize two hills half-way between the firm base and Killi. These were nicknamed East and West Steps and B Company would follow on to land two platoons on West Step and the other two on East Step. The next lift of helicopters would take me, my tactical headquarters including a gunner FOO, and the Firqa al Nasser to West Step. Finally the helicopters would ferry in mortar bombs and spare water to the firm base. All this seizing and securing of ground would take place during the afternoon of the first day. That night 'Killiforce' comprised of B Company, my tactical head-quarters, and the Firqa al Nasser would move forward from East and West Steps to the higher ground overlooking Killi. From there we would ambush the waterhole that night and patrol through the next day before returning in darkness through the Steps to Kumasi. Having covered us through the two MR platoons were to follow us up as rearguard.

One of the problems of the bare moon country of the Jebel al Qamar was to recognize the ground from the air which one had previously seen only on air photographs, or in profile from a distant vantage point. I had evolved a method of getting the right troops to the right spot in helicopter operations of this sort, which I believed was both simple and effective. In addition, and this was to prove important, it allowed for sudden alterations to the plan! My idea was to use a 206 Jet Ranger as a pathfinder, flying in it myself just in advance of the first wave of troop-carrying choppers, each of which was designated a colour. In this case the ones carrying troops for East Step were given 'Red' and those for West Step, 'Blue'. My pathfinder was to fly low, following the contours of the ground, thus presenting a difficult target; I would throw a red smoke grenade onto East Step and a blue one onto West. The troop carriers would then 'sycamore' down to land on their colour, having flown in at high altitude.*

*I used this method again the following year when I was working with the Iranian Special Forces. It was to prove most useful in overcoming any language difficulty in explaining where I wanted them to be.

I believed my plans were as foolproof as they could be and Operation Sikkeen (knife) was launched on 27 October 1972.

Having seen the Firqa Socotri and the Frontier Force platoon at Adonib, and the guns safely into their area, I climbed into the waiting 206 Jet Ranger and off we flew down the wadis. It took us only a few minutes to reach the area and, looking up, I saw with satisfaction four 205 helicopters coming in very high. From the map on my knee I could identify the two Steps, and I asked the pilot to fly low over both – East first. I had the smoke grenades ready, the pin out of the red one.

We clattered out of a small finger wadi and zoomed towards Eastern Step, a few feet from the ground. There was a peculiar fluttering sound and the pilot said, 'Can you confirm that is small-arms fire, Colonel?' which jolted me back in my seat. I had always been told that it was impossible to hear small-arms fire from a chopper if it were directed at you. There it was again – and there was absolutely no doubt. 'Yes I can,' I said and then held on as best I could, still clutching my grenade, as the pilot took violent evasive action. He asked politely what I'd like to do next as we thundered round a rocky cliff at breakneck speed. What indeed? 'The best laid plans,' I thought wryly. Were I to bring the bigger choppers in on the original East and West Steps they would be horribly vulnerable as the small-arms fire was, as far as we could judge, coming from the western one itself. Anyhow, the firers were bound to have a fine view of both Steps. I stood to lose a whole chopper load, or worse, and there could be chaos before there was any chance for the platoons to organize themselves, which was quite unacceptable. Yet to abort the mission with the resulting loss of morale to us and delight of the *adoo* was unthinkable. I told the pilot to give me a view of the ground between the firm base and the Steps. Meantime a plaintive voice from the circling troop-carriers came through on the radio asking about the delay as they were using up a lot of fuel. I spotted two fairly commanding hills and we swooped low over each while I deposited the red and blue smoke. At the same time I explained the situation to the MR platoon commanders via the aircraft radios. Down spiralled the 205s and out leapt the two platoons. They deployed quickly on their positions and I joined them on the western one. The Steps were nicely visible and we waited for the enemy to fire so that we could pinpoint their position. Silence ... broken before long by the returning helicopters, as B Company build-up started. By this time we had put down air panels and they came smoothly into the secure position.

Once the FOO was with us we engaged East and West Steps with neat patterns of shells from the Adonib guns. We received a few convenient bursts from an *adoo* machine gun as the guns were ranging and were able to switch our fire onto that. The firer was undoubtedly impressed no end with the speed and weight of our return volley, because his weapon spoke no more.

As darkness fell Killiforce moved forward, the Firqa al Nasser scurrying out to our front as a screen of scouts. Salim Ghareeb's Bait Kathir tribesmen knew every crack and crevice, every tiny trail of these mountains – the Qara was their country. After our initial hiccup our operation progressed according to plan. We secured both Steps with no opposition and went on to piquet and ambush the waterhole. But the *adoo* had fled. B Company left one or two interesting booby traps, but I forbade poisoning the water.

The next day we patrolled and searched the area, but with no success and so, as darkness fell, we commenced our withdrawal phase. The climb up to the dominating feature of Kumasi, the firm base, proved to be as exhausting as we had expected, especially at the end of a lengthy march. However we made it to the top without mishap and managed to get some rest before the helicopters destroyed the peace of the early morning to lift us back to Adonib.

After the experience of the Midway diversionary operation and now of Operation Sikkeen I could see that the chances of bringing the *adoo* to battle against a comparatively large SAF force on the best ground were slim. All war is a risk and on future battalion-sized operations I trailed my coat by introducing a smaller force in the first stages, with a strong reserve positioned to exploit any contact. It was a fascinating game we played. One important benefit from Operation Sikkeen was to emerge: it increased our knowledge of that particular piece of ground enormously, which was to pay off to a very large extent later on.

Soon after this A Company replaced B at Adonib. Simon Hill immediately continued with vigorous patrolling, concentrating on the country between Kumasi and Mughsayl on the coast. Just before Christmas his efforts were rewarded. One night a patrol from the Company was picking its way silently forward, on the alert but not necessarily expecting to meet any enemy, when suddenly some shadowy figures appeared in front of the leading scouts. Both parties, surprised, halted abruptly. An A Company scout recovered first. 'Who comes?' he called softly. 'Who are you, brother?' And peered through the gloom at the whispering figures in front. He had seen enough to be certain and fired a split-second before an *adoo* Kalashnikov ripped off a long burst. The others from the Company in a position to do so fired too and the night became a hell of confusion, shouts and the crack of weapons. Pressing forward, A Company captured one wounded *adoo* and another one, surrounded, surrendered. It became clear after the captured man had been interrogated that the PFLOAG party was the advance guard of a camel supply train.

Encouraged by the successful night contact, Simon mounted an operation the next day to locate the camel train. He patrolled intensively and found recent evidence of enemy occupation near a waterhole, including copies of Mao's 'Little Red Book' in Arabic script, ammunition, food supplies and a seven-month-old grave. He increased his activity and two days later one of the company ambushes surprised a group of twenty-five enemy – part of the camel train escort. Four *adoo* were killed in the exchange of fire and one seriously wounded; one of Simon's soldiers was also killed. Two groups of enemy were spotted moving into a cave and Simon called in a pair of Strikemasters which fired some very accurate rockets indeed. A Company followed up the air attack with a search of the cave and surrounding wadis, and found an enemy body, some packs, an interesting sack of documents, which were handed over to the intelligence cell in Salalah, and a heavy weapon sight. Sensing that the rest of the camel train stores must have been dumped close by, Simon stepped up his patrols and searches. After two more days his persistence was rewarded when a patrol found the remaining stores, later estimated at forty camel loads. They included sixty-seven sacks of rice and sugar, small-arms and mortar ammunition, documents, another heavy weapon sight and a sack of tobacco. The fact that so much of the load was devoted to food and not to ammunition spoke well of the effectiveness of Operation Hornbeam. Some Eastern Unit *adoo* would be going hungry.

I spent Christmas Day 1972 with Viv Rowe and C Company on Operation Sycamore. It had been an eventful year, I mused, settling back comfortably in a corner of Viv's sangar with a seasonal can of beer. The sun dipped – a fiery red orb – behind the *jebel*. A cool wind, the *shimaal*, took over from the heat of the day and a small flock of brilliant blue-black birds, with vivid orange splashes, wheeled and darted in perfect formation along our wadi with plaintive and rather eerie cries. They were Tristan's Grackle, a much smarter-dressed starling than his drab European cousin. A clattering helicopter appeared, a small dot high in the evening sky, and the pilot's voice asked permission to land. 'Don't hang about,' replied Viv. 'We're liable to small-arms sniping.' Down came the chopper and out leapt Jack Fletcher with a box filled with Christmas fare. 'It's Father Christmas,' said Viv, and off went the Brigadier again to complete his seasonal round-up.

Chapter 11

Enter the Iranians

His Imperial Majesty Mohamed Reza Pahlavi – the Shah of Iran – saw clearly the threat to the Gulf ('Persian' or 'Arabian' depending on which side of it you lived) posed by Russia via PFLOAG. After a highly successful visit by the Commander of SAF, Major General Tim Creasey, he agreed to help Qaboos with material aid. This came in January 1973, in the shape of an Iranian Special Forces Battalion and, to the delight of the Dhofar Brigade Commander, a substantial number of Augusta Bell 205 helicopters, complete with Iranian pilots and servicing back-up. This generous Persian package also included hard cash.

Like the 7th Cavalry in the old Western films this aid arrived in the nick of time. Oman, spending nearly half its annual income on defence and at that time with comparatively small revenue from its oil, was fast running out of cash. Without the Shahanshah's timely help, helicopter operations, which were currently giving SAF the edge over the *adoo* in the war, would have had to be severely curtailed. Indeed, the whole question of sustaining operations such as Simba was in the balance because of the enormous cost of air resupply. SOAF helicopters were long in the tooth and fast going 'off the line' for repair or replacement, but the cost of buying new ones was too much for the creaking economy. The desirable further expansion of the government forces had also been ruled out because of the cost.

The clarion call of the cavalry trumpet and the appearance of the Iranians over the hill (or more correctly out of the belly of C130 Hercules transport aircraft) was a heartening sight for those concerned with the running or financing of operations in Dhofar. I watched the fly-in to Salalah Airport as Jack Fletcher had asked me to take on the training of the new arrivals – the Iranian Special Forces Unit (ISFU) in our Dhofar War procedures.

They looked very impressive – and rich! Every man was beautifully turned out, with the latest American equipment – those familiar helmets with the aggressive chinstraps, the high, heavily laced, black boots, the impeccable and beautifully laundered combat fatigues. All were dressed exactly the same and appeared to be identical in size and shape – boxes of ten. I shuffled uncomfortably; perhaps I should have put on something else. My camel-leather sandals, drab slacks and shirt (home-dyed with nasty black and green spots) and a *shemagh* seemed hardly the dress to meet these shiny new Persians. I glanced at my companions in the landrover: Jebali, who was picking his nose, was wearing baggy Baluchi bloomers with a uniform shirt on top and on his head – oh my God – on his head he wore a civilian pork-pie hat. Abdullah was properly dressed in SAF olive drab with issue gym shoes. Mohamed looked very good in neatly wound *shemagh* and a khaki shirt, providing he remained at the wheel of his vehicle – if he didn't, his ragged shorts and desert boots worn without socks would not look well.

I snarled at Jebali, 'Take that bloody thing off your head,' and he looked startled.

'But I often wear this on operations . . .' he started.

I hadn't noticed he had, but said thinly, 'It will be you who will be operated on, Jebali, if you don't remove that thing and replace it with a *shemagh*'.

He looked very hurt indeed – for two days; after that his hat reappeared.

I turned to greet the Iranian Special Forces Commander who appeared startled. 'The Commanding Officer?' he asked uncertainly.

'Yes, it's me,' I confirmed. 'Welcome to Dhofar.'

I introduced him to Jack Fletcher who looked excellent in a crisply fresh shirt and slacks, and a nice beret. The Iranian, relieved, greeted him warmly. It was going to be all right after all.

I arranged the familiarization training for the Iranians at Adonib with A Company, where they would get the feel of an operational area and see how a SAF rifle company worked and lived. The first difficulty to be overcome was that of language. We had expected that a good percentage of the newcomers would speak Arabic, but we were wrong. None could, or would not admit to it, and only one or two understood English. Luckily we had an Iranian Baluch soldier who spoke the Farsi tongue fluently and could also speak Arabic passably well; he acted as our interpreter.

We showed the senior ranks how to control a Strikemaster in the FGA (Fighter Ground Attack) role, and scrambled a jet from Salalah so

Sergeant Mohamoud
Egeh (right), the
author (centre) and
Corporal Mohamed
Saleh (left) at Awareh.
(note matching legs!).
(Author's collection)

Corporal Dahir Egal at Awareh.
(Author's collection)

The author at Awareh wells.
(Author's collection)

Abdi Farah, the author's syce, with 'Saharadide'.   (*Author's collection*)

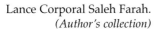

Lance Corporal Saleh Farah.
(*Author's collection*)

Dahir Elmi, the author's
orderly at Borama.
(*Author's collection*)

men of the Habr Awal at Awareh wells.

(Author's collection)

dad (mullah). Prayer mat over shoulder
nilitary water bottle at hip.

(Author's collection)

Warriors of the Hawaye Clan at Villagio.

(Author's collection)

Bait al Falaj fort, Headquarters Sul of Oman's Armed Forces, Muscat.
(Author's collec

Author (right) with Arthur Brocklehurst, the Second in Command of NFR, at the recruits' passing out parade in Ziki, 16 August 1973.
(Author's collection)

Sheikh and retainers in northern Oman.
(Author's collection)

Adam: gateway to the south.
(Nicholas Knollys)

Bedu in the Wadi Mansah.
(Author's collection)

...de the gates to Nizwa. The ancient tree where ...s, goats, vegetable and fruit were bought and
(Nicholas Knollys)

Lieutenant Ali Obaid (centre), NFR Signals Officer, and NFR signallers training in the Wadi Mansah. Oman Artillery officer on the left.
(Nicholas Knollys)

Captain Mohamed Said Raqaishi and Sergeant Abdullah of the Reconnaissance Platoon, NFR.
(Author's collection)

The Reconnaissance Platoon of the Northern Frontier Regiment heads back to Bid Bid after a bus[y] operational tour in Dhofar. *(Author's collecti[on)*

The author's capsized landrover (see page 176) with Driver Mohamed and signaller Abdullah.
(Author's collecti[on)

Salalah in the 1970s.
(Author's collection)

Khareef (monsoon) on the Dhofar jebel.
(Nicholas Knollys)

The fort at Umm al Ghawarif Camp in Salalah. NFR Battalion Headquarters.
(Author's collection)

NFR soldier at Sarfait (Operation Simba).
(Author's collection)

A motley crew back from an ambush patrol
(Nicholas K

Morale was high – as reflected by this Omani
soldier. *(Nicholas Knollys)*

It's not much – but it's home! *(Nicholas K*

Strikemaster over Salalah Plain.
(Nicholas Knollys)

Patrol leaving Mughsayl –
Operation Hornbeam.
(Author's collection)

Hard landing on a makeshift
airstrip for a Skyvan.
(Nicholas Knollys)

The Boom, Gordon
Gillies's pride and joy.
Used for coastal patrols.
(Nicholas Knollys)

A Battery Oman Artillery in action at Mughsayl. *(Author's collection)*

NFR load carriers and handlers. *(Nicholas Knollys)*

HM the Sultan visits A Company at Adonib. *(Author's collection)*

Kingscote. NFR Operations Officer and only ...ryman adds a little tone … *(Nicholas Knollys)*

Nicholas Knollys enjoying a quiet moment on the favourite adoo target – Ashoq. *(Nicholas Knollys)*

...r) Tony Heslop, Angus Ramsay, Hamid Salim (seated), author, Mohamed Haji and Ian Gardiner ...atting). All very alert! *(Nicholas Knollys)*

Typically tough going for this NFR patrol. *(Nicholas Knollys)*

B Company NFR 81mm mortar base plate position on the jebel. *(Nicholas Knollys)*

Two soldiers of the Northern Frontier Regiment at Sarfait (Operation Simba). *(Author's collection)*

Angus Ramsay, B Company Commander (left) with the author.
(Nicholas Knollys)

Mike Kingscote (nearest to camera) and Johnny Braddell-Smith take it easy.
(Nicholas Knollys)

Charlie Daniel moves off on operations (not the normal Royal Marine dress …) *(Nicholas Knollys)*

Viv Rowe (left) with Mik Kingscote board a Gemir for a coastal reconnaissai
(Nicholas Kno

Major Christopher Kemball (Royal Greenjackets), C Company Commander NFR.
(Author's collection)

Major Tresham Gregg, B Company Commander NFR on the jebel. (Author's collection)

Major Vivian Rowe looking lethal.
(Author's collecti

...tenant Colonel Nigel Knocker, the Desert Regiment (extreme right), Johnny Braddell-Smith (next ...m) and others in the 'Grotto' on Sarfait (Operation Simba). *(Author's collection)*

...the Sultan visits a mortar base plate position. *(Author's collection)*

The author at Sarfait (Operation Simba). (*Author's collection*)

Jebali, the author's orderly in Oman (who features on a number of pages in the book). (*Author's collectio*

Abdullah, right, the author's radio operator. (*Author's collectio*

that they could practise doing this. They were also taught how to correct artillery fall of shot onto a target. After a couple of days or so we decided it was time that the Iranians gained some experience in the operation we had achieved some success with in Dhofar – the night ambush. They had already been given a lecture on this and had carried out some training close to the camp. I therefore felt it would be a good idea to take them out into the *jebel* foothills to lay a live ambush on one of the known *adoo* resupply routes. We would take some of the Firqa Bait Said with us as guides so that they could work with the Iranians for the first time, and vice versa. I decided to go along myself to see how the new boys performed, and Johnny Braddell-Smith (who had returned to NFR and A Company, having completed his duty with the Firqa Tariq bin Zaid) was detailed as patrol leader.

Before leaving Adonib we reiterated the paramount need for silence during the approach march and in the occupation of the position. Since we had a long way to go, however, we emphasized that speed was essential too, in order that we could leave Adonib after dark and yet still spend a significant part of the night in the ambush position. The British Army handbook on minor tactics stresses the fact that commanders should travel in the centre of their troops, where they can control things best. In SAF, however, there was only one place to lead from and that was the front! We had found time and time again that the leader, who carried a map and compass, needed to literally lead, otherwise things went wrong. So Johnny and I moved ahead with the *firqa* who set off at their normal fast pace, a tireless, ground-consuming stride, their rifles balanced on their shoulders and their bare feet leaping nimbly over the rocks. In a long thread behind us wound the Iranians – officers, NCOs and a number of soldiers from each company, about sixty or so in all. It was many more than we normally took for an ambush such as this, but our aim was to show as many as practical our procedures. Later these could pass on details to the rest.

'God, what a racket', complained Johnny to me. And it was: the rattle of stout boots – lots of them – against stones and rocks in the wadi bed; the clatter of weapons against equipment; and the chatter of hoarse whispered words of command that grated jarringly in the dark still evening. I dropped back to the senior officer of the Special Forces and whispered that his men should make less noise or surprise would be lost. He, however, was surprised and expressed the opinion that the advance was, in his view, already very quiet. Then he cleared his throat with an alarming hawking and split the air with a muted bellow in his own language, presumably asking for less noise. I crept back to Johnny and the *firqa*.

'What has happened?' hissed the Bait Said leader, 'Is anyone dead?'

I explained that the noise was simply the *Iraniyeen* ensuring there was less noise ... but met his eye and gave up. We moved off once more and after some time at a good pace, Johnny whispered that they were much more quiet now. I glanced back and couldn't see the first Iranian.

'Hang on here,' I said, 'they've dropped back a bit.'

We waited ... nothing, no sound. We started to retrace our steps. They were a dramatic distance behind, sweating in their steel helmets as they clambered over the rocks. We heard them coming for some time. Chink! rattle! thud! click! curse! chink!! The *firqa* started to laugh and we told them to shut up.

'The pace is too fast,' panted. the senior Iranian when they eventually caught up. We slowed down.

'*Wallahee!*' said the Bait Said. 'Firstly, everyone will hear us coming. Secondly, by the time we get there it will be too late.'

They were right on both counts but, for the sake of the training, we pressed stubbornly on. The *firqa* relaxed and chatted amongst themselves as they strolled gently along. They were infuriating, but they could see no point in continuing this noisy and snail-like procession. We played the farce out to the end, ambushed our track for a nominal hour or two and then wound our way back, bumping and clinking over the rough ground. Several men dropped their weapons with a frightful clatter and, towards the end, a soldier slipped down the side of a wadi and broke his leg. Another fired a flare by mistake. We staggered on with our casualty. At Adonib Johnny and I wordlessly opened a bottle of whisky. It was broad daylight and the sun was well up, but we had earned our drink that painful night.

Of course, the Iranians improved, but initially we found them better at holding defensive positions rather than operating in a mobile role. It was my experience too that the Iranians and the *firqas* were best kept well apart – the styles were too different to form a happy liaison. Whatever the initial teething troubles there can be no doubt that the Shah's support to Sultan Qaboos in the Dhofar struggle was a major factor in the eventual successful outcome of the war. King Hussain of Jordan, a close friend of Sultan Qaboos, also assisted greatly. First of all with army engineers and later with special forces and a number of Hunter aircraft. The King's and Shah's support came at critical periods in the struggle. The Emirates provided help in addition by sending a company sized force to garrison the town of Sohar in Northern Oman.

By the time we had completed the familiarization training of the Iranians, NFR's Dhofar tour was nearly at an end. The Battalion would fly to northern Oman in the last week of January, back to Bid Bid for leave and to recruit replacements for our casualties. We would return to Dhofar following this. It was time now for me to review our activities in Dhofar over the past nine months. There was no doubt that Operation Sycamore was a success. A number of enemy groups had been mopped up by the two NFR companies, *firqas* and SAS, while a steady stream of SEPs* were coming over to the Sultan's side. But it was the Hornbeam patrol activity which seemed to me to provide the most significant pointer for the future.

The first and last NFR Company to operate from Adonib was Simon Hill's and he came to see me in Umm al Ghawarif Camp. Over the past months he had walked over most of the barren neck of *jebel* known as the corridor, to the immediate west of Adonib and north of Mughsayl. He knew all the significant trails, wadis and commanding heights. It was country that I had become familiar with too, from Operation Sikkeen and from my own participation in Hornbeam patrols. Simon, his eyes darting and sparking with fervour, stabbed the map with his forefinger. 'If we were to put static positions here, here, here, and here,' he said, jabbing in a vicious way at the features, which would become well known, at Kumasi, Killi, Ashoq and Mughsayl, 'and patrol between them, the *adoo* couldn't get through at all – ever. At the moment, despite our intensive patrol pattern, they are bound to be able to slip through. We were damn lucky to hit that camel train,' he went on vehemently, 'and that put them off more than a bit. They get through now by breaking the stuff down earlier, and man-packing it through in small groups. But ... put a line across here,' and the brown stubby digit slashed the map between Mughsayl and Kumasi, 'then ... nothing could pass. Salalah would never be hit again.' He glared at me balefully, daring me to deny it. But there was no argument – I already agreed wholeheartedly with what he was saying.

Although the 'Leopard Line' achieved some success it was sited in thick country and the *adoo* could always get round to the north. But a line further to the west and sited north of Mughsayl would cover a much more narrow neck of *jebel*. There was little undergrowth and, with the open desert to the north, concealment for the enemy would be impossible if they tried to by-pass it. I liked Simon's ideas and said so. We would need to extend the line further north than Kumasi, and perhaps put further static posts in between, but yes, I liked it very much. We drew up a plan in some detail and then went to sell it to the Dhofar Brigade Commander.

* The SEPs included the chief political commissars of the 'Ho Chi Minh' Unit and the 'Lenin' Eastern Unit. These defections were highly significant as the job of the commissars was to ensure that the hard-core rebels toed the party line.

Jack Fletcher was interested and listened quietly, interjecting now and again with a question or relevant comment. In retrospect, I am sure he was already thinking on the same lines himself; and had it in mind when he first ordered the Hornbeam patrols. We knew we could safely leave it with him to look at in detail and, no doubt, he would float the idea for comment by the Commander of SAF and of 22 SAS and others before making a decision.

In fact it didn't take Jack long to decide and I later heard that the 'Hornbeam Line' was to be established. Jack said, 'The Frontier Force are going to hold the Hornbeam until you return in the autumn, Bryan. NFR can then have it for themselves as it's really your baby! No doubt,' he added pointedly, 'you'll want to do some operations from it.' So the scene was already set for our next visit to Dhofar – but first, a total change of scene in Bid Bid.

Before leaving Umm al Ghawarif Camp I received a signal from Headquarters Dhofar Brigade and a letter from Jack Fletcher. The signal read:

F/F Sunray and all ranks stop (From Brigade Commander to Commanding Officer and all in NFR) Our congratulations and admiration on a very successful operational tour in Dhofar stop Best wishes for a happy and peaceful spell in the North stop See you later in the year.

And the letter:

Now that the time has come for the battalion to have a well-earned break in the North, I would like you to know how much I admire their performance over the last nine months in Dhofar. Their task has not been an easy one, and they have seldom operated as a battalion. They have had their disappointments, and it is sad that some fine soldiers will not be going back to Bid Bid with you. Nevertheless the battalion's record is one of which you can all be proud. You have inflicted heavy casualties on the enemy and by the relentless pressure maintained on him have made a major contribution to the successful progress of the war. I have been greatly impressed by the leadership displayed by your Officers and NCOs and by the courage and cheerfulness of all ranks. I congratulate all of you and wish you a happy and less eventful tour in the North.

I decided to travel back to the north with Mohamed Said Raqaishi and the Reconnaissance Platoon, by Landrover. It would give me a chance to unwind after Dhofar and to see the desert on the far side of the *jebel*. Also, it seemed to me that it was a good time for the Commanding Officer to slip quietly away, while the move was on, leaving it to the more-than-capable Arthur to settle NFR back into Bid Bid camp. Medhi expressed a wish to drive back too, and so, when the companies had all handed over to the Desert Regiment, and were down from the *jebel* waiting for the aircraft shuttle, we slipped quietly over the hill to Thamarit in a Beaver aircraft. Raqaishi and his platoon were waiting at Midway Garrison having driven in from their base camp at Mudhai. I had seen a bit of Raqaishi and his men over the past months, as I had visited Mudhai a couple of times and stayed overnight. I had thoughly enjoyed doing so – Raqaishi and his Platoon Sergeant Abdullah were excellent hosts and my appearances had prompted evening *fuddles* with the platoon, and a freshly killed goat. The country on the north side of the *jebel* was ideally suited for Landrover patrols and I went with a couple of these, cruising through the sand in quite a dashing manner. Mudhai, being an important watering place, was visited by a variety of Bedu, and Medhi, who accompanied me on one occasion, was kept very busy treating illnesses, particularly trachoma, which was very prevalent. I slept in Raqaishi's tent and retain a vivid memory of waking in the early dawn to hear a Koran *sura* being softly recited by a recumbent Raqaishi, sharp, bearded face intent and serious, a forefinger diligently following the written Word in the Book open on his chest. This was his unfailing everyday routine, wherever he was – tent or house, sangar or hole in the ground.

Anyhow, here was the Reconnaissance Platoon at Midway and in high spirits at the prospect of eight months in the north, with home leave and weekend visits to their tribes – the prospect was good. The next day, early in the cool of the morning, Raqaishi proudly paraded his men for my inspection and then, this formality over, we climbed into our six Landrovers and, leaving the Jebel Qara, Dhofar and the war behind us, headed north towards Muscat.

We deliberately took our time to drive the 600 miles through the desert, and diverted to run along the edge of the *Rhub al Khali* (the Empty Quarter), which I particularly wanted to see. Raqaishi drove me in his Landrover and was an entertaining, lively and interesting companion. I enjoyed his company enormously and learnt a great deal from him.

Our first stop after leaving Thamarit was for water at Shisur where:

The ruins of a crude stone fort on a rocky mound mark the position of this famous well, the only permanent water in the central steppes. Shisur was a necessary watering place for raiders and had been the scene of many fierce fights. At the bottom of the large cave which undercuts the mount there was a trickle of water in a deep fissure. This could only be reached with difficulty – down a narrow passage, between the rock wall and a bank of sand, thirty feet in height, which half filled the cave.

Thus wrote Wilfrid Thesiger in his book *Arabian Sands* about a visit to Shisur in 1946. It was unchanged twenty-seven years later when Raqaishi showed it to me.

We halted that night at Dawqa, where there was a pool of clear water at that season, following the rains. We weren't the only visitors for a Bedu family was camped by the water and Abdullah walked over to squat down with them to exchange news. The shadows lengthened and we were suddenly joined by more visitors, hundreds of them, sandgrouse flighting into the still pool. I seized the shotgun, which I had borrowed for the trip, and was in time to bring one or two down. We had them the next morning for breakfast, with our chappatties and dhal.

Our route on the second day ran alongside the great dunes of the Empty Quarter. These – the Ghanim Sands – first appeared as an orange thread, bright on our north-western horizon, but as we approached this shimmering line of colour, the great size of the dunes became apparent. I was intrigued by the abruptness with which the firm yellow ochre plain upon which we travelled so easily gave way to this softly rolling waste which now loomed so large, a brilliant ridge, in front of us. We halted the vehicles – indeed it would have been impossible to have taken them up the soft flanks of the dunes, four-wheel drive or not. I climbed up through some stunted salt bushes and tamarisk trees, which marked the limit of even that sparse vegetation, and gazed across a petrified sandy ocean. It stretched endlessly, its horizons vague in a sandy haze which blurred their meeting with the sky, rose-tinted by the sun. On the dunes close by I could see the miniature terracing – ridges as on a whale's back, carved by the wind. This same restless sculptor even now played tricks within the vast scene before me as whirling dust-devils (*habebo* to the Bedu) got up and rushed about their sandy stage before sinking to the floor as quickly as they had grown, their lonely performances over.

I could see, and yet could not explain, why men like Thomas in 1931, Philby a year later and Thessiger more recently had been motivated to attempt the crossing of this desert by camel. It held a strong fascination for me too – I knew enough of the real discomfort of living in the wilderness, eating little food and drinking brackish water, and not enough of that. I knew, too, of the different traits in the nomad character to be under any romantic false illusions about the Bedu. Yet ... I would have liked the time, there and then, to attempt such a journey, with such companions, into that arid but beautiful landscape. Raqaishi gave a shout. Someone had made some tea and I snapped out of my daydream to share a battered tin mug of a scalding brew which burnt the lips and was thick with sugar; but tasted wonderful. We travelled on, alongside the Sands to Mughshin where the well is surrounded by a tangle of date palms and where the great Wadi Umm al Haiit (Mother of Life) peters out against the wall of the Sands.

We spent our second night, 25/26 January 1973, at Haima. Sergeant Abdullah disappeared shortly after we made camp to shoot a gazelle for our supper, but returned empty handed. The small goat-kid which had travelled, bleating, in the front of one of the vehicles was slaughtered and we ate royally – goat again! Medhi opened a bottle of whisky strictly for the non-Muslims (him and me) but we passed a surreptitious tot to Raqaishi for him to drink purely by mistake. In those days he enjoyed a guilty whisky or two.

Before the sun was up we started our final leg of the journey heading for the tiny village of Adam. This settlement lay between two isolated mountains, Jebel Salakh and Jebel Madhamar, which formed a majestic gateway to the massifs of northern Oman. These two hills, standing as they did in the plain like becalmed warships in a still sea, reminded me of the 'Lion's Tooth' hill near Awareh which formed our landmark in our drive back from Danot. The circumstances then were similar too. I often had that feeling of déjà vu in Oman.

We stopped at Adam by the side of the *falaj* and I was intrigued to see that it was full of small grey fish. I had heard Arthur talk of *falaj* fish but I hadn't seen them myself before. I still don't understand how they existed in irrigation channels which carried the rainwater from the mountains to the plains and wadis, and were frequently, therefore, dry. But exist they did – yet these were far too small at an inch or two to have fried for breakfast as in the stories told by some! We motored on, the scene changing dramatically as we moved deeper into the familiar mountains, and the Jebel al Akhdar, its crown lost in cloud, came majestically into view.*

I left Raqaishi, Abdullah and the Reconnaissance Platoon at Ziki – happy companions of the last four days – and Medhi and I drove on to Bid Bid. 'Al Qaa'id, Al Qaa'id,' called the sentry and the quarter guard turned out. Saif Ali and Arthur appeared, and passing soldiers saluted

---

*There is now a fine metalled road covering the 600 miles from Muscat to Salalah. The journey can be done in a day and there are rest houses if one wishes to stage overnight.

smartly before calling, '*Kaif Halak, Seedi? Ahlan wa Sahlan!*' (How are you, sir? Welcome!) It was good to see my *bait* again, and the Jebel Fanjr opposite. A new Officers' Mess had been built in the months we had been away, with a plunge pool in its garden. Nasser, the Mess Steward, brought me an iced loomi in a frosted glass. The first one disappeared rapidly settling the dust; the second I drank slowly but steadily. Yes, it was good to be back!

The next morning my new Adjutant, Hamid Said,* issued our first Battalion Routine Order since our return. It included a message from me, in English, Arabic and Roman Urdu, as was our custom:

> The Northern Frontier Regiment has returned from nine very successful months in Dhofar. All Ranks in the Battalion have performed their tasks extremely well, whether on the *jebel* or in support in Salalah. On its previous tour in Haluf and Akoot the Battalion earned for itself a name for aggressive and vigorous action against the enemy. I am proud that this fighting spirit has been proved again in the past months. Thank you all very much for your excellent work.

---

* This brilliant young Omani officer, who had proved himself on the Dhofar *jebel*, was to become the General commanding all the Sultan's Forces – Land, Sea and Air. He was later appointed a government minister.

Chapter 12

A Busy Time in the North

The *adoo*, in pursuance of their overall aim to 'Liberate the Occupied Arab Gulf', had always been anxious to initiate anti-government operations in northern Oman. They had experienced difficulty in getting such activities properly going, however, due largely to a severe setback which their plans suffered in 1970. At that time preparations for attack against military camps and civil installations were well in hand, and a 'hit list', on which a number of significant government personalities featured, had been drawn up. Arms had been hidden close to target areas and the hard-core rebel leaders were busy recruiting followers sympathetic to their cause in each of their particular areas of responsibility. (Where this sympathy was in rather short supply it was found that a little pressure brought to bear on his family normally helped a potential recruit to see the Party point of view. If not, then the man himself might serve as an example to the others. A number of mysterious disappearances occurred.) To round off these preparations it was decided to group the leaders together in order to give them experience in a 'live' operation before they returned to their own groups to do likewise. The target selected was the military camp at Ziki.

In June 1970 B Company NFR was stationed at Ziki. One day its routine was violently disrupted when the camp came under withering small-arms fire from a low hill close by. Bullets snapped overhead, and howled away off the hard ground; it was totally unexpected and the first reaction of the British company commander and his soldiers was stunned disbelief. But not for long. All SAF camps had a stand-to procedure if attacked and Ziki was no exception. Soon the enemy group was coming under much heavier fire than it could return. The isolated hill was quickly identified as their position and it disappeared in a hazy dust screen under the impact of bullets from the *jaysh*. The *adoo* felt that training was over for the day and slipped away down the

127

far side of the hill from the SAF camp, and into the Wadi Mahram. Confidently they loped along, talking about their experience. No one had been hurt and the further they left Ziki behind, the safer they felt.

Meanwhile, when the *adoo* fire ceased, Captain Charles Hepworth (King's Regiment) of B Company quickly assembled a strong patrol, and included in it two camp followers who were known to be good trackers. He then set off in pursuit of the enemy. Twelve hours later this patrol took the *adoo* group completely by surprise and most of the rebels were either killed or captured; a few horrified survivors fled, but were rounded up later. Charles Hepworth was awarded the Sultan's Bravery Medal for this action.

This severe jolt lost the enemy a good proportion of its hard-core leaders in the north. This fact, together with the coup in which Sultan Qaboos replaced his unpopular father a little over a month later, caused support for the *adoo* to wither. SAF received a number of tip-offs which resulted in the discovery of arms caches from time to time. A year later NFR and MR inflicted major defeats on the enemy in Dhofar. The former, based at Haluf and under Karl Beale, virtually destroyed an enemy *firqa* on the *jebel*; the latter recaptured the coastal town of Sudh which had earlier fallen to the Front. Later the same year, after Operation Jaguar had inflicted losses on their Eastern Unit, and Operation Leopard had restricted their resupply, the PFLOAG need to divert SAF attention to the north became even more intense.

Early in 1972, therefore, PFLOAG activity began again in northern Oman and in June, shortly after I had taken NFR from Bid Bid to Dhofar, a large consignment of Chinese arms, supplied by the People's Democratic Republic of Yemen, was smuggled in and distributed to fresh caches. The guerillas once more stepped up their recruiting and training activities, working towards a Christmas target date, when operations would begin. These operations were planned to include the assassination of key government and military figures, and plans were worked out in meticulous detail. By a combination of sound intelligence work, cool thinking and one extraordinary piece of sheer good luck, SAF penetrated the plot. On Christmas Eve, in carefully co-ordinated swoops, a total of thirty-nine PFLOAG members were arrested in Muscat and Muttrah, Nizwa, Rostaq, Izki and Mutti. Subsequently a number of arms caches were uncovered, and four 60mm mortars, a hundred automatic rifles and a number of light machine guns fell into SAF hands, together with mines, grenades, explosives and thousands of rounds of ammunition.

Amongst those arrested were three officers, a sergeant major and a sergeant, all of SAF. The Sergeant Major was in the north, although his battalion was in Dhofar, on the pretext of sorting out his family affairs.

He was Hamood Hamed al Rahby of A Company NFR. The mystery behind Hamood's application for compassionate leave was solved.

In February 1973, Captain David Saunders, a Scots Guardsman and Bid Bid area Intelligence Officer, came into my office and asked if we might speak very privately. We went to my *bait* and armed ourselves with an ice-cold loomi apiece.

'You'll know about the Christmas Eve arrests,' David began without preamble. 'Well, we have the names of some more. Quite a few more, in fact, and some of them live in the NFR area of responsibility, including Sumail and Fanjr.'

Between us we worked out a plan to arrest these additional members of PFLOAG, using NFR soldiers moving in on the different targets at the same time on the same night. It went without a hitch. I accompanied the Fanjr 'lift' as I had a personal interest in a cell located on the other side of the wadi which ran past my *bait*! (I had once been woken up from an afternoon siesta by a rough shake. I looked up to see two armed tribesmen who had wandered across the wadi to register a complaint and to have a general chat.) Everything went smoothly and without a shot being fired. The only shooting which occurred was later. Seventy-seven people were tried and found guilty of having actively taken part in a PFLOAG plot to overthrow the Government by force. Some were incarcerated in Jelaali Jail for life. Those sentenced to death were executed by SAF firing squads. They included Sergeant Major Hamood.

With the bulk of the Battalion back at Bid Bid, and C Company installed at Ziki, our main activities were split into four. The first was easiest to achieve: leave. The soldiers went away in happy batches, staggered so that there were never too many away at any one time. Where possible I authorized 3-ton trucks to take the soldiers to their tribal areas and these departed noisily with much banging on the sides and shrill calling and singing, watched morosely by those whose turn was yet to come or, much worse, those unfortunates who had only just got back!

The second matter of NFR concern was recruiting – we needed to replace those who had left the *jaysh*, or were about to, and also the casualties in Dhofar. Generally we were able to combine this recruiting with our third activity – 'flag' patrols within the vast chunk of *jebel*, gravel and sand which was our area of responsibility. These patrols were popular with all. The British officers saw a great deal of a fascinating and little-known country; the soldiers, proud of their status in the Sultan's army, looked forward to the *fuddles* which welcomed their visits to villages deep in the wadis or far out on the plains.

In addition to bringing in potential recruits, these patrols increased our knowledge of the country considerably. Each patrol commander was required to complete a detailed report on his return. This showed: the number of men, women and children in each village visited; the quantity and quality of stock; availability of water; the state of the tracks; medical problems; and so on. They were valuable exercises from a military point of view, and for the Government too. Some of the more remote villages were visited for the first time and there were many stories told on return. None could quite cap that quoted by Arthur of a visit he had made to the Interior a year or so earlier. He swore that his overheating Landrover, on its arrival over impossible ground at a village perched precariously on a wadi side, was offered a bowl of corn! This, he said, was proffered nervously at the radiator end and shaken encouragingly at the steaming but blank face.

We reached the really inaccessible spots deep in the mountains or desert by helicopter. Even villages on the offshore islands didn't escape our attention; these we travelled to by dhow!

Leave, flag patrols and recruiting, they all took place, but our fourth and final priority increased in importance as our time in the north wore on: training – training to achieve as high a standard as we could before Dhofar again; training of the new recruits by Mohamed Said Raqaishi, now a Captain, at Ziki; training of the replacement British officers in our aircraft and gunner drills; training of new mortar numbers, assault pioneers, radio operators, drivers, all our infantry trades, and then some. It was a familiar infantry training cycle which started at individual and section level, and developed into company battle camps held in that familiar training ground for NFR – the Wadi Mansah.

General Tim Creasey, the Commander SAF, visited one such company battle camp. A Company was conducting a defence exercise and it was Simon Hill's swansong as Company Commander. He and David Nichols were controlling a simulated attack onto the company position. Their idea was to provide realism by firing live rounds to the flanks of the soldiers' sangars, angles of safety having been carefully worked out. General Tim sat with me on the edge of one such sangar in order to gain an overall view of the exercise. Suddenly a burst of fire snapped over the General's head and some rounds screamed off a nearby parapet. Either someone had made a horrible miscalculation in the safety angles or (as later turned out to be the case) a weapon tripod had collapsed or shifted. Anyhow, I didn't wait to find out but instead gave my well-known demonstration of a racing dive and joined two white-faced soldiers on the sangar floor. I could see by their petulant expressions that they were objecting to being put at such risk by their own company having survived a Dhofar tour.

General Tim, still sitting easily on the rock wall, gazed down curiously at my recumbent form. 'Much better up here Bryan', he observed after a bit, gently. And then, in a matter-of-fact sort of way, 'Never does to show these chaps you're worried, does it?'

'Certainly doesn't,' I agreed from my hastily restored position bolt upright beside CSAF. 'My word, no.'

He could have made a legitimate fuss over the dangerously close rounds but, being the man he was, he did not. He knew that the lessons would be well learnt. A rather white-faced David Nichols, who had been alongside (but not firing) the offending weapon, appeared. 'Bad luck, David', said the General. 'You missed me by a mile.'

General Creasey was the ideal Commander for SAF, with exactly the right touch. The men liked and respected him, and the officers had tremendous confidence in him as a leader The incident above is a small example of his personal courage and he was a great advocate of leading from the front. He had a great sense of fun and possessed one of the keenest brains in the soldiering business. Tragically, years later, after having contributed so much to both the British Army and to Oman he became ill with cancer and died. He was a great soldier.

My wife and two children joined me at Bid Bid for a fortnight over the Easter period in 1973. It was a unique experience for them as, at that time, few visitors were allowed into the interior of the country. They flew to Maseira Island off the Oman coast via Cyprus in a Hong-Kong bound RAF Brittania. At Maseira they were picked up by a Skyvan of the Sultan's Air Force, which hammered its noisy way to the new International Airport at Seeb. This airport could take the largest jets and had replaced the Bait al Falaj strip with its hair-raising approach.

Another Mohamed was now my driver; he was an Omani Baluch and had replaced Corporal Mohamed Salim who was undergoing officer training with the SAF Training Regiment at Gallah outside Muscat. This new Mohamed drove me to Seeb to meet the Skyvan and, as always, Abdullah sat silently in the back of the Landrover. Soon we were rattling our way back to Bid Bid again, having collected our tired travellers – although not too tired for comment as we splashed our way across the Wadi al Fanjr and tackled my notorious camp approach road.

It was a very crowded and very enjoyable two weeks that included a visit to Nizwa, where we stayed with the Muscat Regiment and visited the *suk* and the Portuguese Fort. From Firq, near Nizwa, we flew by Skyvan to Saiq, on top of the Jebel al Akhdar. My son travelled in the co-pilot's seat, and the rest of us sat in the back with the fresh rations and stores for delivery to the SAF camp on top of the mountain. Several villagers who had waited at Firq were taken too. On the wonderously cool top of the Green Mountain we called on Mohamed Salim, now a Second Lieutenant, who had a house in Saiq. In his airy *majlis*, which commanded a breath-taking view across the massif, we ate locally grown fruit and exchanged our news. There is a road to the top now but in 1973 the alternative to flying was a day's climb up a precipitious path, large stretches of which, in the rainy season, were washed away by the water rushing down the steep black cliffs.

Our return route from Nizwa to Bid Bid lay via Ziki, where we were due to have lunch with Dick Candlish of PDO. Mohamed Said Raqaishi lived in Ziki too, and we had allowed time to call on him first. We took the Landrover as far as we could through the tortuous winding passages between the mud buildings, but soon we could drive no further and continued on foot, Mohamed and Abdullahi having arranged to take it in turns to look after the vehicle.

Raqaishi's house was one of the largest in the village, nicely situated beside some green gardens and a pelmet of date palms. He welcomed us delightedly and, as it was the first time my family had been inside a typical Omani house, proudly showed us around. Upstairs, in the main room, we were in for a treat. There sat Raqaishi's mother – a great character with a personality we were to remember vividly. A vibrant, sparkling-eyed woman, she had passed on her love of life and sense of fun to her two sons Mohamed and Abdullah.* She was a wonderful hostess to my wife and daughter, and her total lack of English and theirs of Arabic made not one jot of difference to the strong and immediate rapport which sprang among them. A memorable woman, she was built on generous lines, with a mind and character to match: *Umm al* Raqaishi (Mother of Mohamed).

There was naturally no question of leaving Raqaishi's house without refreshment. He had produced, in his terms, a light snack: halwa, fruit and a mountain of chicken and rice – a light snack ... before lunch with Dick Candlish!

Dick acted as liaison officer between the oil company and the tribes. He was well placed at Ziki for his journeys into the desert, but not too far from his head office near Muscat. He had built a pleasant bungalow with a flourishing garden next to the army camp. Dick was an Arabist, born in Egypt, and one-time officer in the Grenadier Guards who was later seconded to the Trans-Jordan Frontier Force. He had wide interests and loved animals – in his garden were a couple of tame gazelles and some monkeys.

* Abdullah was a sergeant in SAF at that time. In Dhofar he had been severely wounded in the stomach which was to prove a severe physical handicap.

He used to have an Egyptian Vulture too, called Draculus. He had found this unlikely pet with a broken wing and had cared for it until it healed. The idea was to release Draculus back to his natural element once he was fit and strong. But the bird knew a good thing when he saw it and never did manage to fly again, despite Dick's great efforts to teach it. Once the wing was better Dick placed the untidy looking bird on top of the high wall which surrounded his garden. He then gave a demonstration of what was required, leaping up and down in front of Draculus, flapping his arms vigorously all the while. (Unfortunately I hadn't witnessed this performance myself, but received a full report from Peter Tawell, the Ziki Company Commander at that time.) Instruction over, Dick move to the rear of Draculus and pushed him off the wall. With an outraged shriek and a dust-and-feather-raising thump, the vulture hit the ground. Three times this performance was repeated, but not once did the bird show any signs whatsoever of becoming airborne. Eventually Dick accepted defeat and they both walked away together. Draculus continued to live the life of Riley, with regular meals on a plate and the occasional stroll in the cool of the evening. Until, one day, curiously, the bird was stolen. Who would want a vulture, especially one like Draculus who went by road and not by air? Suspicion centred on a SAF officer stationed in Ziki and a well-known practical joker as the kidnapper. But Dick missed his Draculus and it was a very poor joke.

Dick was a good raconteur and we heard about the exploits of his vulture over the enormous lunch which eventually sat uneasily on Raqaishi's chicken and rice. We were FULL.

General Creasey's family was in Oman too, and one day he invited us to join forces in a motor-launch trip from Muscat harbour to Bender Cassim, a little bay further down the coast from the capital. A memorable incident occurred while we were wading ashore from the launch, carrying our picnic baskets and cool-bags. General Tim's son was moving behind his father, when suddenly the great man gave a mighty roar. We all stopped short. Sharks? Or, at the very least, stingrays?

'That's what they do!' shouted the General bitterly. 'You spend all your money on an expensive education; you arrange for them to spend a holiday in a little-known and exotic part of the world; you take them in motor launches to secluded golden beaches. And what do they do?' He paused, then started to wade shorewards again, a wide-brimmed peon-style straw hat on his head, arms wrapped round an enormous picnic basket. 'They slip jellyfish into your swimming trunks!' he ended morosely. 'That's what they do!' His son, Patrick, shouting with laughter, had meanwhile splashed his way well out of range.

Our other activities during the two weeks included a trip along the Wadi Sumail in a 205 helicopter (piloted by Tony Nicholson of SOAF, at an altitude varying from 2 to 3 feet); attendance at the Bid Bid school open day; and for my son, a conducted tour round his fort by the *Wali* of Bid Bid. We were invited to lunch with the British Ambassador and his wife, Sir Donald and Lady Hawley, in their elegant Embassy overlooking Muscat harbour. And we climbed to the highest point in Fanjr village in an afternoon temperature of 114 in the shade.

One of the main items on our programme was a *fuddle* in the house of one of the Omani soldiers, in Sumail village. It was unusual for women to be included in such an invitation and for my wife and daughter it was to be a unique experience. Arthur was invited too, and Saif Ali who was the soldier's company commander.

The centre of Sumail seemed to consist of a huge mud block, mouse-holed with numerous dark tunnels and passages. Into this cool shadowed labyrinth our guide dived, and we followed closely, twisting our way deep into the centre. In dark openings and behind latticed windows we could hear women chattering shrilly as we passed and behind the carved wooden and ancient doors came the smell of spiced cooking.

Somewhere inside this maze the sexes split. My wife and daughter, both looking rather apprehensive, were led away by a smiling silent woman, while the men were introduced to the Elders of Sumail and joined them, sitting on a carpet in a large bare room, backs to the wall. After half an hour's talk and fortified by dates, coffee and halwa, we assembled in an adjoining room. A huge copper and brass tray was brought in by two young boys, who staggered slightly under the weight of their burden. From the centre of the tray a mountainous heap of rice and meat towered like the Jebel al Akhdar itself. Around the edge of this mammoth platter were dates, raisins and choice pieces of goat on beds of long-grained rice, all soaked in a delicious stock. We tucked in without more ado. Our host pressed selected morsels on us while Saif Ali made sure my son Anthony, who was enjoying every minute of it, was also kept well supplied. On the periphery of our seated and busy circle were a number of spectators, one of whom stepped forward and lifted a goat's skull delicately from the pile. With a deft crack from the butt of his ancient Martini-Henry musket, he spilled the brains, a grey sludge, onto the tray. Pinches of this, the juices well squeezed out between the fingers, were offered for our further enjoyment. From time to time portions of meat were whisked away by the boys who waited on us. (I was soon to discover where they went). Despite these withdrawals the pile of food did not dwindle as replacement pieces, freshly cooked, were thrust into the cooling rice mountain.

We had been going at it for some time when I became aware of a whispering behind me, then someone plucked at the sleeve of our host and murmured into his ear. He turned to me and said apologetically that there was a little difficulty with regard to the women. A question, he said, of communication. Perhaps I would go along and help? I was led to another building by a shy but matronly lady who pushed open a door and I saw a room bare save for a carpet on the floor and a centrepiece consisting of a tray of rice and meat similar to the one I had just left. I noticed an enormous bone sticking out from the rice, and, a familiar exhibit – a goat's skull lying amongst other debris. The women were feasting on the meat the men had finished with! Seated behind this majestic but second-hand meal, and peering uneasily round it, were my wife Paula and daughter Julia. They were flanked by two Omani women who, perhaps as a demonstration of the problem, now pushed forward some generous pieces of meat, nodding and smiling. With rather fixed smiles their guests politely refused.

'We've eaten as much as we possibly can,' said Paula rather plaintively, 'but they keep pressing more and more upon us – we simply can't eat another thing.'

'They're so kind, but we can't make them understand,' explained Julia, 'and Mummy's zip has broken on her slacks!'

I explained to the hostesses as well as I could, but left them amazed at the tiny appetites of the Western World.

The memory of those two forlorn figures seated behind that vast dish is as clear now as it was then.

Before my family returned to England, we were invited to Saif Ali's quarters in Bid Bid for tea. Once we were all seated, Khalfan, one of the Mess waiters, came in bearing a plate of hot cross buns. It was Good Friday! Such a gesture from Saif, a Muslim, was very touching, and it was a happy tea party in his *bait*.

My family left Oman on 23 April and soon afterwards the Sultan held an investiture at his palace in Seeb. A number of NFR officers and men were decorated for their recent service in Dhofar. Amongst those who received awards were Said Nasser and Saif Ali, Hamed Hamdan, Christopher Kemball, Tresham Gregg and Simon Hill; I was fortunate in receiving the Distinguished Service Medal. Men of other regiments were there too and the long queue wound slowly past the compact, bearded and very dignified figure of Sultan Qaboos bin Said. He pinned the gaily coloured ribbons to the uniforms of his soldiers who gripped his hands and swore their allegiance before saluting smartly and moving proudly on.

Mohamed Said Raqaishi was making a very satisfactory job indeed of training our recruits at Ziki. In order to practise them in as many tactical and weapon training lessons as possible he organized a gruelling end-of-course exercise, which involved an overnight climb to the top of the Jebel al Akhdar, followed by section and platoon attacks the next day. I visited this training and was impressed with the keenness of the recruits and with the way Raqaishi, assisted by Said Nasser, had planned and carried out the exercise. It ended in a glorious battle with the young soldiers joyously firing off the remainder of their blank ammunition and Raqaishi and Said hurling thunderflashes among them with gay abandon.

For the recruits' passing out parade on 16 August we invited the Minister of the Interior and the *Walis* and Sheikhs from the tribes and villages of the new soldiers. Arthur had arranged for these dignitaries to be collected by 205 helicopter, and had worked out carefully the number of elders to be lifted, and thus the number of trips to be made. It was a novel experience for these greybeards and they waited eagerly to be picked up. Alas, we had forgotten about their retinues of *askars* and servants, and had not allowed for them. The first tribal chief, Sheikh Sultan of the Hawaseneh, was followed into the chopper by five tribal warriors and two servants. Seeing this, Mohamed bin Zaha, the *Wali* of Sumail, immediately assembled eight henchmen in order to be one better. The one chopper was thus full and we had only two guests aboard. Eventually all agreed to travelling with only three of their households, but we still had to make four times as many trips as we had previously planned. The pilot muttered darkly about 'flying hours' and 'pay loads' but, being SOAF, he completed the job perfectly.

Soon we had all the great men sitting quietly in a long line of chairs beside the airstrip at Ziki Camp, which also acted as a drill square. Following the parade and a speech by the Minister of the Interior, a grand *fuddle* was held in the camp to which all the recruits and our guests were invited. It was a day which helped to foster the growing sympathy with the Sultan's cause held by the tribal chiefs and certainly enhanced the standing of NFR in those tribal areas which supplied our young men.

'March in, please, Regimental Sergeant Major,' I ordered. With a crashing of highly polished sandals, Dad Mohamed roared '*Sahib*' and directed his ferocious attention to a miserable-looking wretch who was clad solely in a shabby green *wazr* and closely attended by a smart Regimental Policeman.

'Regimental Orders' were held when I was required to deal with offences considered too serious to be handled by the company commanders, whose disciplinary powers were more limited than my own. Luckily there were few such cases in NFR and thus Orders were only necessary about once a week or so; in Dhofar, even less frequently.

This case was of particular interest as it concerned a camp follower who, although a civilian, was also subject to military law. The man concerned, Hassan Obeid, was a cook who had had a heated quarrel with a soldier and, as a means of settling the argument, had struck the unfortunate man over the head with a handy meat axe. It was a miracle that the soldier survived, but he did, and sported an impressive but neatly stitched wound. Hassan had been placed in the cells in the Battalion Guard Room pending his appearance on Regimental Orders.

Dad Mohamed was a fine RSM on the *jebel*, and a respected father figure (as befitted his name) in the Battalion – a grand old Baluchi warrior whom I would not have swapped for the world. I had long suspected, however, that drill was not his strong point, and this he now began to prove – noisily.

'Accused and Escort 'Shun!,' he bellowed. 'Quick March! Left wheel; right wheel; left ... er ... right ... no, left wheel! As you were ... right, I mean left ...' Order and counter order were shrieked by Dad as he tried desperately to position the man in the required place in front of my desk. There was little room to manoeuvre in my office and the confined space offered no scope for the activities Dad was now indulging in. The unfortunate Accused – perhaps believing this was all part of his punishment – cannoned smartly off one wall, only to be marched at high speed into the opposite one. Reeling back he was prodded none too gently in the back by the RSM's pace-stick and propelled forcefully in the general direction of my desk – but ended up behind me, having overshot the mark. The escort, meanwhile, had quietly detached himself from his charge and, disassociating himself from the whole proceedings drifted outside and sat down in the sand.

Eventually, after the Accused had shot through the door by mistake and had been retrieved, we started all over again. This time, when the dust had cleared, Hassan was left standing reasonably near the required position; the fact that he was facing the wrong way was quickly rectified, and we were ready to proceed. Slowly we worked our way through a lengthy procession of witnesses and it transpired that there had been fault – and blows – on both sides. There were powerful mitigating circumstances (apart from those springing from the evidence of those with tribal affiliations to Hassan and which I tried

137

to ignore). I decided not to remand Hassan for court martial, after which, no doubt, he would have disappeared into Jelaali Jail, but instead to award him the maximum detention possible in Bid Bid cells.

Clearing the room of all save the Accused, which took much longer to do than it does to write, I addressed myself to the dejected-looking cook.

'I find you guilty of the offence of which you stand accused,' I said, 'and I am about to pronounce sentence.'

'Before you do that,' interrupted Hassan, despite a powerful thrust into the small of his back from the RSM's pace-stick at his first utterance. 'Before you do that I must sit down!'

'You can't sit down,' I explained. 'The accused always stands for sentence.' I felt rather aggrieved at having to explain – such behaviour was not catered for in the Manual of Military Law.

'Nevertheless,' continued Hassan, 'I am sitting, as my legs will no longer bear me'. Having said that, he disappeared from my view as he sank purposefully below the level of my desk. 'I am now ready,' he called from below. 'Go ahead.'

I stood up. Things were getting out of hand and a strong element of farce was there to stay. I peered down at the figure sitting comfortably on the floor. He peered back. I could see the whites of his eyes in the shadows.

'Come back!' I commanded.

'No,' he replied. 'I cannot.'

'Then I shall sentence you down there,' I said sternly, giving in.

'Do it then.'

So I did. Six weeks. On learning his punishment Hassan recovered his strength, his legs became those of a young man, he leapt to his feet and, evading Dad Mohamed, seized my hand in both of his.

'My God!' he said, fervently. 'God is generous. His blessings on you,' he announced. 'Praise be to God!' He then turned on his heel in front of the outraged RSM and strode out, heading purposefully for the Guard Room.

He was a model prisoner who thoroughly enjoyed his spell in the cells. He was the only incumbent and I visited him from time to time. Whenever I appeared he greeted me warmly, showering me with both his and God's good wishes and bidding me welcome. On his release, much rested, he returned to his job as a NFR cook with enthusiasm and, for all I know, is there still.

Another nice story involving Dad Mohamed comes to mind. While we were in Dhofar the Battalion main headquarters was located in the fort in Umm al Ghawarif Camp. One morning Arthur Brocklehurst came into my office and handed me a very small and dog-eared piece of paper on which was written (badly) in block capitals: 'ME RSM ME WANT BEER'.

I should explain that at that time, as a special privilege to the British officers, the Sultan had allowed the officers' messes in his military units to provide wines and spirits, which had to be drunk on the premises and not in public places. This concession had not been extended to the warrant officers' and sergeants' messes where there were no British members. However, in NFR Sergeants' Mess there were a number of NCOs who liked a drink and RSM Dad was now producing a case on their behalf. His many attributes did not include writing English – why should they?

I examined this terse document and decided that an equally terse reply was appropriate. I wrote underneath his words: 'ME CO ME SAY NO'.

It did the trick and I never heard another word on the subject.

There had been quite a lot of movement and changes among NFR officers since our return to Bid Bid. Seconded officers only served a period of eighteen months with SAF before returning to their respective regiments, and Simon Hill, Tresham Gregg and Christopher Kemball had all left, having completed their tours. A, B and C Companies were now commanded by Johnny Braddell-Smith, Angus Ramsay and Viv Rowe respectively. Angus was a newcomer, a large and happy Scot from the Royal Highland Fusiliers, with an ebullient personality and bubbling vitality. He possessed a huge sense of humour and noisily settled into our team. He was to prove an excellent company commander.

Among other newcomers was Ian Gardiner, bringing the total of Royal Marines in NFR to five. Already with us were Viv Rowe, Charlie Daniell, David Nicholls and Bob Hudson. I had cornered the market in SAF – they were all excellent.

Also joining us about this time were Mike Kingscote from the 17th/21st Lancers, Charles Ogilvie-Forbes, ex-infantry and on contract, Christopher Barnes from the Royal Signals and Mike Bourne, a Sapper. Later, Tony Willis from SOAF was also posted to the Regiment. All quickly mastered the necessary infantry skills. With Dhofar looming the incentive was there! All were to prove valuable additions to our close-knit Battalion.

After the recruit training was over I appointed Raqaishi to command Headquarter Company. This post had become vacant as that stalwart of NFR, Saif Ali, had been selected by the Sultan to serve in his Royal Guard. This was a sad loss, only made easier by the feeling that a man of Saif's integrity and character could only have the very best influence in circles close to the Ruler. We couldn't blame the Sultan for wanting him, but we missed him sorely in NFR, none more than Arthur.

Said Nasser was appointed Second in Command of C Company, a significant move, as I had in mind his eventual takeover when Viv Rowe left. He would thus become our first Omani rifle company commander but, in the meantime, would learn a great deal from the way Viv handled things. Hamed Said, the Assistant Adjutant, was appointed Adjutant in his own right and a British officer was withdrawn from that appointment too – a popular move all round as the Brits all wanted to be with the rifle companies and not in an office anyway.

A new word had arisen to describe a subject which was giving General Tim Creasey, and all of us in SAF, a lot of food for thought at that time. It was 'Omanisation'. In other words, the gradual taking over of SAF key appointments by Omani officers. Everyone knew that this must happen – it was only right and proper that as the Omanis gained experience and promotion they should assume increasingly more responsible posts. The first major step in this direction had already been taken a couple of years earlier – the appointment of the first Omanis to commissioned rank. Inherent in this move was the knowledge that a time limit had thus been placed on the continuance of non-nationals in command posts – these new Arab second lieutenants would be captains, majors, colonels and brigadiers one day.

There were, however, good reasons for not moving too quickly, especially while the Dhofar War was on. One of the major reasons why SAF was beating PFLOAG was our ability to use fighter ground attack aircraft, the pilots of which were British. One or two could speak Arabic, but the majority could not. Orders to them, on the ground, in the briefing room, and over the radio net when they were airborne had to be given in English. Senior commanders' briefings were also conducted in English. This would change of course once the senior commanders themselves became Omanis, but it would be some time, even with accelerated promotion, before they could handle these higher appointments.

CSAF was therefore thinking in terms of a gradual takeover by the Omanis, as and when they became ready. This process could be speeded up, no doubt, once the war was won, but in the meantime, progression by the Omanis was important and must be seen to be happening. The Sultan was aware of the critical eye cast at his British leaders by the other Arab League countries, but was conscious of the need to move at the right pace. One of the most professional and experienced armies in the Middle East was being forged on the anvil of Dhofar, assisted by experienced British soldiers.

Thus, in 1973, we were much concerned to place the right Omanis in the right appointments – these were the men who would one day command the SAF battalions and brigades. I felt pleased with the three moves just made for Raqaishi, Said Nasser and Hamed Said. It subsequently worked out well. Raqaishi became the first Omani Commanding Officer of NFR in 1976; he was relieved by Said Nasser in 1978 who, in his turn, was replaced by Hamed Said in 1980.

While the Battalion was in Bid Bid, NFR sent out companies from time to time to round up parties of illegal immigrants who were reported to be wandering in the Regiment's area of responsibility. These unfortunates usually fell into one of two categories. Either they were *Haj* pilgrims with the aim of visiting the Muslim Holy City of Mecca, or they were anxious to settle in the Gulf and seek employment. Most of the former came from Pakistan, but a number of Indians were included amongst those seeking a new life in a fresh country. Whatever category, they had one thing in common: they were the victims of a well-worn and vicious confidence trick run by the shifty captains of the battered and overcrowded boats which bore them to the shores of Arabia. Fed on stories of easy jobs in the Gulf States, or of a simple trip to Mecca, their life savings were exchanged for a fearful trip across the Indian Ocean to a parched and deserted spot on the coast of Oman. A number of suitably shelving beaches – between the Musandam Peninsula in the extreme north and Sudh in the south – were known to the skippers of the boats; they were all miles from the nearest settlement. Once ashore the bewildered would-be pilgrims and settlers were left to fend for themselves. Few knew the name of the country they were in, let alone the direction in which they should head. Some died of thirst before reaching any settlement; others were driven off by suspicious Omanis as they descended, parched and starving, on a village; one or two were killed by tribesmen in the desert or *jebel* as they staggered hopelessly along. Most were eventually rounded up and shipped back to Pakistan, penniless and sometimes broken in spirit.

Those hoping to make the *Haj* were faced with a walk across the Arabian Peninsula in order to reach their destination. It is a miracle that one or two made it all the way – most did not, and many perished. The story of 148 Pakistani men, women and children who landed in the Kuria Muria Bay in Dhofar in the autumn of 1972 is typical. After landing by night they walked for several days along the coast until they reached a tiny village, where the majority rested and waited. Four men set off into the desert to summon help from an oil survey camp some days march inland. Three died along the nightmare route; the surviving man reeled into the camp, delirious and only half-conscious.

141

The oilmen signalled Headquarters Dhofar Brigade and transport was sent to bring the pilgrims from the coastal village. They were housed, watered and fed in the Frontier Force Camp at Raysut before being shipped back to Karachi.

In Bid Bid, in 1973, we had news of a party of some 600 Pakistanis who had beached at Sur, on the coast south of Muscat. Some had already been apprehended by the Oman Gendarmerie, others had been rounded up by the Oman Artillery battery from Rostaq. A number, however, had escaped to the mountains and were heading west into the Interior and NFR's area. They had the totally hopeless aim of reaching Mecca.

Our sweeps and searches in the foothills of the Jebel al Akhdar proved fruitful and a number of pitiful scarecrow figures were brought into Bid Bid Camp. I talked, via a Baluchi soldier who spoke his language, to a grey-bearded and emaciated Pashtun who was a leader of the group. The old man told me that his family had sold all they possessed to buy a passage on a launch across the Indian Ocean to Mecca. The voyage, he said, was best forgotten – there was insufficient room for the adults to lie down and everyone was sick; the stink was fearful. On being put ashore at Sur they had no idea where they were, but understood that Mecca was 'south-west'. When the *jaysh* came and detained a lot of them, the rest struck inland. They walked for several days and, being mountain tribesmen, had survived a fearful route over rocky passes in temperatures which reached 130 degrees in the mountain defiles and gorges. Eventually, continued the old man, they had arrived by night in Sumail (we identified the name of the village later) where they had begged for water, but the local tribesmen of the Beni Hinnah had chased them back into the hills, refusing them any. 'They fired at us,' said the Pashtun matter of factly – treatment not unknown in his own country where tribal squabbles were rife. He told me that they became so hungry and thirsty that some died – they had only eaten grass since they had landed. Then, he explained, the soldiers had come. We were sad for these tribesmen and they were fed well that night, but the next day they were taken by trucks to Muscat to await shipment back to Pakistan.

Medhi was fond of animals, a kindness that extended even to the large rock lizards common around Bid Bid. He kept one of these beasts, which was about 3 feet long and weighed as much as a small dog, in a pen by his quarters. The soldiers, particularly the Baluchis, would not touch the thing as they believed that the spirits of djinns often inhabited these scaly bodies. Also common in Oman were the horrible-looking camel spiders, hairy creatures that grew to as much as 12 inches across, with furry legs as thick as a man's finger. It was not uncommon to find oneself sharing a sleeping bag with one of these, and they frequently scuttled from one's path in the stony desert. Their appearance, luckily, was more ferocious than was the case, although they could inflict a very nasty bite. More dangerous were the scorpions which abounded, and which I found from time to time in cupboards in my bait, and snakes, particularly a very venomous form of sand viper. We had a number of cases of snake bite among the soldiers training near Bid Bid. One unfortunate, who was bitten on an exercise in the Wadi Mansah was in a very bad way indeed. Medhi rushed him to hospital in Bait al Falaj in the nick of time.

By the end of August 1973, after NFR had been in the north for seven months, the preparations for our next Dhofar tour were going so well that I felt I could take two weeks leave in England. There was a very good reason why I wished to do this at that time – my wife and I had bought our first house. After many years of living in other people's houses and flats, and in army quarters, we had felt it was time for us to establish a firm base. We had already decided that this would be in the North Yorkshire countryside and my father-in law had found the very place. He had kindly said he would keep an eye open for us and I had given him my criteria which included: 'Not being able to see anyone else's washing' and 'small, old, but with a spot of land'. The impossible dream perhaps, but he had found it – an old stone cottage deep in the country with a couple of acres of ground which included a paddock and a small copse.

My first news of this success came when I was sitting on the Dhofar *jebel* during my reconnaissance for our next operational tour. A soldier came up to me with a letter which had arrived with the last resupply helicopter. It contained some colour photographs and a note which began: 'You are now a householder.' I sat on the hot sangar wall and gazed at this cool and picturesque English country cottage. Something to look forward to ... we would keep hens ... perhaps a horse.

I reached Canterbury in time to screw down the final packing cases and, a few days later, we drove to Yorkshire. It was everything we had hoped for.

Back in Bid Bid once more I started a series of company test exercises to satisfy myself that we were fit for operations, and before the soldiers went on pre-Dhofar leave. These went well and I was particularly pleased with the way in which the new British officers in NFR had learnt our procedures. One of these was Charles Ogilvie-Forbes, a quiet, thoughtful man of considerable charm. He was on contract to the

Sultan, having been pointed in the direction of SAF by Colonel David Stirling, the founder member of the SAS. Charles was eager to get to Dhofar as he had heard a great deal of that fascinating province and wished to see it for himself. But he never did. Instead, he became the subject of a number of newspaper articles, mostly under dramatic headlines, such as the one from the *Daily Express*: 'I Was Put in Irons – No-Trial Briton's 73-Day Ordeal in Desert Jail'. Or, from the *Daily Mail*: 'Monk Fights to Free Nephew in Arab Jail'.

In the middle of September Charles was driving a Landrover when the clutch went. He swerved and hit another Landrover which over-turned, killing three of its occupants. The Minister of Defence, Said Fahar, ordered Charles's imprisonment in Jelaali Jail for one year. Once in Jelaali the luckless Briton was clothed in a *wazr* and his ankles were shackled by a solid iron rod 14 inches long and weighing some 6½lb. Later this ironmongery was replaced by a chain and then, after SAF representation through the Embassy, was removed altogether.

Charles shared a cell with a murderer and a sheikh who had been jailed for political offences. He ate the standard Jelaali fare – goat meat and rice, or fish and rice – twice a day. By Omani standards it was quite good food, and certainly as good if not better than the meals he would have got with NFR on Dhofar operations!

In the medieval surroundings of the ancient Portuguese fort time stood still for the jailed officer. At night he could hear the clanking of chains as new prisoners were shackled; by day he squatted in the shade with his fellows, moving position from time to time as the sun swung across the sky.

At last, after two months of representation by the Ambassador, Sir Donald Hawley, I was allowed to visit Charles, on 12 November. I took with me a parcel of things to eat and read, and a very large and very glittery picture of the crucifixion. This was a present from Medhi which caused enormous interest and prompted much discussion amongst the inmates during the weeks that followed. I found Charles to be very philosophical about his plight. He told me that he was sorely saddened by the deaths in the accident and, if he was guilty, he did not object to imprisonment in Jelaali. Indeed I could see what he meant. Although primitive it at least was different, and later, rightly or wrongly, would not bear the same stigma. 'I was in Brixton' or 'The Scrubs' was surely more damning than 'I was in Jelaali Jail in Muscat.' He bore it stoically, but resented not having received a trial.

I was in touch with Charles's wife, Camilla, by letter and sometimes telephone, and knew that the wheels were turning in the UK to secure his release. Eventually, after a personal intervention by the Foreign Minister, Sir Alec Douglas-Home, and the payment of over £7,000 'blood money', Charles was released on Boxing Day and flown straight home. He would not be returning to SAF.

By the time that Charles flew his stony cage NFR were well established on the Hornbeam Line in Dhofar. It felt as if we had never been away. The varied happenings, and coming and goings in Bid Bid seemed like a curious dream. Once more we were faced with the firm reality of the *adoo* and a war to be fought and won.

Chapter 13

Life on the Hornbeam Line

Brigadier Jack Fletcher had quickly recognized that the best place in Salalah from which to conduct operations was not Umm al Ghawarif Camp, but alongside the Sultan's Air Force on the airfield. As soon as the necessary new building had been completed, he bundled his staff into it and set up shop. It was a much more efficient and slick emporium than it had been possible to run in the previous string of dusty offices.

It was to this shiny new Brigade Headquarters that I first made my way on my arrival in Dhofar in early November 1973. My plans for the NFR takeover of the Hornbeam Line had been carefully laid and there was time for me to bring myself and my new Intelligence Officer, Mike Kingscote, up to date on the war. A new Brigade Operations Officer – shiny and smart to match his surroundings – took us efficiently across the Dhofar scene, moving briskly from west to east on the master operations map which was supplemented by a neat formation of air photographs stapled to its margins. He gave us a detailed briefing on events from January to October 1973 while NFR had been in Bid Bid.

At Sarfait, Operation Simba had continued with little change. As it was virtually on the PDRY border there were no problems for the *adoo* regarding their resupply of ammunition. Consequently the resident battalion, the Jebel Regiment, had received a daily ration of mortar and artillery 'incomers'. Some of the heavier stuff was brazenly delivered by 85mm guns located just outside Hauf itself. In a six-month period some 2,300 assorted shells and mortar bombs fell on the SAF position, but caused few caualties and little damage to the strongly constructed sangars. A Caribou resupply aircraft was hit and destroyed on the ground at Sarfait, however, and thereafter all resupply was done by helicopter via the airhead at Manston.

On 6 February, JR had mounted a company sized operation out of Manston against a PFLOAG position in the area of Janook. Major Paul Wright (known as 'Tiger' Wright to all), a tough and experienced officer seconded from the Royal Engineers, was in charge of this. Having first established a firm base, he led forward a fighting patrol to overlook the enemy on the coastal plain. The route was a difficult one, and speed and surprise were important factors. Successful operations often also depend on a certain amount of luck, but this time the luck was not on the side of SAF. An advancing soldier stepped on a carefully concealed PMN anti-personnel mine and was badly wounded. The shattering detonation also alerted the *adoo*, who reacted with extreme speed and ferocity, like hornets roused from their nest. Groups of them raced onto the surrounding heights and swiftly opened withering small-arms automatic fire onto Paul's patrol, which was pinned down. The enemy lost no time in exploiting their advantage and heavier weapons were rushed forward, including a mortar. SAF casualties began to mount. The bitter fighting continued over six long hours, at the end of which Paul, who had darted backwards and forwards between his men's positions, encouraging them, attending the wounded and coolly directing fire, was killed by a mortar splinter. His Second in Command, Captain Mike Austen, took over and eventually the patrol was extracted with the help of a second JR company. For their actions that day Paul and Staff Sergeant Salim Khalfan, were awarded gallantry medals. Mike Austen and six others were also decorated. There was a significant number of SAF casualties.

So there was still a lot of sting left in PFLOAG and some nasty hornets' nests remained to be cleared out, particularly in the Western Area.

Further east the Hornbeam Line was beginning to bite hard – things were going well here for the Sultan. The enemy presence had dwindled by a marked degree on the *jebel* north of Salalah and in the Eastern Area. This was due not only to the continuing drain of defectors to the Sultan, and to the casualties suffered in clashes with SAF,* but also to the extreme difficulty the *adoo* experienced in passing men and supplies through the Hornbeam Line. Some enemy parties got through, but not many. Those that did had not enjoyed their trip, none were without incident and most of the few groups which did penetrate took

* A total of 115 enemy surrendered during 1973, most bringing their weapons with them; 63 *adoo* were confirmed killed during the same period but probably twice that number actually died; 32 were confirmed wounded, although the true figure was about 100.

casualties. The defectors reported shortages in two vital commodities: food and ammunition. The grape was withering on the vine.

SAF success on the *jebel* was reinforced wherever possible by Civil Aid Teams, which were rapidly established in 'liberated' areas. These teams were provided with suitable buildings and vehicles, and consisted of a schoolmaster, a shopkeeper and a medical orderly who plied their respective trades under the overall control of a team leader.

It was therefore not surprising, one way or another, that attacks on Salalah Plain had been few in the last nine months. Even the anniversary of PFLOAG Revolution Day in June had passed without incident. The year before this had been marked by the RCL attack on RAF Salalah in which Peter Hulme and others had been wounded. Earlier in the year, however, there had been one effective stand-off attack which took place in broad daylight. On 8 March, a number of RCL rounds were fired at Salalah Airfield from the mouth of the Wadi Jarsis. Three helicopters and two Strikemasters which were standing on the dispersal pad were badly damaged.* To counter any future attempts on these lines the Desert Regiment had established two new positions on the *jebel*, known as the 'Dianas', after the Huntress. Diana One covered the Wadi Jarsis and Diana Two was placed astride the Midway Road.

With the Hornbeam Line severely limiting the provision of men and supplies from the west, and the new Dianas denying favourite gun positions to the *adoo* who were already in the Central and Eastern Areas, life for the rebels was becoming very frustrating. The number of mortar and RCL rounds which were fired at the Hornbeam positions, all from the west, were a measure of this.

It was a very useful briefing and gave Mike and myself plenty to talk about during the short helicopter flight to Mughsayl, our future tactical headquarters, at the southern end of the Hornbeam Line.

There were 33 jagged and bumpy miles of the Hornbeam Line – a wide front for a single infantry battalion. Spaced along it, like beads on a meagre necklace, were nine positions sited on commanding hills which enjoyed excellent all-round views and good fields of fire. They were permanently manned by a platoon or more, all housed in strongly constructed sangars, some with thick overhead cover. The ground in between these positions was vigorously patrolled by day and night to prevent enemy infiltration. The next development, therefore, was a

---

*Thereafter aircraft were effectively dispersed to protective bunkers which were scattered round the airfield. These were constructed with remarkable speed following the attack!

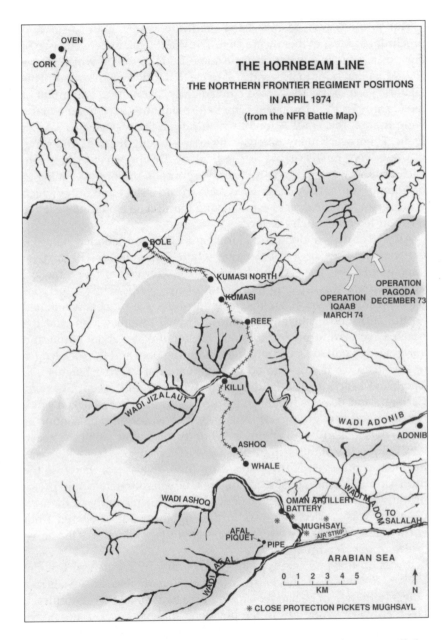

THE HORNBEAM LINE

THE NORTHERN FRONTIER REGIMENT POSITIONS
IN APRIL 1974

(from the NFR Battle Map)

OVEN

CORK

BOLE

KUMASI NORTH

KUMASI

OPERATION
PAGODA
DECEMBER 73

OPERATION
IQAAB
MARCH 74

REEF

WADI JIZALAUT

KILLI

WADI ADONIB

ADONIB

ASHOQ

WHALE

WADI ASHOQ

OMAN ARTILLERY
BATTERY

WADI MADOM

TO
SALALAH

AFAL
PIQUET

MUGHSAYL
AIR STRIP

PIPE

WADI AFAL

ARABIAN SEA

0 1 2 3 4 5
KM

N

✳ CLOSE PROTECTION PICKETS MUGHSAYL

logical one: to erect a barbed-wire fence and lay mines between all the
positions. This task had been given to me as a high priority by Jack
Fletcher. In theory it sounded simple enough – in practice it was a
formidable undertaking.

The ground was granite hard, and the wadis were deep and precipitous; some of them were vast. The Wadi Jizalaut between two of our positions was a major obstacle some 2,000 feet deep which took a soldier half an hour to descend and twice that time to climb out of. This gigantic gash of a wadi passed conveniently, from the enemy point of view, through the Hornbeam Line before handing over to an equally large fissure, the Wadi Adonib, which ran all the way east to Salalah Plain. There were many other wadis criss-crossing the area and some of these were nearly as big as the Jizalaut. Driving steel pickets into such ground was not going to be easy; concealing mines was going to be equally difficult. A sharp-eyed *adoo* would detect any mine which was less than perfectly laid – and having found it he would move it to a position likely to catch the layer.

All the positions along the Hornbeam Line were allotted names – either nicknames or a tribal name where one existed. The map at page 149 shows the SAF positions on the Hornbeam Line. Tactical Headquarters was sited in the mouth of the Wadi Ashoq which debauched into the sea at Mughsayl, with protective piquets positioned on the surrounding heights. Where the wadi mouth widened at the beach a *khor* had formed, a still blue stretch of water about a hundred yards across. It made an admirable swimming pool and the rock ledges of the steep wadi side formed diving boards at varying heights. On Mughsayl beach itself a landing strip which would accept Skyvans, Caribous and Beavers had been marked out on the hard-packed sand. It was a good enough runway, but one which was used with caution as it was overlooked by an enemy position further west along the coast. Any regular use of the strip earned a few RCL rounds, a fact which was inclined to put even SOAF pilots off a little. It was not therefore the most popular landing site in an area which boasted some pretty primitive ones! The helicopter pad, from which resupply of the *jebel* positions was carried out, was further up the wadi, sheltered from enemy view, and was opposite the operations tent which was the nerve centre of the Headquarters.

It was on this pad that we landed to be met by Lieutenant Colonel Vivyan Robinson of the Frontier Force. Vivyan was an ex-Ghurka officer (with whom he had won a MC) who had joined SAF on contract. His men were strung out in the positions snaking away to the north, but at Mughsayl itself the local defence was carried out by my old friends the Iranian Special Forces Battalion, which looked after the Afal piquet position as well. 'They're not bad,' said Vivyan, 'but noisy at night – if they hear anything at all they shoot in that direction! They've lost one or two of their own men as a result,' he added, 'but luckily they don't shoot at us much, probably because we're careful not to make any noise.'

When the NFR company commanders arrived later we arranged for them to be taken by helicopter to the positions their men were to occupy in a couple of days' time. The company commanders would get to know their areas and see the Frontier Force routines while making their own plans for their areas of responsibility. They knew they would be patrolling aggressively in addition to holding the static posts. (It was lucky that this was what I wanted to do, as it would have been very difficult to restrain these enthusiastic and very capable officers – sit still they would not.)

I allotted Johnny Braddell-Smith and A Company the northern sector – Oven, Bole, Kumasi and Reef. B Company, under Angus Ramsay, was given Killi and Ashoq. C Company, commanded by Viv Rowe, was to be responsible for local defence at Mughsayl, and the position at Adonib, which formed a long stop for any PFLOAG parties which had survived the crossing of the Hornbeam Line. Adonib was important as there was permanent water there and it was a tribal watering place. C Company would also provide a reserve which could be used to exploit any success by our aggressive patrolling, or to counter any unusual move by the *adoo*. The Iranians were to remain where they were at the moment, and we would all keep our heads down at night!

The planned air move for NFR was by Viscount from Seeb to Salalah, by Skyvan from Salalah to the Mughsayl strip, and then by helicopter from the Mughsayl pad to the *jebel* positions. Timings had taken some working out, as did the number of Skyvan and helicopter shuttles, and fuel resupply. There was enormous scope for chaos, error or, at the best, irritating delays, yet it all went smoothly and without a hitch – thanks to the good work by Mike Kingscote and our logistics king, Tony Willis. Each Viscount load of soldiers and supplies was split on arrival at Salalah into Skyvan lifts, and these versatile aircraft plied briskly to and fro with the minimum of fuss – especially at the Mughsayl end, where the chances of a sporting shot or two by the *adoo* increased as the shuttle continued.

The company commanders collected their men at Mughsayl, briefed the platoon commanders and despatched them, platoon by platoon, in the clattering choppers. Those with furthest to go went first and so we started with the delivery of men to Oven and worked south. The Frontier Force Baluch soldiers were brought in on the returning helicopters and despatched to Salalah aboard the departing Skyvans.

The Operations (Ops) Tent was something of a misnomer. In common with all the other positions in Tactical Headquarters, it consisted of stout, splinter-proof rock walls, and a tent pitched incongruously on top, in the case of the Ops Tent, a marquee. This was sited like all the rest, under the protective western side of the wadi so that no RCL shell could possibly reach it and only a lucky mortar bomb could inflict damage. Mike Kingscote was Lord of the Ops Tent and spent most of his day there. (He occasionally escaped to join a rifle company patrol, but I always managed to recapture him, despite a lot of slippery wriggling, and place him back in his own pool). The Ops Tent housed our control radio sets. From it we could speak to every Hornbeam position and patrol, HQ Dhofar Brigade, SOAF and supporting Strike-masters and, directly or indirectly, to every unit in Dhofar. It was Mike's calm clipped tones which could normally be heard on the Battalion control set. Those who heard it learnt to rely on what was said. A cavalryman, Mike Kingscote became a very good infantryman indeed. Another, highly different, personality was also normally to be found in the Ops Tent. Tony Willis was a contract officer with past experience in SOAF, whom I had placed in charge of resupply. He was at least twice Mike's age, but they got on well and each had something in the way of experience (military in Mike's case, life in Tony's) to offer the other – chalk and cheese. Later, Tony was to become enmeshed in the mammoth task of moving many tons of metal pickets, barbed wire and mines as we spun our web more thickly.

Round the corner from Tactical Headquarters, in a small tributary wadi, was A Battery, Oman Artillery, which was assigned to the Hornbeam Line and now came under my command. The Battery Commander was a very co-operative and pleasant officer who got on well with everyone. He did, however, have his leg pulled rather unmercifully for a reason totally out of his own control. To explain this it is necessary to know that an artillery shell which drops short of its target is known, logically enough, as a 'short'. It is obvious that such a mistake can be costly to one's own troops, who could, for instance, be advancing under an artillery barrage aimed at enemy to their front – a 'short' under such conditions would not be too popular. Sometimes the Artillery are known, rudely, as 'Drop Shorts' by rather cruel infantry-man. (The gunners have equally unflattering terms for infantry.) To get to the point, Major Adrian Short was definitely at a disadvantage where his name was concerned – especially with NFR, a rough lot. He took it well, and did well, too. He used his battery, which consisted of a troop of three 25pdrs, a light troop of three 75mm pack howitzers, and one aged 5.5-inch gun, with professional skill and imagination. We enjoyed excellent support from Adrian, who never lived up – or down – to his name with NFR. Also in the battery was Tony Smith, another sound gunner and popular man.

152

I inherited three other bands of warriors from Vivyan: three *firqas*. The Firqa Ummr al Kitab (Mother of the Book) was positioned at Oven, the men being recruited from the gravelly sandy wastes to the north of the *jebel*. The Firqa Bait Said was based at Adonib. This *firqa*, named after its sub-tribe, drew its members from those who lived on the Jebel al Qara immediately to the north. Most had served at one time with the *adoo*. It had a sound reputation, but I was to find it more difficult to activate than most. The third *firqa*, the Firqa al Nasser, named after the Egyptian leader, was positioned at Mughsayl. This *firqa*, under its impressive young leader, Salim Ghareeb, was well known to NFR. It was, in my experience, one of the best and most reliable of the tribal units. The Firqa al Nasser lived in the wadi just above my tactical headquarters with its families. Every evening the young boys brought the camels and goats past my sangar down to the waterhole, a daily event which grew to be a familiar and welcome sight.

All three *firqas* sprang from the same mother tribe, the Bait Kathir, but this did not mean to say they could operate well together. In fact, the opposite was true. My one attempt to position some of the Ummr al Kitab men together with a few of Salim Ghareeb's warriors at Reef ended in bickering and a spate of French leave on both sides. The *firqas* were strongly individual!

Oman National Day was celebrated on 18 November and in 1973 was marked by a curious little incident. Mike and I were sitting in the Ops Tent listening idly to the messages being passed on the Brigade radio network – a useful way of keeping in the overall Dhofar picture. Suddenly voice traffic was ordered to 'minimise' – something unusual was coming through from Makinat Shihan. This is a spot on the Dhofar border with Yemen some 35 miles north-west of Habarut. A watering place of long standing, the wells there were being improved and a SAF protective base had been set up which included a squadron of the Oman Gendarmerie, the Assault Pioneer Platoon and a Mortar Section (two mortars) from JR and a troop of armoured cars. It now reported that it was under air attack! We sat up sharply as did many others in a variety of *jebel* locations who were tuned in to the Brigade net. The *adoo* had no air support, or so we had thought up to then.

It transpired that an Illyushin 28 'Beagle' bomber had flown majestically across the border from the west and dropped eight bombs which were aimed at the well-head. Only five of these exploded, however, and those harmlessly in the sand several hundred yards from their target. Having made this gesture the elderly aircraft banked ponderously and rumbled back into PDRY territory. It did not reappear again on that day or any other.

153

The SAF aim in improving the Makinat Shihan wells was to provide an alternative watering place to the sensitive Habarut for the Dhofar tribes. If PFLOAG hoped to prevent this by their show of air might, they had failed badly. I believe it was another measure of their frustration caused by the Simba, Hornbeam and Diana operations. They needed success, somehow, somewhere.

If air attack was luckily not to be a regular card played, the *adoo* did have a sinister new one which they were already dealing. For sometime we had realized that the Russian 'Katyushka' 122mm rocket was a weapon well suited to the enemy mode of operations. It could be fired, in the absence of a launcher, from two sticks tied together in the form of a cross. The projectile itself was sophisticated and had a shattering effect – literally. It could penetrate up to 4½ feet of overhead cover. Luckily the size and weight of each rocket was a limiting factor in its liberal use for it took two men to carry one. The weapon had already appeared in the hands of Mozambique guerillas and, in the normal course of events, we could expect it in Dhofar too. We were not mistaken. During October and November a total of ten Katyushkas were fired from extreme range at RAF Salalah and the Diana positions. However they all landed harmlessly, well clear of their targets. There was no doubt in NFR minds that if we prevented any further Katyushkas being smuggled through the Hornbeam Line, which we were determined to do, we would be the obvious target for the next batch. We examined our overhead cover thoughtfully. Even Tactical Headquarters was vulnerable.

Once the companies were settled, and I had visited and spent a night in all the battalion positions, I decided that there was only one way in which I could get to familiarize myself with the lengthy expanse of my responsibility – on foot. I decided to start at Oven in the north and walk to Mughsayl, spending one night in each position en route. Thus I would get to know each ridge and wadi, and the time and effort necessary to cross them. Mohamed, my new orderly (Jebali was on long leave in Baluchistan), would accompany me, and I decided to take the Battalion Operations Officer too. Mike Kingscote had a fine taste in tinned food and, in typical cavalry fashion, had recently received a hamper from Fortnum and Masons. It contained, amongst other delicacies, quails in aspic, tinned grouse and a Dundee cake. He was therefore the ideal man to be included on the trip. (Also, as Lord of the Operations Tent, the more he knew about the ground the better.) We flew to Oven by helicopter and I was glad to see that Mike's Bergen rucksack bulged in an interesting way and gave an optimistic and metallic chink or two as he settled it on the helicopter floor.

In our original concept of the blocking positions, Oven had not been included. It was well clear of the *jebel*, some 12 crow-flying miles north of Kumasi, and it was felt that any enemy party attempting to outflank the Hornbeam in that direction would be quickly spotted by SOAF on the gravely, waterless plateau. Now, however, as we passed over Kumasi and Bole, and followed the Wadi Armat which snaked whitely northwards, I could well see the need for this extra outpost. The naked brown surface of the ground was riven by numerous small wadis and fissures. Although most of these ran generally north to south – and thus would make any west to east crosser's task doubly exhausting – they could, nevertheless, provide adequate cover from view. A small party could, given luck, escape detection by a helicopter or Strike-master if it lay low in the shadows at the bottom of one of these cracks in the rocky landscape. There was another good reason, too, why ending the Hornbeam Line further north would pay off: we could keep in regular touch with the nomads who wandered for many miles in these wastes; the Bedu would know of any *adoo* party attempting to cross north of the *jebel*. Based at Oven, in addition to the platoon from A Company NFR, was the Firqa Ummr al Kitab, together with four SAS. It was the brothers and cousins of this *firqa* who watered their stock near Oven – we should quickly get to hear of any enemy presence.

My thoughts were interrupted by the pilot reporting that we were nearly at Oven and he would approach at low level. We dropped abruptly below the dark wadi sides and raced along a few feet above the light-coloured sand of the valley floor. The wadi had widened considerably at the point we had descended into it and now, banking steeply round a bend, we arrived suddenly over our destination. A small tent, flapping vigorously under our rotor wash, was pitched in the centre of the wadi bed and nearby a helicopter pad had been marked out with a large letter 'H' in white stones; by it an SAS trooper, arms raised in a letter 'V', was directing us in. We passed overhead and then made a steeply banked turn for our approach. Looking up through the side windows now pointing skywards I could make out the sangars of the NFR platoon on the crest of a small hill alongside the wadi. I would be visiting this piquet later. Ahead the trooper was making the customary (and rather soothing) downward flapping movements with both arms, indicating that it was clear for us to settle. Some empty plastic water jerricans* tumbled merrily away from the side of the pad

---

* The standard SAF containers for water and fuel which could be thrown into a helicopter without damage.
Sometimes speed was essential!

as we eased down, and a whirling cloud of choking sand gradually subsided as the rotors stilled.

Oven was well named – it was baking hot in that wadi, without a breath of wind. A few parched thorn bushes clung to the valley sides but it was an arid and desolate spot. The SAS NCO in charge showed us round his small empire. The tent which had trembled under our rotors was a new school, established by one of the recently appointed Civil Aid Teams. We watched a small group of Bedu boys being taught Arabic script – an incongruous sight in that barren wilderness.

I was introduced to a group of the Ummr al Kitab who wandered over and I pondered on whether to broach the subject of our move to Bole the next day. We would need an escort, and if this was provided by a few of the *firqa* under their leader it would give me an admirable opportunity to get to know them. 'Leave it to us, Boss', said our SAS friend. 'We'll chat them up in the morning. They'll be seeing some of their tribe tonight and the fewer who know there'll be a Colonel on the loose the better!' I took his point. After a cup of tea in the SAS sangar, a magnificent affair dug into the wadi side, roofed with timber and floored with concrete, Mohamed and I set off to climb up to the piquet.

Mohamed was a member of the Ma'mora sub-tribe of the Hawasaneh and his home was in a rock-strewn wadi north-east of Ibri in northern Oman. It is easy to pick out wadi-dwelling tribesmen – they walk with a high-stepping gait which has resulted from the need to clear the large stones and small boulders which cover the wadi floors. Moving at night, when the ground cannot be seen, one finds oneself adopting a similar movement automatically to avoid tripping over the rocks. A desert-dwelling Bedu on the other hand – or foot – walks with an economical heel-dragging pace; why waste energy lifting the feet up in sand? Mohamed must have lived in a very rocky wadi for his feet moved in an almost rotary way, as if he was riding an invisible bicycle. A small man, just 5 feet tall, he had a wrinkled, benevolent face and a wispy beard – a sunburnt leprechaun in his dark green shemagh and clothing. Anyhow, he now covered the ground very well and we were soon with the NFR platoon. After several cups of cardamom tea in a number of different sangars, I knew that I need not worry about NFR morale at Oven. It was a good position, too. The hill, although small, commanded excellent all-round views and there should be no danger of the SAS position down below being surprised. Up on top there was a light breeze which relieved the worst of the heat.

Mike and I spent that night under a low tent roof pitched by the helicopter pad. We had eaten well from a sophisticated and royally crested tin or two kindly provided by Mike. Perhaps I should have had a nagging conscience at failing to pull my weight in the provision of food, but I didn't feel bad at all, just full; and pleasantly tired.

The next morning we were up with the sun and, after a powerful cup of tea, strolled over to where the *firqa* were squatting round their fire. The leader rose as we approached and greeted us traditionally. He had agreed to providing an escort to Bole and announced that he and six men were ready to move. Before any more attractive way of spending a *firqa* day could materialize, I quickly said, 'Good, lead on.'

The unwritten SAF law for a small party moving by day across country where there could be a contact, was to stick to the high ground. If it was necessary to move along or search the wadi bottoms there were two alternatives. Either do it by night or, if the force was big enough, provide 'rolling piquets' on the high ground flanking the soldiers moving below, in which case it could be done by day. With a total of only ten men, we would be walking along the ridges to Bole. The Ummr al Kitab set off at a smart pace, climbing rapidly out of the wadi along a small goat track. Once on top they sent two scouts forward who moved about half a mile in front. The rest loped along in an irregular pattern but keeping several yards between each man. The three of us brought up the rear, Mohamed keeping an eye on our left flank, and Mike watchful on the right. We had with us a radio tuned to NFR command net and a small 'Sarbe' beacon for contacting strike aircraft.

The sun swung up and it became very hot as the hours passed. Each of the small wadi tributaries which originated on the flanks of the successive ridges we moved along looked exactly the same. The country was a map-reader's nightmare. Pinpointing one's exact position in Dhofar, especially in this bleak moon country, was an often reoccurring problem. It could be a dangerous problem too – part of the information required by aircraft, guns and mortars, before they engaged a target, was a six-figure grid (map) reference of one's own position. Quite often it proved necessary to resort to the method of getting a round on the ground as quickly as possible, and then correcting the subsequent shots from that until the target was engaged. But there were obvious hazards in this (such as the first round landing on oneself!). At noon we stopped for the first time on a small crest and drank from our water bottles. One or two stunted bushes survived on the rocky surface and, following the *firqa* example, we spread our *shemaghs* on these and rested in the tiny squares of shade. One of the Ummr al Kitab men squatted on the highest point to keep watch. These tribesmen had eyes like hawks and could detect movement in the far distance much earlier than any European.

In the late afternoon we set off again at a steady pace and could soon see the SAF position at Bole in the hazy distance. A mile or so short of our destination we picked up a well-marked camel trail and one of the *firqa*, a youth of about sixteen, started to move along it. A sharp word from his leader made him jump hurriedly to one side. The Front were apt to lay mines on the approaches to SAF positions, working by night and cunningly concealing their efforts. In the early days they had some success with this, but not any more. Every SAF recruit was taught to avoid tracks in the Dhofar mountains and the *firqa* were learning too. For the same reason old sangars once left were never reoccupied without being carefully searched for mines or booby traps first.

At Bole we were met by Captain Tony Heslop, a contract officer in A Company. Tony had a platoon plus two 81mm mortars and their teams under his command. It was an ideal spot for the latter as besides enjoying uninterrupted views to the north, Bole also covered a known enemy route which lay along the tail of the Wadi Jizalaut – running west to east at that point – and thus into the Wadi Qa Bakish which petered out just north of Kumasi. A few days earlier this NFR platoon had surprised a small PFLOAG resupply party using that approach and a sharp firefight had resulted in the *adoo* disappearing fast the way they had come, having almost certainly suffered at least one casualty, as there was a blood spoor. Despite a swift follow-up the fleet Dhofaris slipped away.

The following day the Ummr al Kitab returned to Oven, and we moved on to Kumasi, with an escort of a couple of men supplied by Tony. He also accompanied us some distance along the route to point out the scene of his encounter with the enemy in the Qa Bakish.

Johnny Braddell-Smith was well organized at Kumasi, where he had his company headquarters plus a platoon on top of the hill. Tucked in below the crest were a couple of 25pdr guns detached from A Battery. These could cover all positions in the northern half of the Hornbeam Line which were out of range of Mughsayl, except for Oven, where contacts were less probable.

Johnny was a man who had adapted easily to his Omani and Baluchi soldiers' way of life. He lived simply and ate the food his soldiers ate, even when it was possible to supplement this monotonous diet with European rations. His ration store reflected his splendid disregard for British Army routines and order. It consisted of a small compound contained by a concertina fence of coiled barbed wire; so far so good. Inside this arena a canvas awning was rigged to keep the sun off a great heap of SAF issued rations: tinned herrings, Chinese biscuits in small packets, bales of compressed dates, sacks of flour, and drums of ghee and rice. Picking around on top of this small mountain of foodstuffs were a number of scrawny hens – bartered from the Bait Kathir. Some goats pulled delicately at a few meagre salt bushes in the same pen, farting comfortably as they munched. Not too hygienic, but as Johnnie pointed out, all the food was in containers. Weeks later, after Johnnie had carried out a particularly aggressive and successful patrol, the Dhofar Brigade Commander visited Kumasi to offer his congratulations. I saw him wilt visibly as his horrified eye took in the food storage arrangements – the chickens and goats had not been idle since my last visit. The Brigadier swallowed hard.

'Get it tidied up, Johnny,' he ordered. Then, seeing a query in Johnny's innocent eye, 'The ration stores I mean.'

'Yes sir', said Johnny Braddell-Smith. But he never did.

I spent that night in Johnny's sangar and we worked out a few routines to cover the Wadi Qa Bakish area with ambushes. He also outlined his patrolling ideas to me and my confidence that the northern part of the Hornbeam Line was in sound, if unorthodox, hands grew. This confidence was soundly based as events in the next few months were to prove.

One short story lingers in my memory from that night at Kumasi. We had eaten and settled down in sleeping bags. A cool breeze came in through the apertures in the rock walls and Johnny, lightly primed by a nightcap of a shared enamel mug of whisky, was telling me of his youth in Ireland. In particular about the village policeman. 'We used to puncture the tyres on his bicycle when he left it unattended from time to time. You know, that man's regular beat included an uphill gradient and I swear he used to *freewheel* up it every day. Now you wouldn't be able to do that anywhere else but in Ireland, would you?' He laughed his rather foxy laugh, both front teeth well exposed.

Our port of call the next day was only a few miles' walk, but to get to it we had to first climb down the steep escarpment below Kumasi and then over a ridge before descending into the Wadi Urzuq. Finally, there was a steep haul onto the Jebel Da'at on top of which was the spot we called Reef. Johnny came with us to the bottom of the Kumasi scarp – there were some new mines which he had laid at the foot of the cliff and which he wanted to inspect. I suppose he wanted to make sure we didn't walk through them as well.

Captain Ian Gardiner, a Royal Marine, was in charge of the position at Reef. In addition to a platoon of A Company NFR he had a section of the Ummr al Kitab and a few men from the Firqa al Nasser and its associated SAS team. He therefore had enough men to allow him to patrol out from Reef for a limited way as well as look after the blocking position itself. He was a large and cheerful Scotsman whose exuberant manner masked a thoughtful and imaginative personality – a delightful companion. We shared a mess tin of something or other that night in the darkness of his sangar – we had delayed the meal rather and lights were not a good idea in that particular position. We each had a spoon. 'Dig in, Colonel,' said Ian. 'I made it myself.' To this day I have no idea what that meal was. There was lots of it and once I think I caught a flavour of rabbit; I may have been wrong. It was a featureless and lukewarm stew and one needed to be really hungry to tackle it. We were and the spoons scraped away busily.

Two SAS men escorted my small party from Reef the next day as far as the Wadi Jizalaut. At the bottom of that vast valley we waited while some soldiers of B Company climbed down to meet us. It gave me a chance to look around. The wadi floor was strewn with huge boulders and was several hundred yards wide. The only possible way of ensuring no enemy could penetrate it was to erect a physical barrier of wire and mines. This, of course, we planned to do and I could see it was indeed going to be an extremely difficult job to build that barrier down the steep sides of the Jizalaut; in places the slopes were sheer.

It was a testing climb out of the Wadi Jizalaut, especially carrying equipment and a rifle. I was glad to get to the top after an hour's long slog. The Killi position was held by B Company less one platoon which was detached at Ashoq. The feature was large and to cover it properly the Company Commander, Major Angus Ramsay, had split his force into two, one half dominating the Wadi Jizalaut where it joined the Wadi Adonib, the other some distance to the west covering another major wadi junction and likely enemy approach. He thus overlooked two principal enemy resupply routes. Angus had rigged trip flares in the wadis and these were activated by jackals, wolves and *adoo* alike. Nights on Killi were thus inclined to be noisy – days too, as the Front expended a lot of RCL and mortar ammunition against the stout bunkers of B Company. Angus had arranged the tail fins and nose cones of these projectiles in orderly rows on the ground, and it was a steadily growing area.

It was an amusing night in the roomy sangar which doubled as the Company Operations Room and sleeping quarters. Angus, beard bristling and blue eyes gleaming with enthusiasm, propounded a number of schemes he had for aggressive patrolling to the west. Given his head he would have been in Hauf, or possibly Aden, by sunup. I think I must have irritated him as I vetoed some of his plans. I did not want to dampen his ardour but I need not have worried – he and Charlie Daniel, his Second in Command (another Royal Marine), were to perform some very adventurous and successful forays deep in *adoo* territory before long.

The next day Mike Kingscote remained at Killi to take part in a forth-coming patrol, while I pushed on with Mohamed and a B Company escort to Ashoq. With the Jizalaut behind me this was a comparatively easy leg. Ashoq was a bare dome, the top of which had been hammered white by many RCL shells and mortar bombs. It was our most heavily bombarded position and the sangars built on this bald peak had an impressive thickness of overhead cover as a result. Most days the cry 'Incomers!' was heard and there would be a mad scramble as everyone in the open dived for the nearest cover, like so many prairie dogs disappearing into their holes. No one lingered long in the open on Ashoq and there were very few visitors indeed. The helicopter pad was sited in ground out of view to the enemy, on the eastern slope, but even so the resupply aircraft was often greeted with an optimistic mortar bomb or two.

Ashoq was hammered because our presence upon it hurt the *adoo*. Like Killi, it dominated a favourite enemy resupply route, this time along the Wadi Ashoq which looped round to its south side. Before occupation by SAF it had been a favourite enemy stamping ground – literally a stamping ground. Simon Hill, on patrol during NFR's previous Dhofar tour, had watched the *adoo* through his binoculars doing foot drill on Ashoq, marching up and down, halting and turning. (And wheeling and running when Simon's guns and mortars started to register.)

Captain Nicholas Knollys, an effervescent Scots Guardsman, was Squire of Ashoq and gave me a warm welcome. It was no easy thing to live for weeks on end under bombardment – or the threat of bombard-ment – but Nicholas was weathering this ordeal cheerfully and well. My visit was a good opportunity to discuss some future plans. We had suspected that the enemy had managed to slip one or two men through the Hornbeam Line between Ashoq and Mughsayl at a spot which neither position could quite cover. Nicholas agreed that a platoon placed on a feature we were to call Whale should successfully plug that gap. I later gave the task to C Company and the stern Said Nasser was sent to command the little force on Whale, past which no *adoo* would dare to scamper.

After Ashoq I dropped down the comparatively gentle inclines to Mughsayl. The remainder of the positions which were held by C Company – at Adonib, Afal and protecting Mughsayl itself – I already knew well. After my walk from Oven I felt confident that I had a sound knowledge of the ground on which to base future operations – both defensive and, more importantly, offensive.

Chapter 14

Operations Pagoda and Thimble

After my walk along the Hornbeam Line I was very much aware of the difficulties inherent in the task of building a barbed-wire fence from Oven to the sea at Mughsayl. It was going to take an enormous amount of defence stores, and even more sweat. There were rumours of forthcoming specialist army engineer support, both from the UK and from Jordan, but, in the meantime, I would start with the labour I had: Pindook Murad and the trusty Baluchi Assault Pioneer Platoon.

Initially materials were going to be very short and we made a careful work programme to ensure that the most vulnerable parts of the Line received early attention. Clearly the Wadi Jizalaut provided the enemy with their best approach, but I felt it wiser to break in the NFR pioneers over easier terrain than that – they needed to attain a high standard of expertise before tackling the precipitious sides of the Jizalaut. So we started with the gap between Ashoq and Whale – another known *adoo* route, but over less fierce country. This was a shorter and easier lift for the helicopters too, and would give the pilots a chance to increase their skill in managing underslung loads, for this was how we planned to deliver the tons of heavy metal piquets and rolls of dannert wire to the work sites.

After the Ashoq to Whale fence was done we would turn our attention to the Jizalaut between Killi and Reef, before filling in the whole of the centre stretch. North of Kumasi could wait a bit, as could the southern end from Whale to the sea.

Our very efficient Brigade Major, Peter Sincock, scrounged, begged and borrowed until he had assembled enough defence stores for us to begin. The stuff was delivered by vehicle convoy along the dusty tracks from Salalah to Mughsayl – the limit of road movement. Gradually an impressive pile of piquets and wire grew alongside our helicopter pad. Tony Willis sweated blood for hours on end within the Operations

Tent, emerging eventually with a helicopter lift and refuelling programme. The long gruelling task, which was to take many months, got under way.

Driving those heavy piquets into the iron-hard surface rock was spine-jarringly heavy work. In some cases Pindook used plastic explosive to crack the ground first; in other areas the piquets were driven into fissures and rammed home until they were immovably gripped by the rock. Foot by foot, yard by yard, the fence grew, coils of wire held in place by a double apron of strands, all firmly secured to those back-breaking piquets. The pioneers tried not to remember that they had started with an easy stretch and that there were 33 miles to do! All of us were spurred on by the sure knowledge that every day's work made the Front's task harder. We were sewing up Salalah, stitch by metallic stitch.

The wiring had just got nicely under way when I was called in to a Brigade Commander's 'Orders Group' (O Group) in Salalah. I flew in with our daily resupply helicopter and joined a number of familiar figures in the Brigade Operations Room. Bill Kerr of the Muscat Regiment was there, as well as Patrick Brook, the Commander of the Armoured Car Squadron, all the Dhofar unit commanders, as well as principal SOAF officers and, I was interested to see, a brace of senior Iranian officers whom I had not met before. Something was very much in the wind.

Jack Fletcher did not beat about the bush. Now that the *adoo* were finding it impossible to reinforce and resupply properly their Central and Eastern Units because of the Hornbeam Line, he explained, he felt that the time had come to make things more difficult for those rebels who were already east of the barrier. At the same time, to make things easier for ourselves, we would open the Midway Road. Having done so, it would never again close. That well-known rustle moved through the audience – the Brigade Commander had everyone's total attention.

The difficulty in the past had not been so much the opening of the road, but the fact that SAF could spare insufficient troops to keep it open for any length of time. All the dominating ground along the road's tortuous meandering through the mountains had to be held, and this took a lot of soldiers. The custom had therefore been to mount an operation to secure the road whenever it was necessary to send a vehicle column with supplies from Thamarit to Salalah. As SOAF airlift capability increased the road convoys became proportionally fewer, but they were still necessary from time to time.

SAF road-opening procedures normally fell into four phases. First, the commanding heights were piquetted, the troops having moved in

163

by night; secondly, the road was swept for mines; thirdly the convoy motored rapidly through; and the fourth phase covered the withdrawal of the protective parties. This last could be the most tricky as by that time the *adoo* would undoubtedly have gathered in, and they were skilled ambushers. Most operations of this sort resulted in a skirmish or two and the rebels normally brought forward some heavy weapons to attack the road convoy. SAF replied by directing artillery fire or Strikemasters onto the gun or mortar positions.

The reason why we were now in a position to keep the road open, Jack explained, was the provision of an extra 1,200 infantrymen by the Shah of Iran for the Dhofar campaign – in addition to the Special Forces Battalion which I had under my wing on the Hornbeam Line. The Shah was proving a staunch friend to Sultan Qaboos. This final opening of the road link from Thamarit to Salalah was to take place in late December and was to be known as Operation Thimble. It would be preceded by a diversionary operation to draw the *adoo* off and to give the troops on the Midway Road piquets a chance to establish themselves firmly. The diversion would involve the seizure of an area of *jebel* to the east of the Hornbeam Line and holding it for a five-day period; this was to be nicknamed Operation Pagoda.

There followed a wealth of detail on how Operations Thimble and Pagoda were to be carried out; everything had been worked out meticulously by Jack and his staff. The newly arrived Iranian infantrymen, with elements of SAF, including the armoured cars, SAS and *firqas*, would open and hold the road. The diversion would be mounted by the Iranian Special Forces from the Hornbeam and I would receive a platoon from MR to help plug the resulting gap in the Line.

After the O Group was over the Brigadier had a private word with me about Operation Pagoda. The ISFU would need some help in preparing for this operation, he explained, as they hadn't been on the *jebel* on their own before and would not be too familiar with our procedures. He therefore asked me to plan it. I returned rather thoughtfully to Mughsayl and had a long talk with the ISFU Commander. My fears that he would object to having someone else telling him how his Battalion should carry out its task were short lived. He eagerly handed the whole thing over and said simply, 'Just tell us what to do, please.' And that was that. I had a very free hand indeed.

The spot selected for Pagoda was known to SAF as Idlewild. It was an old airstrip, originally used by the oil exploration parties and sat on top of the escarpment overlooking the Wadi Sha'ath. It was some 8 miles north of Adonib and 7 miles east of Kumasi. It had been a long time since the Sultan's soldiers had set foot on that particular piece of *jebel*, but many an enemy party had crossed it in the meantime.

A substantial number of helicopters, all with Iranian pilots, had been allotted to the ISFU for the initial landing to seize Idlewild. Once the area was secure and the airstrip cleared of mines, resupply would be done by Skyvan; these versatile workhorses would also be used to fly in a troop of the new Indian light guns. These were the latest toys of the Oman Artillery, and could be easily dismantled and fitted into the aircraft. Some NFR assault pioneers would need to accompany the Iranians, not only to check the airstrip for mines, but also to clear any booby traps from the old sangars which littered the area. Some *firqa* guides would be useful too – I hoped the Iranians would be doing some patrolling from the position.

Peter Sincock arranged the provision of some air photographs of the Idlewild area from Headquarters Dhofar Brigade and I pored over these for hours as I worked out the details of Pagoda. I flew as unobtrusively as possible across our objective in a 206 Jet Ranger, heading purposefully for another spot entirely, over which innocent area the pilot circled once or twice for good measure. The plan really wrote itself. There were the obvious things that needed doing: the securing of the dominating ground, the sweeping of the airstrip, the fly-in of the light guns to a suitable gun position and so on. The ground lent itself admirably to our purpose. There were four convenient hills roughly one at each corner of the strip, which screamed for protective piquets, and a comfortable little knoll for the ISFU Headquarters. Alongside the airstrip there was a broken area which would afford cover and concealment for the light guns. The whole thing, I decided, could be wrapped up very nicely.

I drew up an operation order and presented it to the ISFU commander. 'Carry on,' I said hopefully.

He retired for some hours with his majors and eventually emerged. 'We agree with your plan,' he announced blandly, 'and look forward to accompanying you to Idlewild'. So saying he bounced off to the Khor to join his soldiers sporting by the sea. Their tans were coming along nicely.

I accepted the inevitable and the responsibility for the execution of Operation Pagoda. Command of the ISFU would be a new and rather unique experience, especially as I couldn't speak one word of Farsi. Brigadier Jack Fletcher seemed suspiciously unsurprised. 'Yes, I thought you might decide to go along,' he said. 'I'll come and see you once you're settled on the *jebel*.'

I decided that, in addition to the NFR Assault Pioneers, I would take with me a small party of my own experienced soldiers with a GPMG or two. A section of C Company from Mughsayl was available, and, even better; so was Viv Rowe, their Company Commander. He was itching to come anyway. I was to appreciate his presence no end.

The first day of the Operation, 14 December, dawned and the morning peace was soon shattered as the first flight of helicopters clattered noisily into Mughsayl. The Iranians were lined up neatly in 'sticks' of a dozen men, with spare ammunition and water jerricans stacked on the airstrip ready for the Skyvans. C Troop of the Oman Artillery were also on the airstrip, their light guns stripped and ready for loading. I was thankful that I had evolved a simple method of directing helicopters onto their right objectives. My coloured smoke-grenade routine from Operation Sikkeen the previous year would be an ideal way of making sure the piquets around Idlewild were secured. Bearing in mind the language difficulty, it was the simplest and best plan for seizing the objective. I therefore flew in the first 205 helicopter from Mughsayl, some three minutes before the first troop-carrying flight became airborne. With me I had Abdullah my radio operator and the Assault Pioneer Platoon Staff Sergeant with seven of his soldiers, leaving Pindook and the rest to battle with the Hornbeam fence. Viv Rowe and the C Company Section would come in with the initial Iranian lift.

Within ten minutes we were circling over Idlewild and I pointed out the objectives to the Iranian pilot who nodded and smiled politely. Eventually, communicating in a series of exasperated grunts and gesticulating with a quivering forefinger or two, I managed to get the chopper to fly low enough over the hills flanking the airstrip for me to hurl the appropriate coloured grenade on each. The smoke blossomed gaily on the barren brown terrain and the circling helicopters started to spiral in. I didn't wait to see any more, but pointed vigorously at the airstrip. Our helicopter deposited my party onto the ground and wheeled away over the edge of the scarp. It would join the second lift. Once the dust had cleared I ordered the pioneers to start sweeping the strip while I kept a sharp lookout and an ear cocked for any *adoo* who might be in the area. If there were then they soon made themselves scarce – we were unopposed. Fanning out in line abreast with their mine detectors the pioneers moved steadily down the airstrip. There were one or two false alarms, but no mines were found. Next the strip had to be cleared of boulders and rocks, but luckily there weren't too many of these. While this was going on the ISFU build-up continued, helicopters flying busily to and from Mughsayl. Viv and his party arrived on schedule and he sprinted to a neighbouring knoll to give local protection to the airstrip operation. It was a relief to see the GPMGs quickly mounted with the gunners lying purposefully behind their weapons and I was heartened to see my professional NFR! Viv told me afterwards that the troop-carrying helicopters had a shaky start due to overloading and had difficulty initially in gaining height. His aircraft approaching Idlewild was much too low and hit the face of the scarp with its skids, the pilot managing to scrape clear and pulling away to gain height (and composure!)

I was soon able to speak to the Brigadier on my radio, report Idlewild secure and to ask for the Skyvans to be released. Despite the mine-sweeping it was with a certain amount of anxiety that we watched the first Skyvan line up for its landing. The aircraft was heavily loaded with one of the howitzers, and the runway was rough to say the least – and short too. In came the dumpy aircraft and we waited with bated breath. It bounced a bit and there was a huge churning dust cloud, but it was safely down and the pilot grinned and waved at me from the window. I blessed SOAF and watched with interest as the Omani gunners unloaded, assembled and trundled away their charge with unbelievable speed. There was a sense of exhilaration in the air which was caught by the normally rather dour Baluchi assault pioneers – I heard a whoop or two and an excited shout as the Skyvans came lumbering in, one after the other.

The mission given to the ISFU by the Dhofar Brigade Commander was: 'To seize the area of Idlewild airstrip and hold it for a five-day period'. After the unopposed landing this aim was easily achieved. From 14 to 18 December we sat on that feature; but not one *adoo* did we see, which was surprising because some admirable targets were presented from time to time. I was, for instance, relieved that there were no enemy about on the morning following our arrival when I visited a company position during dawn 'stand to'. This period, as the sky brightens, is a popular one for any attacking force. There is enough light to identify and assault one's objectives, but sufficient darkness remaining to provide stealthily advancing troops with some cover from view. (Evening dusk is another vulnerable period for the defender, for similar reasons). As I arrived at the Iranian sangars the sun was peering over the *jebel* edge and its warm rays were dispelling the night's chill air. 'Stand Down' was ordered and the Persians swung into their morning routine. Viv Rowe was with me and was equally rooted to the spot, jaw agape, as the soldiers stripped off their drab shirts and in gleaming white singlets sat up on the sangar walls as they started to strip down their weapons for cleaning. Not one weapon per section at a time, not half the company weapons first, not even just leaving one LMG intact. No, the whole lot, simultaneously. 'Good God,' murmured Viv and we scanned the surrounding country anxiously. Our eyes took in the other ISFU piquets. Each had sprouted its own crop of distant white vests – weapon cleaning was going on there too. For a single

Front marksman it would have been a field day. It would have been like falling plates on the rifle range, with all the ISFU weapons in little bits – bright, clean and slightly oiled! Later that morning we watched as long and close-packed queues formed at the cooking areas for breakfast. Marvellous linear targets these, but again, praise be to God, no *adoo* machine gun spoke to rudely interrupt the orderly scene.

That night I quietly approached the ISFU Commanding Officer in his Tactical Headquarters, guided by a great avenue of light which spilled out of the command sangar, generated by a chorus of hissing pressure lamps from within. As tactfully as I could I raised one or two points which, it seemed to me, could be important. Perhaps weapon cleaning could be staggered so that some were always ready for action? Maybe white vests transformed the wearer into too fine a target? Might the rations be split down so that they could be cooked and eaten in sangars thus avoiding the long 'chow' queues? The Commanding Officer hooted with laughter.

'You are so anxious,' he told me during a brief lull in the storm of his mirth. 'You are always wondering about the enemy! Pff to the enemy!' he remarked, making a sweeping and very rude gesture with his forefinger. 'The ISFU are more than a match for them.' He glanced quickly over his shoulder. 'There are none here anyway,' he added happily. He reached out a hand. Was he going to pat me on the head? Not quite. He gripped my shoulder. 'Don't worry,' he said earnestly. 'We are fine fighters.'

There is nothing I could do here, I thought. We were poles apart in our military thinking.

I returned to my sangar on the small ridge Viv and I had selected for ourselves and the NFR soldiers. As I left I heard a gale of laughter which I assume followed the explanation of my visit. I hadn't even mentioned the light streaming from the command sangar which now guided me over the rocks to my own dark and silent position.

A voice hissed in Arabic, 'Who comes?'

'It's me, al Qaa'id. Well done my brother, stay alert.' The ISFU would learn the *jebel* lessons the hard way, I thought to myself.

With us in our position was a Bait Kathir tribesman who worked with our Intelligence Branch. He was a fine old warrior who knew every inch of the area and, through his own sources, was well in touch with the movement of the *adoo*. I shall call him Hamid Hassan, although this is not his real name. Hamid told us that the enemy had been keeping the Idlewild operation under careful scrutiny since our arrival. He thought that they would not make any move against Idlewild, but might take on any patrols the ISFU sent out if the ground was favourable. The *adoo* did hit the Iranians a week or so later, but on the Midway Road.

We shared our evening meal with Hamid and he taught us a few words in the guttural Jebali tongue. He had accompanied NFR on a number of operations and was to do so again. He was an excellent guide and a fearless man.

Brigadier Jack flew in jovially the next day, delighted that the operation had gone to plan, and that the Iranians were firm on Idlewild. Later he and I watched some ISFU patrols going out. Long strings of steel-helmeted soldiers picked their way gingerly along the ridges running south on both flanks of the Wadi Sha'ath. Surely the *adoo* couldn't resist a long-range burst or two at these prime targets? But they did.

On the fifth and final day Viv and I, together with Abdullah, Hamid, and a few from NFR, manned a piquet and a GPMG while the entire ISFU assembled on the airstrip to await lifting out by Skyvans. I had drawn up a plan for this which involved a tactical withdrawal with only one Skyvan load of soldiers at any one time on the strip – and they would be lying down, facing outwards, weapons ready. However, here they were now, drawn up smartly in platoons with their kit stacked ready for loading. I pointed wordlessly at their rifles stacked in beautiful, neat little triangles. We waited for the long-expected crackle of Kalashnikov or RPD fire. Nothing. The Skyvans arrived and departed on schedule. Viv and I with the NFR section remained until last, covering the withdrawal from our piquet position. We were accompanied by the ISFU Operations Officer who had decided to remain with us. He had, however, put his rifle and equipment on the last Skyvan and thus was unarmed. A helicopter had been tasked to pick us up, but due to a mechanical fault at Mugsayl there was a long wait. Why the *adoo* did not attack our small and vulnerable party I will never know.

Immediately following Operation Pagoda the ISFU joined the road-opening force for Operation Thimble. Things went according to plan and the first SEPs arriving at the new Midway Road piquets confirmed that the enemy had been diverted by Pagoda. I bet they had – I had too. After a few days the long-expected stand-off attacks along the road started. There were some Iranian casualties and white singlets suddenly became unpopular. Weapon-cleaning routines changed and lights at night vanished to a large extent. They were learning and were good tough soldiers; without them SAF would have had very severe problems indeed.

Back in Mughsayl NFR were settling down well in their Hornbeam Line tasks. All three rifle companies were sending out patrols and ambush parties, and making life difficult for the *adoo*. Pindook and his men were making progress on their mammoth wiring task and, at Battalion Tactical Headquarters, the Headquarters Company Commander, the unquenchable Mohamed Said Raqaishi, was making great improvements to our comfort. A major advance was the Officers' Deep Trench Latrine (the capital letters are deliberate). I have described earlier the normal routine for one's early morning or after-dark functions, but here in Mughsayl's rocky wadi we decided a DTL for the officers was required. That was all very well, but how to dig a deep trench in such country? We left the problem with Raqaishi and forgot about it. One afternoon the peace was shattered by two large explosions. Mike Kingscote, on duty in the Operations Tent, ordered 'Stand to', everyone grabbed his weapon and manned his post. Had the Katyushka rockets arrived at last? Perhaps mortars? A pall of smoke hung over the far side of the wadi. When it cleared Raqaishi's intent figure could be seen inspecting the crater. He had blown a hole in the rock with a shaped beehive charge for our DTL! Work went on apace and a little cubicle was constructed out of an old tent wall. There was even a comfortable wooden seat, and a couple of back copies of *Mayfair* – luxury indeed.

It wasn't the only time Raqaishi startled us in his enthusiastic development of the Mughsayl base. I recall leaping out of my bed one night as shots rang out within our wadi. I tore into the Operations Tent, wild-haired, wearing a green *wazr* and carrying a rifle. A thin bearded face peered through the door. 'It's all right,' said Raqaishi, 'I have been shooting the wolves that have been stealing the sheep. Every night they come. Goodnight.' He left. Soldiering with SAF could often be quite different.

Wolves were not uncommon in Dhofar, where the curious climate contributed to the existence of a wide variety of animals not normally seen in Arabia. They added a gruesome aspect to an incident in the Wadi Jizalaut. Angus Ramsay and Charlie Daniel of B Company had been busy making the bottom of this wadi as difficult as possible for the *adoo* to negotiate. Their combination of booby trapping, mining, ambushing and observing eventually paid off. They had noticed that some earlier west-to-east crossers, who had managed to slip through their obstacles, had felt confident and secure enough to move rapidly eastwards along an old camel trail on the north side of the Wadi Adonib, which junctions with the Jizalaut at Killi. This route was therefore booby trapped by night with 'jumping jack' mines operated by trip wires. This particular device leapt into the air when detonated and was generally a very nasty piece of work indeed. A few nights later a small PFLOAG party escorting a man (who it later transpired was the paymaster for the Eastern Unit with money from Hauf to pay the troops!) managed to penetrate the Jizalaut and, relieved, headed quickly up the same camel trail – as far as the jumping jack, but no further. The leading man tripped the wire and took the main force of the cracking explosion which tore his head from his shoulders. The decapitated corpse collapsed in the centre of the trail. The paymaster, a short distance behind, was injured and, judging by the trail he left, badly hurt, but escaped with his money. Picking their way down the trail, noses scenting the fresh blood and whining in anticipation, came the wolves. They stripped the flesh from that corpse and Angus, leading a patrol to investigate the explosion, witnessed some of that terrible feast. Although he subsequently recovered some valuable documents from the scene of the explosion, which were sent to the Intelligence people in Umm Al Ghawarif, the body had to be left. To try and extricate that pathetic heap of bones from the mined and booby-trapped area would have proved an unacceptable risk, and it would be impossible to bury the body in the solid rock it rested on. It was an unattractive decision for all. Clearly visible from Killi and the Jizalaut it was a dreadful warning to the enemy resupply parties.

Angus and B Company continued in their nightly operations, ambushing and mining, booby trapping and patrolling. An extract from Charlie Daniel's notes illustrates the deadly game that they played with the *adoo*:

They soon learnt to lift our little 'goodies' and even began to lay them against us, so we had to start anti-lifting them with a variety of ideas using white phosphorous grenades, mortar rounds, etc. They later started to lift these as well which shows how quickly a good, determined enemy can adapt and learn with incredible speed with minimum resources. This led us into the game of anti-lifting the anti-lift and after a very short period of playing this game – always at night – my adrenalin supply began to run out. They never lifted any of that ... On one occasion I remember getting very excited as a patrol reached the trap in the middle of the night and with great self-control I waited till the last possible minute, activated the circuit and ... no boom at all. The connections had got sodden in the monsoon! However, all this aggressive mining made life pretty unpleasant for them, particularly when travelling by night and having to be alert for our ambushes as well.

Much later, in the middle of 1974, Angus and Charlie were lucky to escape with their lives while patrolling to the west of the Hornbeam Line in the mists of the monsoon. They were working in two separate parties, Angus with one and Charlie with the other, when they were surprised by several groups of enemy. Then began a battle of fire and movement, a lot of it fought beyond the range of the NFR mortars and the Oman Artillery covering fire. B Company suffered and inflicted caualties. At one stage both officers thought that they would have to make a 'last ditch' stand with their small patrol, but a lull in the fire enabled them to scramble into cover dragging their dead and wounded with them. From there they got back to Ashoq now under the close support of the Omani gunners and most ably supported by a Wessex helicopter which picked up seven casualties from the forward area at night and in thick monsoon. I have not described this action in any more detail as it occurred after I had left Oman. It has been fully covered in John Blashford-Snell's book *A Taste for Adventure* and by Ian Gardiner in his book *In the Service of the Sultan*. Angus was awarded the Sultan's Bravery Medal for this action and Charlie Daniel, together with two others of C Company were awarded the Sultan's Distinguished Service Medal for gallantry.

During NFR's previous tour in Dhofar, Medhi had been placed in charge of the hospital at Umm al Ghawarif Camp, which was the normal task of the medical officer with the Plains Battalion. The hospital dealt with all routine cases of sickness and also received the wounded from the *jebel* after their first emergency treatment by the Field Surgical Team on Salalah Airfield.

Medhi had been sorely missed in Dhofar when, with NFR, he returned to Bid Bid. It came as no real surprise, therefore, when, shortly after my arrival at Mughsayl for our second tour, Brigadier Jack Fletcher asked for Medhi to be released from NFR in order to be the permanent Senior Medical Officer at Umm al Ghawarif. Of course I hated to lose him and he was sad to leave the Battalion, but he obviously had to go. Medically it was a more responsible and demanding job, and he was the right man for it. But we missed him enormously. In Medhi's place came a neat and happy Sikh, Captain Manjit Singh, like Medhi seconded from the Indian Army Medical Corps. Manjit fitted in quickly and served NFR well for several years. Fairly soon after his arrival we persuaded him to replace his bright blue turban with a dark green *shemagh* wound in the Sikh fashion. Pastel shades on the *jebel* were definitely not NFR style!

Chapter 15

Accidents, Sappers and an Island Adventure

'Harassing Fire', as far as we on the Hornbeam Line were concerned, meant lobbing artillery shells onto favourite enemy haunts – water-holes, gun positions, meeting places, trail junctions and so on. Most mornings, soon after dawn, Adrian Short's elderly 5.5-inch gun gave its throaty early morning coughs, and a hopeful shell or two whispered off to the west.

One such morning, very early in the New Year of 1974, the roar of the 5.5 sounded different, wrong. A splitting, cracking sound, once – then silence. I turned over uneasily in my bed, and stared at the rocky blast wall of my sangar. A snake lived there somewhere and, since its arrival, the rats which had hitherto shared my accommodation, had vanished, eaten or fled. This snake left its curving graceful spoor on the sandy floor of the boulder-edged square patch in front of my quarters, fashioned by Raqaishi – 'a *majlis* for the Qaa'id'. I saw my snake only once, a flickering tail for a second against a rock. Live and let live. But that 5.5 had sounded strange.

Mike Kingscote poked his head through the tent flap. 'Sorry, Colonel,' he said tersely. 'It's the gunners. There's been an accident.' I tumbled out of bed, shouted for Manjit Singh and drove my battered Landrover fast up the Wadi Mughsayl and round into the tributary wadi where A Battery was positioned. The old 5.5 had spoken for the last time. A shell had exploded in the breech – the nightmare of gunners in every army since the invention of gunpowder. The barrel of the huge weapon had been torn from the gun and hurled many yards across the wadi. Incredibly it was stuck in the sandy soil, for all the world like a javelin thrown by a giant hand. The Number One, the gunner who had pulled the lanyard to fire the piece, lay in a crumpled heap some yards from the weapon; mercifully he was dead. The Bombardier in charge also lay nearby and was badly wounded in the head. Swiftly Manjit rigged a saline drip and prepared him for a helicopter move to the Field Surgical Team in Salalah.

Later that morning Adrian did what had to be done and ordered his men to stand to their guns. 'Take post!' NCOs shouted orders and the gunners ran to their familiar positions, kneeling upon one knee, alert for the orders to come. A comprehensive harassing shoot got under way. Soon the barrels were scorching hot, the gunners slick with sweat, and the thick dust swirled round the echoing reverberating wadi. Throats ached with shouting orders or their acknowledgements; the acrid smoke stung the eyes. It was the old story: if you're thrown, get on again – quickly. It was a good battery.

About this time I was told by Headquarters Dhofar Brigade that the long-rumoured help by British Army engineers to build the Hornbeam fence was at last on hand. Very tangible evidence of this appeared in the enthusiastic, extrovert and ample form of Major John Blashford-Snell who arrived in our early morning resupply helicopter from Salalah. At first he was treated with a certain amount of caution by NFR. His flair for publicity, which had helped to get many of his past exploration expeditions off the ground, was rather at odds with the slightly laconic and 'throw-away' manner of some officers in the Regiment. (A notable exception was the exuberant Angus Ramsay who had an immediate and strong rapport with our visiting sapper.) John, however, proved very rapidly that he was a practical, up-to-date and excellent combat engineer with a tremendous flair for improvization. He was also a charming and amusing man, and a brilliant raconteur. In brief, he couldn't lose, and didn't. He swiftly assessed the requirement – wiring, mines and booby traps – and allotted a troop under Lieutenant John Hoskinson for the task. After a little initial problem with heat exhaustion, these sappers worked magnificently and to good effect. The fence grew apace. Meanwhile John turned his own attention to the problem of the Katyshuska rockets. The ones which had been fired at SAF positions had proved that they could penetrate thick sangar walls with ease. Worse, their trajectory meant they would fall from above, so that is where the protection needed to be. Ashoq was an obvious target and had already received a number of Katyshuska 'incomers', although luckily there had been no direct hits. John was able to help enormously by arranging for electrically driven hi-cycle drills to be made available. These clawed down into the solid rock and thus stronger, deeper sangars with stout rock roofs were built. The silhouettes of these new positions were lower too, thus making them less easy targets to hit.

John had been given Dhofar-wide tasks by the Brigade Commander and so disappeared to the central *jebel* once he had got all his work under way on the Hornbeam Line. He returned from time to time, always with helpful advice, and gave his already hard working soldiers added impetus. Elsewhere his men were busy building schools and digging wells for the Civil Aid teams. The war to win hearts and minds was also gaining impetus.

I allowed myself a little quiet satisfaction with the way things were going along the Hornbeam Line. Company patrols and ambushes were well organized and followed a vigorous programme. Wiring and mining with John Hoskinson's men, aided by Pindook's pioneers, were going well. Few, if any, *adoo* were getting through. I decided that I could afford the time to go to Salalah by vehicle – something I hadn't done up to then. This would give me the opportunity of visiting the Adonib platoon on the way in, and then of discussing future plans with Jack Fletcher. Above all, I thought to myself, I could get a bath and pick up some clean clothes in Umm al Ghawarif. I did, however, break one of my own rules and decided against taking a second Landrover as an escort vehicle – a silly omission which could have had very serious consequences as I was to find out.

I set off in the cool of the early morning, Mohamed at the wheel and Abdullah in the back; silent as always, radio headset over his ears. In common with all the *'jebel* runners' the vehicle was stripped down to the basic chassis – no windscreen, side screens or superstructure. Riding in it – on it – was rather like being served on a tray carried by a drunken waiter.

The first part of our route lay east along the coastal strip. It was exhilarating driving along by the sparkling sea, a swirling cloud of dust behind us and a smooth expanse of firm sand in front. After a while, however, this coastal strip gave way to increasingly more difficult rocky outcrops and we swung away from the sea and threaded our way through some low hills. When we were about halfway to Adonib the ground became very broken and we were confronted by a steep ridge. Both flanks of this feature dropped steeply into rocky wadis. There was no way round and so our only route lay straight over the top. Mohamed looked rather thoughtful and I knew why. Although the obstacle presented no great difficulty to a reasonable Landrover, our vehicle was really rather unreasonable. Its weary old engine was developing roughly half the horsepower it should. Mohamed put the vehicle into four-wheel drive, stamped on the accelerator and gunned it up the slope. The engine howled, the wheels churned up the slippery, gravelly incline and we very nearly made it to the top – nearly, but not quite. We gradually slowed down and, as the gradient neared one in two, we slewed sideways and sickeningly, with ever-increasing speed, started to slide backwards down the hill! The brakes were useless and we hurtled downwards, bounding into the air from time to time as the wheels hit large boulders and rocks strewn on that fearful scree. 'Jump,' I yelled. Easier said than done with the Landrover travelling at the speed it was. I recall hurling myself from my seat assisted by a last tremendous bound in the air as we bucked across a small gully.

There was a tremendous crash and when I recovered my senses again I could see the vehicle upside down with its wheels pointing skywards. Mohamed, Abdullah, what of them? They would have had no chance if they had failed to leap clear. I heard a sound behind me. There they both were, God be praised, sitting up and looking as bewildered as I was. As one man we muttered '*Allah Kareem*!' He was – very generous indeed. Especially so when, having first recovered our rifles, we found that the radio set, miraculously, still worked perfectly. I was soon speaking to Mike Kingscote. 'We'll get someone to you as soon as we can,' he said. 'In the meantime keep a sharp lookout'. A good point. We toiled up to the top of the ridge and built a sangar. We had two full water bottles apiece (and there was the radiator water as a reserve) and fifty rounds of ammunition each. Things could have been much worse and we settled down to wait.

At last we saw a smudge of dust from the west and soon heard the sound of Landrover engines. Two vehicles drew up at the bottom of our ridge and Raqaishi leapt out from the first one, grinning from ear to ear. 'My God, Sahib', he said. 'What have you done to your Landrover?' And then, seeing blood on my leg, leapt at me with an enormous field dressing which he clapped over a minute cut on my shin! Soon I was continuing my journey in Raqaishi's Landrover leaving that admirable officer organizing the recovery of my wretched vehicle to Mughsayl.

In Salalah Mary Fletcher, Jack's pretty wife, invited me to dinner in their bungalow on Salalah beach. First I bathed luxuriously in my old *bait* at Umm al Ghawarif, now occupied by Bill Kerr. It was a different world only a few miles from the Hornbeam Line.

On one such evening, some time earlier, my fellow guest at dinner with Jack and Mary turned out to be Sultan Qaboos himself. He arrived in a Range Rover convoy, his bodyguard occupying the vehicles surrounding his own. Clad in white *dishdashas* these silent, intent men flitted like wraiths to positions completely surrounding the bungalow. There they remained unmoving while the Sultan was within. The Sultan was easy and charming to talk to. He possessed the dignity and courtesy of his race aad had a shrewd and delightful sense of humour. Now, however, there were no guests other than myself. Just a warm, pleasing evening with two strong friends.

The next day, after a session in the Brigadier's office on future operations, I returned to Mughsayl by Landrover; stopping once more at Adonib to talk to the Firqa Bait Said. The trip back was uneventful and I was soon back in my familiar wadi. Mike Kingscote brought me up to date with Hornbeam happenings as we sat in the cool evening in front of his tent. 'Have a curried mussel', he said, passing a plate of those delicious delicacies which had been prepared by Nasser, the Mess Steward. Mike collected the mussels from the beach at Mughsayl where the sea teemed with crayfish, barracuda and turtles. Fresh turtle soup was another of Nasser's dishes, and once we tried turtle curry, but only once – it was quite disgusting. Sharks also abounded and could be seen clearly from a helicopter as they turned effortlessly in the blue waters.

Viv Rowe joined us and the talk switched to plans for the immediate future. He wanted my permission to execute a plan which he had been hatching for some time. Choosing his words with care Viv outlined his idea, keeping it brief, in a rather nonchalant, matter-of-fact style which did not deceive me for one moment. 'A routine affair', his manner indicated.

'Shall I go ahead then?' he asked. 'Yes? OK?'

'Just a moment, Viv,' I said. 'Let's have it again, shall we? Only this time in detail'.

Slowly the highly imaginative (and potentially highly dangerous) scheme was unfolded. Part of Viv's company's operational task in the southern Hornbeam was that of coastal patrol, to ensure the *adoo* were not slipping past our defences by sea. A motorized dhow or 'boom' had been made available for this, and the ancient craft was skippered by Gordon Gillies of the Sultan's Navy. A year earlier Gordon the Boom (as he was referred to by all in SAF) had been sailing along the coast west of Mughsayl, just out of small-arms range, when he sighted a group of *adoo*. These men were on the beach below the Jebel Afal which lay just to the west of Mughsayl. Gordon noticed that a few hundred metres out to sea from this beach was a tiny island, a sea-washed rock only a few yards across, ringed by smaller rocks – a vicious assortment of jagged satellites. The Afal beach, although close to Mughsayl, was totally concealed from it by the curving sweep of the coastline round the Jebel Afal itself. It was from the top of this craggy feature that the PFLO gunners engaged the Mughsayl airstrip. Later, their mortarmen used the same area from which to strike at the SAF positions on the southern Hornbeam. Gordon thought no more about this until some twelve months later when he and Viv, while carrying out a coastal reconnaissance, sailed past the same spot. The idea was then conceived that an observation post (OP) on the tiny island could observe and also, with the necessary communications, direct aircraft and artillery fire onto any *adoo* using the beach. Thus the seed of the plan was sown.

Viv proposed to me that he and one other should land on the island by night, paddling ashore by Gemini rubber dinghy from the boom which would stand well off the coast. Once on the rock they would conceal themselves before daybreak and remain for several days before being withdrawn – again by night. Any resupply necessary would be done by using the Gemini in hours of darkness. A pre-arranged code would be used with the Strikemaster pilots so that the OP's position would not be compromised.

As Viv explained, '*Adoo* intercepting our radio conversation would have no trouble working out that we were sitting on the only rock off their coastline if I gave the usual "left" and "right" corrections [to guns and aircraft]. So that's the plan, Colonel', said Viv, 'Is it on?'

I delayed my reply until a day or so later, after I had taken a look at the minute island from a Jet Ranger helicopter. There it was, a grey, white-rimmed dot in the deep blue-green sea, close, oh very close, to the Afal beach. If the *adoo* detected the OP there would be no hope of rescue or survival for Viv and his companion. But, if the observers remained unseen there was a chance of dealing the Front a hard and totally unexpected blow – especially to their morale.

'It's on,' I said to Viv later. He had by then decided that the chances of my agreeing were nil. He grinned, nodded and commenced detailed planning the same day. All was ready by the time the moon state was right – we didn't want a bright night for the landing, and one February afternoon saw Viv and Tony Smith of the Oman Artillery, who was to accompany him and direct fire, embarked on the boom at Mughsayl. Also aboard the wooden vessel were the stores and equipment, including the all-important radios and water supplies.

For two, maybe three nights running, Gordon, Viv and Tony attempted the landing , but the sea swell was too great. The sea foamed round that jagged ring of minor rocks which guarded the main one, and it was impossible to paddle the black Gemini close enough to disembark the two officers and their equipment. During one such attempt, luckily with the Gemini still inboard, a searchlight stabbed out of the darkness and illuminated the boom. It was a Sultan's Navy fast patrol boat on a routine trip along the coast. The Navy was swiftly and rather colourfully warned off and steered well clear thereafter.

Shortly after this Tony Smith was redeployed elsewhere and Christopher Barnes of C Company volunteered eagerly to replace him. Chris was from the Royal Signals and so would be an ideal man on the radio. After another unsuccessful attempt the sea calmed and the following day the swell had gone. The boom rocked gently in a near placid sea and the water slapped softly against the wooden planking of the hull. The moon state was right too, being not too bright. There was no doubt that the landing was on for the coming night so Viv decided to tie in a land operation with the landing on the island. He briefed his Company Second-in-Command, Said Nasser, to carry this out with half of C Company. Said and his men were to scale the precipitous cliffs of the Jebel Afal after dark and conceal themselves on top to act as an observation post.

The afternoon saw Viv and Chris embarked with all their supplies, and me too. I wanted to see the operation launched and the landing on the island. The sun beat down and the boom bobbed in the swell. Everyone felt rather soporific and relaxed. We would sail after dark. Suddenly the peaceful afternoon was destroyed by the most appalling crashes and explosions on the shore. Not only on the shore, but on my Tactical Headquarters in Mughsayl! Large puffs of smoke bloomed suddenly and violently amongst the sangars and tents. They were far too noisy and earsplitting for mortar bombs or RCL shells. There was no doubt in anyone's minds that Katyshka rockets were landing on NFR Battalion Headquarters! It was clear where my place was and it wasn't on the boom. Wishing Viv and Chris good luck I went ashore by Gemini, the flat bottom of the craft slapping the water with a crack like a giant beaver's tail as the Omani crewman gave the powerful outboard motor full throttle.

At Tactical HQ everyone was in their stand-to positions, and Mike Kingscote had already alerted the jets; one was circling overhead. Each time a rocket fell we worked feverishly with binoculars and compasses to try and detect the position of the firer. Mike directed strikes onto possible areas, but we had little to go on and were not optimistic of any success. After a while the rockets ceased and it turned out to be the one and only Katyshka attack on Mughsayl. It certainly resulted in a keener interest in overhead cover for our sangars thereafter.

Meanwhile out at sea the Gemini headed softly for the island, while Said Nasser's men commenced their climb up the Jebel Afal. Silently Viv and Chris steered the rubber craft between the satellite rocks until it bumped gently against the minute island. This still night there was no problem and the two officers and their equipment were soon safely ashore. They were to remain for four long days and nights.

Viv and Chris concealed themselves as best they could that night and tried to snatch some sleep before dawn. The next day they were able to take stock of their surroundings, but dare not move from their rather exposed position on the southern flank of the rock for fear of being detected. On that first day there was no enemy activity on the beach and that night the cramped observers were able to move. Cautiously they worked their way round to the north (enemy) side of the island and found a fissure, too small to be described as a cave. They were able to use this on the following days as it not only gave them good cover from view, but also protected them from the burning sun. On the second day four armed men with four heavily loaded donkeys appeared on the beach and moved to a large cluster of rocks where they disappeared from view. Several hours later the men emerged without the donkeys and Viv assumed the rocks concealed a supplies dump of some kind. This first piece of useful information was filed away on the OP log.

That night the sea swell returned and the two were drenched to the skin with the flying spume as the waves broke over the tiny rock. The third day was uneventful and that night, the sea being calm once more, Nick Knollys of B Company landed some fresh radio batteries, water and other supplies by Gemini. On the previous night Said Nasser and his men had withdrawn from the Jebel Afal, taking a shorter, more precipitous route which entailed roping down the cliffs using a number of rifle slings buckled together. He was a good soldier, Said Nasser.

On the fourth day, which was to be the last on the island, there was more activity culminating in the late afternoon, with the appearance of a group of armed men moving through some scrub at the far side of the beach. Members of this party bathed rather cautiously in the sea. Those who weren't in the water kept a sharp lookout as if expecting trouble. Perhaps Said Nasser's recent sojourn on the top of the Afal had made them nervous. Viv realized that this *adoo* group probably represented the best target he would get and alerted SOAF by radio. Soon two Strikemasters were airborne and awaiting his directions.

Surprise was of course essential in that thick and rocky country if the *adoo* were to be caught in the open, and Viv was careful in his briefing of the lead pilot. In his account after the operation he described what happened next.

A certain amount of bad luck set in. The first aircraft missed the target by only 100 metres with his marker rocket. The second air-craft was given the coded correction and went the wrong way! Its pilot was new in SOAF and had arrived only that afternoon from the North. He had been tasked at short notice when a previously briefed pilot's aircraft had become unserviceable. The new man had not been briefed on the control code. There then followed a fairly frustrating sequence of orders, guarded explanations and, very nearly, swear words. We solved it by directing the lead pilot as arranged, and he then gave translated directions to the number two using the pilot's line of approach as his correction line.

The enemy disappeared into cover, not surprisingly, after the first rocket was fired but thereafter, having briefed the second pilot, the OP was able to bring the aircraft in more and more accurately onto the area where the rebels lay. Viv had opted to use aircraft rather than artillery, as he had worked out that the target was 300 metres beyond the planning range of Adrian Short's guns at Mughsayl. However, after the jets had completed their strike, he decided to try the guns in order to keep the *adoo* pinned down, or perhaps cause casualties to them should they attempt to withdraw. To the satisfaction of the two observers the first round landed accurately in the centre of the target. It afterwards transpired that the additional range achieved was due to the fact that the ammunition had been standing in the heat of the sun all day and was baking hot before being loaded into the breech! Viv and Chris corrected the fall of shot onto the stores area behind the rocks where the *adoo* donkeys had been unloaded on the first day. This also was beyond recognized range, but received a very heavy and highly accurate pasting nevertheless. A Strikemaster returned to the scene before dusk and happily thickened up the bombardment using Sura rockets.

Night fell, but Viv found that by using his binoculars he could detect any movement on the beach and was able to carry on using the artillery after dark. As the ammunition cooled, however, it could no longer reach the extreme target areas. At intervals there were bursts of small-arms fire from the *adoo*, but none appeared to be directed at the island.

In the middle of the night the Gemini slid quietly in on a smooth sea with Nick Knollys at the helm. The operation was over and Viv and Chris were lifted back to the boom, to be greeted warmly by Gordon, and also a grinning Ian Gardiner from A Company, who had smuggled himself (unbeknown to me) aboard. Eagerly Ian engaged known enemy positions with the boom's .5-inch Browning, also likely caves which could be spotted by an image intensifier on board the boom. The .5 Browning must have been nettling the *adoo* because a chorus of AK47 fire broke out in response, to be joined by the thudding note of a 12.7 Shpagin heavy machine gun, and what sounded like a 7.62 Gurynov. It was time the boom departed and, cramming on all possible speed, it eased away from the coast at a stately 3 knots flat out, but it took a long time to get out of reach of that Shpagin. Mughsayl looked good to the returning OP officers when they were put ashore the next morning.

As was often the case, there was no immediate feedback on the number of enemy casualties, although it later became clear through intelligence sources that a number had been killed. Certainly the effect on *adoo* morale was significant and I considered the operation highly successful.

181

I believed Viv and Chris had shown remarkable courage. It is easier to be brave in the heat of battle, or on the spur of the moment when one's passions are inflamed. To sit for four scorching days and four drenching nights on a tiny rock close – very close – to the enemy shore, with no hope of rescue if discovered, requires a very special sort of bravery. They had it, but few do.

For this action, and for his courage during his previous tour and the current one, Viv received the Sultan's Distinguished Service Medal for Gallantry.

Chapter 16

A Company's Battle, a Farewell and the End Game

The *adoo* Firqa bin Dhabeeb operated in the savage country of the Wadi Sha'ath east of the Hornbeam Line. Early in March 1974 we received an intelligence report, from a normally reliable source, that a group of about sixteen from this *firqa* were positioned just south of Idlewild Field, probably ready to receive a party carrying supplies and bringing reinforcements, who were about to attempt to cross from the west. This was A Company's area of responsibility and Johnny Braddell-Smith was not one to hang about when such an opportunity presented itself. On the night of 12 March his four platoons slipped quietly down from the Idlewild ridge and ambushed likely enemy approaches in the Wadi Sha'ath. Johnnie was determined to hunt the men of the Bin Dhaheeb down, and bring them to battle.

Nothing was seen that night and so, the next morning, Johnny ordered Ian Gardiner, his Second in Command, to take two platoons and set up further ambushes to the east. The remainder of the company stayed where it was with Johnny, concealed and silent. On the Idlewild ridge the company 81mm mortars were positioned, ready to support operations as they developed. Unbeknown to Johnny and Ian, however, the Bin Dhaheeb had already been reinforced by the supplies party from the west. A Company was not tracking down sixteen or so men, but was facing a much larger enemy group – which meant that splitting its strength would allow the enemy to attack Ian Gardiner's detachment with superior numbers. Events developed suddenly and swiftly on that baking hot March morning.

Any high-circling bird of prey would have commanded a fine view of the drama about to be enacted far below. It was a broad brown stage with two main groups of players: Johnny with his two platoons lay in the dusty scrub, motionless, eyes watching intently through the glaring sunlight as a group of ten *adoo* came towards them. They moved easily yet cautiously, unaware of the waiting soldiers, but alert. Gradually they came nicely into range. The soldiers, fingers curled round the triggers of their weapons, safety catches off, hearts thumping, lay and yearned for the word to open fire, and release them from their stifling tension. It was now 1130hrs.

Stage right, to the east, and Ian Gardiner's platoons were moving tactically forward, in bounds. One platoon lay on a small *jebel*, ready to give covering fire to the second platoon, which, with Ian, was moving across difficult ground; it was a risk, but under the circumstances, seemed acceptable. Ian, accepting it, moved steadily forward with his men. Some stretches of ground they had crossed were better than others, but this was a bad bit, so move on. The ground was difficult because it gave the advantage to any enemy who might take up positions on the rocky ridges covering the SAF approach. That same soaring bird, with its switching, swivelling eye, would have seen that this was precisely what the enemy were doing. One or two had already observed A Company's approach; others, in dead ground, raced to take up positions overlooking the unsuspecting soldiers.

Perhaps, if Johnny's ambush had been sprung first, events would have been very different. As it was, the *adoo* lying in the rocks facing Ian opened the performance with a withering skein of automatic fire, which fell across the advancing soldiers, causing them to drop to the ground and claw their way to the meagre cover offered by the scattered rocks and parched bushes.

When the chatter of small-arms fire split the air, the enemy walking into Johnny's ambush stopped abruptly in their tracks, then, turning, ran sure-footed over the broken ground to swell the numbers now surrounding Ian's men, hammering them with everything they had got.

One of the main tests a soldier faces in war concerns his ability to lift his head, locate the enemy and return fire – despite the screaming, howling nightmare which fills his ears and numbs his senses as bullets hit the rocks and ground around him. It requires a supreme effort of will – some could not, and never would, manage it; the good soldiers did. For the only way to survive the close-quarter firefight was to hit back hard and effectively, and very quickly. The alternative was to lie inert, and probably die. If too many failed to raise their heads then certainly all would die.

Lying alongside Ian Gardiner, and firing back at the enemy with a GPMG, was a SAS man, Trooper Kent. Ian directed and corrected his fire as he too searched desperately for the enemy positions. Suddenly Kent collapsed, dead, behind his weapon. A group of four soldiers dashed across to help Ian. One of these, Corporal Hamid, was killed immediately; another – a SAS trooper – fell badly wounded. Leaving the two dead men, Ian and his group stumbled to better cover taking the wounded with them. To have remained where they were would have proved fatal. In the new position another soldier was shot and wounded. Once again Ian's small party had to seek a new refuge under heavy fire. Ian had already contacted Johnny by radio and now continued as well as he could with the intensive firefight.

The morning wore agonizingly on, the sun passed its glaring zenith, and by early afternoon things were looking bleak for Ian and his men. Despite mortar and jet support the *adoo* were gaining the upper hand. They had outflanked the NFR position and had looted the two bodies still lying in the open. Curiously, however, they had left the GPMG and radio set with the dead men, making off with epaullettes, boots and a self-loading rifle.

The firefight continued unabated, but help for the beleaguered patrol was at hand. Viv Rowe, C Company Commander, had moved forward under his own initiative and had seen Ian's vulnerable position. He asked for part of his Company to be deployed to assist and this was immediately approved. With C Company, Strikemaster and mortar support the firefight finally swung in SAF's favour and Viv, having thwarted the *adoo* attempt to surround Ian's group, took control of all the supporting fire.

Suddenly some figures appeared close to Ian's position, one of whom sprinted across and dived for cover alongside him. It was Johnny Braddell-Smith, calm and laconic, proferring a cigarette and through his very nonchalance bringing a sense of order and sanity to a fraught situation. With covering fire, Ian and Johnny were able to collect the dead and wounded ready for evacuation by helicopter, although they were under fire themselves from the enemy. The helicopter itself was hit by a burst of firing as it lifted off with its casualties, but made it back to Salalah.

With C Company covering them Johnny, Ian and their men were able to complete the long, hot and weary journey back to their position on the Hornbeam Line. Ian told me afterwards that Viv's part in the six-hour battle and the survival of the A Company patrol was pivatol. Although they received casualties NFR also inflicted losses on the enemy, but most importantly had achieved their main aim of discouraging the *adoo* from attempting to penetrate the Line.

I wrote Johnny's, Ian's and A Company Sergeant Major Said Murr's citations that night. I am happy to say that Johnnie received a Bravery Medal, Ian a Distinguished Service Medal (Gallantry) and Said Murr a

Sultan's Commendation for his part in the action. These awards reflected SAF's respect for brave men.*

However, the Bin Dhaheeb's tails were up! Had they not taken on NFR, killed two and wounded two? Had the soldiers not withdrawn? That would teach SAF to meddle in the affairs of the Wadi Sha'ath. Clearly the story could not end there. I urgently asked Jack Fletcher for extra men to man the Hornbeam Line in order that I could take NFR out and sweep the Sha'ath for the Bin Dhaheeb. I had my reply immediately – two companies of the Muscat Regiment were put at my disposal. Operation Iqaab was on.

A few nights later A and B Companies, together with my Tactical Headquarters, walked out from Kumasi along the Idlewild ridge and then dropped south to the Wadi Sha'ath and pre-arranged ambush positions. The next morning C Company flew in by helicopter and positioned itself in reserve, ready to be used to outflank or cut off any enemy we might encounter. The Oman Artillery provided a troop of light guns on a feature we knew as 'Windy Ridge' and we grouped our mortars in a firebase overlooking the Sha'ath.

From intelligence reports we knew that the enemy in the area based themselves on the Hurhurit waterhole, deep in the tributary of the Wadi Nar which supplied it with water in the rainy season. Our Bait Kathir guide knew Huhurit and said he would lead us to it. On the second night of the operation, I therefore left A Company to hold the high ground at Idlewild while B and C Companies moved down the ridges flanking the Wadi Nur. Soon the soldiers were positioned overlooking the Huhurit waterhole. With C Company staying on the commanding piquets, B clambered down to the bottom of the wadi. There, on the sandy soil, they soon picked up the spoor of men and goats. Following these tracks Angus Ramsay and his soldiers found spacious caves recently used as sleeping areas by an estimated twenty to twenty-five men. Further caves were walled off for keeping goats and there was evidence of very recent use of these too, by up to 200 animals. There was a good deal of *adoo* rubbish – tobacco pouches of a type sold in Aden, and so on. Angus moved on north up the wadi and found the well itself, which was reinforced with concrete and fed by a constant trickle from a long cleft in the rock.

I had refused permission to poison the waterhole, but said it should be temporarily destroyed if possible. Angus was the right man for the

* The story of the wresting of the initiative from the *adoo*, the winning of the firefight and the heroic recovery of the bodies and equipment has been written by Ian in his book *In the Service of the Sultan*.

job – a master in the art of improvization. In a nearby cave he discovered, to his huge delight, five high-explosive, 2-inch mortar bombs. Using these, plus an augmenting charge for a 60mm mortar bomb, a fuze fashioned from a bandage and the contents of several rifle cartridges, he made a very satisfactory bang indeed. When the dust and smoke cleared Angus peered anxiously at his handiwork. Not bad – the cleft in the rock was filled with rubble, the bowl of the well itself had been destroyed and there was no trickle of water at all. He estimated that it would take the enemy a week's uneasy digging, tunnelling and concreting to repair his night's work. Having thoroughly searched the rest of the area the B Company men clambered back up the wadi sides to the piquet positions.

For three nights and three days we hunted the Bin Dhaheeb over that savage ground. We saw one or two small groups and engaged them at long range, but it was the old story: we were on the best ground and the *adoo* chose not to close with us. Despite the coat-tailing which we indulged in at every opportunity, they left us severely alone. My mission of bringing the Bin Dhaheeb to battle and destroying the enemy *firqa* was not achieved. But we had retaken the initiative, we were calling the tune and the *adoo* knew it. The lessons I once learnt in those Ogaden villages near Danot were paying off. 'Face' – so important to a Muslim – had been restored for the soldiers of the Sultan.

On 24 March 1974, NFR returned to the Hornbeam Line and the rifle companies resumed their patrolling, ambushing and watchful roles. The wiring and mining was progressing excellently and PFLOAG found the task of resupplying and reinforcing their Central and Eastern Units impossible to achieve. Only a tiny trickle of men managed to get through our defences and even these had some hair-raising stories to tell. The final link of the Hornbeam chain yet to be forged was the northern stretch between Bole and Oven. This was a lengthy part of the front, but it would be the easiest to do. Although riven by wadis the ridges between provided a level enough run all the way and there were no really fierce gradients to negotiate.

There had been a lot of work going on in diplomatic circles which was to help me enormously in the completion of the fence. As a result of this activity a stocky, confident and extrovert Major of the Royal Jordanian Army arrived one morning in my Operations Tent. He commanded a squadron of Jordanian Engineers and had been sent to me by Jack Fletcher to assess the task of completing the wiring. I showed him the northern stretch by helicopter and together we plotted the route for the fence and a road to run along its eastern side. Such a road would be a boon as it meant we could resupply Oven from Bole by vehicle and thus save valuable helicopter hours.

Brimming with confidence the Jordanian Major shook my hand warmly on departure. 'I will return with my squadron,' he announced. And he did – but shortly after I had left Oman so I never saw the northern part of the fence completed.

I have a sharp clear memory from this period of a moment in the wadi at Mughsayl. I had been visiting Raqaishi's Headquarter Company soldiers in their camp, which he had sited some hundreds of yards from Tactical HQ and close to the *khor*. It was a hot still day and the sun was at its zenith. I could see the scarred dome of Jebel Ashoq further up the wadi and, beyond that, the dark and rather ominous-looking masses of the Killi and Reef features. My feet stirred the dry dust in the wadi bottom and I picked them up to avoid the rocks and large stones. It was very silent. A voice inside me said, 'Savour this; enjoy what you are doing; live every moment – it is a unique experience which can never reoccur.' I felt that very keenly. I was happy – not in retrospect, with the bad times clouded, but there, then, in the Wadi Mughsayl.

I walked on to the operations tent where Mike Kingscote handed me a telegram. 'Guess who is going to Sandhurst in April?' it asked, and continued, 'No prizes'. It was from my son Anthony and rounded off a memorable yet uneventful day. I would be back in England for the Sovereign's Parade when he would be commissioned, for I was due to hand over command of NFR to John Pollard (of my Regiment) on 14 April. It would not be easy to leave. I was enmeshed in NFR, in Dhofar, in Oman. Brigadier John Graham had not been wrong in his letter to me at Beaconsfield. I was involved, totally.

Over the next week I travelled the length of the Hornbeam Line and spent a little time in each NFR position, saying my farewells to the Omani and Baluchi soldiers. I shook many a hand and drank so much sweet tea that I estimated I was doing about five miles to the gallon of it as I travelled slowly between the posts.

'Go with God, Sahib,' they said.

'In God's generosity,' I replied, but sadly.

On my last morning I sat in the open doorway of a helicopter while the pilot flew me very low along the Hornbeam Line. The soldiers stood up, rifles pointing in the air and waved as we clattered overhead. Suddenly the pilot looked round, ashen-faced.

'That sounds like rifle fire – they couldn't possibly be crazy enough to be firing in the air, could they?' he asked.

I smiled to myself, listened to the multitude of popping sounds and saw the rifles bucking on the soldiers' shoulders as joyously and dangerously they gave their traditional salute. 'Good heavens no!' I said – but they were.

* * *

Believers! Shall I point out to you
a profitable course
Which will save you from a woeful scourge?
Have faith in Allah and His Apostle
and fight for His cause with your wealth and your persons
That would be best for you,
if you but know it.

The Koran
Sura 61: Battle Array.*

By the middle of 1974 the Hornbeam Line was finally completed. A formidable barrier of barbed wire laced with mines and each of the dominating features capped with a SAF fortress. In the wadis at night the Sultan's soldiers lay in ambush, varying their locations and timings so that the enemy never knew which of their uneasy approach routes were being watched. Patrolling by SAF continued too, deep into country which PFLOAG† had previously thought to be safe. The Hornbeam Line worked. It was an obvious success. Obvious because Salalah received no shells or rockets, which fell instead on the impregnable stone sangars of the Hornbeam.

After the spring of 1974 virtually no Front supplies or reinforcements penetrated the barrier. The *adoo firqas* in the Eastern and Central areas dwindled rapidly. Some of the rebels were hunted down by SAF and killed; others slipped quietly back into the obscurity of their *jebali* tribes. A great many took themselves and their rifles to Salalah and declared themselves to be men of Sultan Qaboos.

General Tim Creasey and his new Dhofar Brigade Commander, Brigadier John Akehurst, were now able to turn their formidable attention to rolling up the *adoo* from the Hornbeam back across the PDRY border. Brigadier Akehurst, who had relieved Brigadier Fletcher after the latter's highly successful tour, was to prove to be an equally brilliant commander.

---

*Translation by N.J. Dawood.
† By this time retitled PFLO by the Front – Peoples' Front for the Liberation of Oman.

To help SAF in their task of pushing the enemy across the border, and taking on those who stayed to fight, were the Iranian soldiers and the swelling government *firqas* with their attendant SAS advisers. As this rolling-up operation moved westwards, so the Civil Aid Teams moved in and established their schools and clinics, wells and shops on the *jebel*. The Hearts and Minds were not being neglected. In some cases the CATs moved in hard on the heels of the skirmishing soldiers while the sound of fighting still split the air.

Further strongly held lines were established as SAF advanced towards PDRY. One, the Damavand Line – west of and roughly parallel to the Hornbeam, and then finally, in October 1975, the position at Sarfait, on the border – was extended to the sea, thus sealing Oman against invaders in the logical place at long last.

Yet the *adoo* had not given in easily, fiercely contesting the progress of the Sultan's forces. In one such battle, on Christmas Day 1974, Johnny Braddell-Smith, detached from NFR to work with the Firqa Tariq Bin Said, took part. His *firqa* were working with an Iranian battalion which came under very heavy fire from an enemy ambush position.

The Iranians were in some confusion and at this point Johnny's *firqa* Sergeant Major was killed. Typically Johnny ran forward to recover the body but tragically fell under a hail of bullets. He was awarded the Sultan's Gallantry Medal (Posthumous) and is buried in the Christian Cemetry in Muscat. Johnny was one of the best and bravest soldiers in the Dhofar War.

It came as no surprise to those involved that the scene of the most bitter fighting in the final stages of the war was the storage cave complex at Shirashitti, an unattractive name for a particularly unpleasant spot. In January 1975, the Jebel Regiment was nominated to attack the caves and the plan was for the advance of this force to be preceded by a *firqa* screen of skirmishers. Disastrously, however, surprise for the operation was lost because of the heavy supporting fire insisted on by the *firqas* before they moved forward. Thus alerted, the *adoo* were ready and waiting in excellent ambush positions which dominated the line of the SAF advance.

It is rare that ambushes work in precisely the way they are planned, but this one did – only too well. As the leading company picked its way forward over the rocks the enemy commander sprang his trap. A hail of automatic fire hit the leading troops so effectively that thirteen were killed and twenty-two injured within the first hour. A British officer, Captain Nigel Loring, was amongst those who died immediately, and Captain MacLucas was one of the wounded. It was a scene of awful shambles. The dead lay where they had fallen; the wounded who could move crawled painfully towards cover from the awful hail of bullets; the cries of the injured could be heard when the din of automatic weapons stilled for a moment. The rest of the vanguard found what cover they could, but were hopelessly pinned down. At last this decimated company was extricated with the help of the SAS and Strikemasters. Fighting continued fiercely for weeks, with the enemy earning respect from their opponents for their courage and tenacity in defence.

Eventually and inevitably Shirashitti fell to the Sultan, with the help of the Oman Armoured Car Squadron under Major Patrick Brook which pounded the limestone caves with their 76mm guns and prevented the enemy approaching them. With their stores complex gone the heart went out of the rebels, although they continued to resist bitterly. The seizing of the ground between the Sarfait feature and the sea in mid-October 1975 spelled the end of enemy resistance and at the end of the year Sultan Qaboos was able to declare that the war was over.

The Sultan issued a medal to his soldiers to mark their victory in Dhofar. The struggle had lasted for ten long years and had been a very close-run thing. The medal is called As Samood which means 'Endurance', an apt name.

Epilogue

After leaving Oman and the Dhofar War I felt that I had achieved a modest peak in my military career. As a subaltern in Somaliland I was lucky enough to have had an exciting and enjoyable time with the Scouts. Much later I was fortunate to have commanded a fine battalion on active service in the Dhofar Campaign. There I had all the toys to play with too: helicopters, artillery, Strikemasters and, at one point, the Iranian Special Forces as well! Therefore, after a spell as a staff officer in Catterick Camp in North Yorkshire, I felt the time had come for me to leave the Army, albeit a few years before retiring age. I did not wish to sit behind a desk for the rest of my service.

There was another reason too. Since our marriage, my wife Paula had lived with me in twenty or so houses in various parts of the world. She had loyally complied with the 'Pack and Follow' code of the army wife in that period. She had lived in Tripoli, Cyrenaica, Cyprus (twice), Germany (twice), Denmark and Northern Ireland during the 'troubles'. Earlier she would have come with me to the Canal Zone of Egypt, but no families were allowed in Tel el Kebir! She could not accompany me whilst I was in Dhofar for two and a half years, and it was then that we bought a house of our own for the first time, in the county of her birth, North Yorkshire. She loved it and although she would have moved again were I to be posted abroad, it seemed to me it was time to settle, and I submitted my resignation.

Alas, our happy life in Scackleton, a hamlet in the Howardian Hills, was not to last. In the autumn of 1980 Paula became ill and died the following year in the house and county she loved.

Some time later General Sir Timothy Creasey, now commanding all the Sultan's Forces in Oman, suggested I applied for a job with the Oman Internal Security Service (known at that time as the Oman

Research Department, or ORD). I took his advice, was accepted and thus I continued my association with Oman.

After finally leaving Oman I worked for a while as Clerk to the Curriers Livery Company. It was a friendly company and I enjoyed my time there. However, I realized that I was not really the man for the job and when an old friend from Oman, Brigadier Peter Stewart-Richardson, suggested that I visited Afghanistan with him, I leapt at the chance. This led to my being asked by the security firm Defence Systems Limited if I would do a job for them in Afghanistan, which I did in 1992 and 1993. Following that I worked as a security advisor under my own name for various NGOs (non-governmental organizations). This work took me to South Sudan, Pakistan, Kenya and, in 1995, back to Somaliland (once more independent).

I had not expected ever to return again to Somaliland for after its independence in 1960 and becoming part of Somalia, the whole country descended into chaos – war with its neighbour Ethiopia and among its own people. However, return I did, in 1995.

Somaliland

Since its formation in 1960 the Republic of Somalia has never achieved lasting stability as a nation. It has been devastated by war with Ethiopia in the Ogaden, trouble on its border with Kenya, and with continual and bloody inter-clan fighting. In 1969, following a coup, an authoritarian regime was established under Major General Siad Barre, but the chaos continued. Barre was ousted in 1991 following which there has been no functional government in Mogadishu.

After the fall of Barre, an independent Republic of Somaliland was declared in north-west Somalia in the former British Somaliland territory, predominately the Isaaq tribal area. This indepency has yet to be recognized by a number of Western countries, including Great Britain. The north-western part of Somalia – Puntland – was declared an automonous region in 1998.

A limited number of aid agencies, some of whom found working in the chaos of southern Somalia impossible, entered the new Somaliland at the request of its president to provide assistance. There was a great deal to do. One of these agencies was a team from the Save the Children Fund (SCF). The years 1994 to 1995 saw a deterioration in the country, with fighting breaking out in the airport at the capital Hargeisa in November 1995, which involved shelling in the city. Fighting also broke out in the town of Burao. Security in the outlying areas of the country fell into the hands of local clan leaders who failed to control the many unruly and armed elements.

In the light of the volatile security situation SCF offered a consultancy to me in order that I might assess the situation and make appropriate suggestions for the security of their staff and their operations. Thus, forty-five years after I had left Somaliland, I was given the chance to return, which I had always wanted to do.

On 25 November 1995 I arrived by air in Djibouti, once the capital of French Somaliland but now a country in its own right. I was met by Ahamed Ibrahim of the SCF and the following day flew by small Beechcraft aircraft to Somaliland. We did not land at Hargeisa airfield as I had years ago, since it was unusable due to the fighting. Instead we touched down on a hammered earth strip at a spot called Kalabaydh some miles from the capital. There I was met by Mohamed Gadaf of SCF and we sped off down a tarmac road to Hargeisa in a Toyota Landcruiser. We passed through the familiar countryside of thorn bushes and acacia trees, sandy soil, with camels and fat-tailed sheep on the sparse grazing. I noticed that many tribesmen were wearing trousers and shirts, with a few in lungis or traditional dress. On the way we had to negotiate two road blocks manned by surly looking characters sporting Kalashnikov assault rifles.

Hargeisa had grown almost beyond recognition and the streets were filled with vehicles, mostly battered and old. There were many signs of destruction and damage from the fighting. My work kept me in Hargeisa for a couple of days and during this time I was able to see something of the town and surrounding area. The SCF camp was sited on the edge of a large sandy *tug* – a dry river bed or wadi – and, accompanied by two members of SCF, I went for a stroll along the *tug* as far as the British cemetry which had been established in the time of the Protectorate. A sad sight it was, too. Savagely desecrated, the tombstones were smashed and scattered, the tombs broken. It was wanton destruction and, one of my companions said, still going on as more stones had been broken since his last visit a year earlier. I took a photograph of the broken gravestones of a Scouts officer who had died in 1947. There were graves there of East African Armoured Car soldiers and others who had died in, and in some cases for, Somaliland. We walked on. A group of boys who were kicking a ball about in the sand started to follow us and jeered, calling us names. I thought of the old days when, during the time I spent in Hargeisa before moving to Awareh, I had ridden down this same valley. Then small boys greeted me shouting 'Ma nabut ba?' saluting and grinning.

I also thought of the disastrous intervention of the UN-led intervention in Mogadishu. One could see why feelings could run high against the West. The *Somaliland News*, published by the Ministry of

194

Information in Hargeisa (an A4 six-page, photocopied document dated 1 December 1995) carried the following notice:

For your Thought. *(sic)* Which of the two AIDS hinders a Nations Development
  HIV Virus Aids or Foreign Aid???

While in Hargeisa I also visited the area south of the town which had received a severe hammering in the recent fighting. It had been shelled, mortared and swept with bullets. It was a mess, especially the side opposite to the airport. This area included the old Hargeisa Club, now battered and bullet scarred. It was difficult to recognize the place where I had once relaxed and eaten many a curry lunch! Also included in my tour was the State House built in the early 1950s by the British as the new Government House. Obviously once a beautiful building, it was now ruined and vandalized. In retrospect it is incredible that such an expensive project had been undertaken only a few years before the country received its independence. The foundation stone laid by the Governor stood forlornly in the once-grand grounds.

Later I went to the airport. The buildings had been vandalized and stripped, and two damaged MIG fighters stood in the hangar. However, the runway itself was in good order and the shell holes had been neatly repaired. On the way back to the SCF camp we passed a group of men who were demonstrating in the town and were protesting at the price of *qat*, the drug which so many men chewed. The Government had fixed it at one hundred Somali shillings a measure, but the day before it had risen to one thousand. The men were not happy. Further on in the town we stopped by a shop where a man reached in through the car window and grabbed my shirt. I knocked him away but it illustrated the sort of tension that aid workers there experienced. I deserved what I had got as I had broken one of my own rules and had the car window open in the town!

On 2 December, I travelled by car to Berbera on the northern coast. Mohamed Gadaf, who had been allotted to me as my guide during my visit, was with me. I asked him about his name – Gadaf was unusual for a Somali. He explained that his father was a sailor and after visiting Tiger Bay in Cardiff, he was nicknamed 'Cardiff' or, as pronounced and spelt by the Somalis, 'Gadaf'. He was a good man and a fast but safe driver. The port of Berbera lies 120 miles from Hargeisa and I had travelled there in a 15cwt Bedford truck over a bumpy graded track when with the Scouts. It had then taken me five hours, but now the trip took only two hours on a tarmac road and on a more direct route, although we had to pass through a series of six check posts, each manned by National Army soldiers or by the police. All were armed with AK47 rifles. The main difference I noticed was the almost total lack of wildlife – in the late 1940s the country was alive with game, including a number of varieties of gazelle; there was also a good chance of seeing lion and certainly cheetah, which abounded. The only wildlife I saw in the whole journey was a group of warthogs. Sadly I was to find this on all my journeys during my visit and it was easy to know why – an abundance of Kalashnikovs were to blame.

Halfway to Berbera we passed an obelisk erected by the side of the road. The inscription had gone, but it still bore the dates '1939–45' at the top. It is the memorial to Captain Wilson of the East Surrey Regiment who won the Victoria Cross with the Camel Corps in the campaign against the Italians. His son still visits the country from time to time.

Berbera bore many battle scars with rusting bits of armoured personnel carriers and tanks here and there. Apart from this there was little change from when I had been in the town before. At the docks were many camels being shipped to Saudi Arabia and the Gulf States for meat – a major industry now in a country with many camels and a greatly reduced number of nomads.

Two days later Mohamed and I visited Borama on the border with Ethiopia. This was once the site of the Scouts Depot where I spent about six months at the end of 1949. It was a little over two hours drive from Hargeisa via Kalabayth Airstrip, Dilla and Garyaul where the Depot used to be. The tarmac ended at Dilla and I had a strong sense of the Somaliland I once knew as we drove down the dusty track. The sights were much the same including the women who wore very much the clothing of half a century earlier. The men, however, wore shirts and trousers now, but still carried a stick across their shoulders, a hand on either end, as they walked, in the same manner that they once carried their spears. From Dilla west is Gadabursi country and the road snaked along the Ethiopian border into the hills around Borama. The town had grown, but not a great deal. There were still a number of *ghurgies* around the edge of the town. The hospital, where I had once seen Edum Clarke amputate a man's leg, had grown too and its facilities improved. On the return journey we visited the Depot site at Garyaul, but little remained of the old buildings. There were some recently built huts which were occupied by Somali families. During this trip too there was a dearth of wildlife; we saw a number of baboons but little else.

The following day I flew to Erigavo, in the Eastern part of the Republic, in a Cessna Caravan light aircraft. There had been a number of incidents in this area including shots fired at the Cessna when it landed there earlier in the year. The aircraft was holed and flights suspended for two months. Having seen the aid agencies and held discussions with them, I returned to the airport for the flight back. Some armed, self-appointed 'aircraft security guards' demanded US$70 from me for looking after the aircraft! I refused and, evading clutching hands and much abuse, the pilot, a few passengers and I climbed aboard and took off. The name of the head 'security guard' was handed to the Hargeisa authorities.

On 8 December, I flew back to Djibouti from Karabagh, my work completed. Sitting in the aircraft I reflected on what I had seen of the new Somaliland. My overwhelming feeling was one of sadness. Sadness for the people who had suffered so cruelly through so many years of bloodshed. Sadness for generations of Somali youth who had grown up with the Kalashnikov and no prospect of work, and who spent many an afternoon chewing *qat*. Sadness for the women who struggled in such circumstances to provide for their families and whose status in society was low. Sadness too for the Government striving with few funds to establish a viable state. Lastly, sadness for the decimation of so many animals in a country once almost unique in its richness of wildlife.

Oman

In early April 1982 I was once more in an aircraft flying over the familiar landscape of the Dhofar *jebel*, following the route of the Midway Road far below to Salalah. But there were differences – this time I was flying out as a civilian to take up my appointment with the Oman Research Department. This time there was no Dhofar War and the mountains below showed tarmac roads where once there had been tracks or nothing at all. And, the biggest difference of all, this time I was accompanied by my wife who would be in Salalah with me.

Brigadier Jack Fletcher, the youngest brigadier in the British Army on his promotion, was tipped for the top. He had done brilliantly as Dhofar Brigade Commander and had been given the Order of Oman by the Sultan. On his return to England this was swiftly followed by a CBE and he was informed that he was to be promoted to Major General. Shortly after this, and tragically, Jack was taken ill and died. Jack and his wife Mary were great friends of my wife Paula and I. We had all been in Northern Ireland together – Jack as Commanding Officer of the Second Battallion of the Queen's Regiment, and I as one of his company commanders. Some time after Paula's death Mary and I re-met and later we were married.

Sadly, General Sir Timothy Creasey had died too. They had been a great pair to have guided us through a crucial part of the Dhofar War, the country was lucky to have had them and so was SAF.

197

So Mary was with me in the aircraft; we were both returning to a country we knew and loved. Mary had lived in Salalah with Jack and had worked as a nurse in Salalah military hospital treating our sick and wounded with Medhi. She had made many trips into the *jebel* to attend to sick soldiers and civilians in remote places. For this work in the war zone she had been awarded the Sultan's Commendation Medal.

We had arrived at Seeb International Airport about ten days earlier, and the dramatic development in the country since the war which had ended six years earlier was immediately obvious. The airport set the standard – it was modern and highly efficient. Quite a change from the old one at Bait al Falaj! Good tarmac dual-carriageways led to the capital. On either side new buildings were being erected – well-designed dwellings, ministerial offices, shops and mosques, all built with traditional Arab design in mind and many surrounded by well-watered areas with palm trees, lawns, shrubs and flowers. This development had been undertaken with both efficiency and the Arab delight in beauty and lush gardens. The roads too were lined with young palms and we noticed some impressive hotels under construction. It was difficult to recognize the city itself – it had expanded beyond belief, and was continuing to do so. The old fort which had been the headquarters of SAF at Bait al Falaj, and which once stood some distance from the city centre, was now surrounded by the smart new buildings of modern Muscat. In fact, it was difficult to find and now, appropriately, houses the military museum. In Muscat and Muttrah there were new bridges and flyovers, modern shops and superstores. The Sultan's palace was being grandly expanded. There was only one word for all this activity: impressive! I was, however, glad to see that the forts of Marani and Jelaali still guarded both flanks of the harbour of Mina Qaboos.

When we arrived in Dhofar we found the changes in Salalah were not so dramatic. It had expanded and the *suk* had been modernized, but we were still able to find our way along familiar streets. There has been a good deal of development since with smart houses and even five-star plus hotels – the Crown Plaza and the Hilton included. We did notice a huge change in the roads, however. These were now tarmac and the *jebel* itself was criss-crossed with new and fast routes. There were many cars, including Japenese four-by-fours, and every type of expensive saloon where once battered Landrovers struggled over the tracks. We often travelled down those new roads. Ground that had taken SAF a day to clamber over could now be covered in a quarter of an hour. There was even a good road under construction to Sarfait, an undertaking over jagged ground once considered impossible. In later years I travelled that road, stood on the cliff at Sarfait and gazed across to 'Capstan' and the sea. I could hardly believe that soldiers had been roped down that steep escarpment.

There were changes in the lifestyle of the *jebalis* too. Many had houses in Salalah and most now wore the traditional Omani dress of *dishdash* and headcloth. They still grazed cattle, goats and camels in the mountains, but life generally was much easier for all. The cash to provide for this development throughout Oman came from its oil revenues. Tourism was also carefully being introduced and expanded, and this was was also becoming a major source of income for the Sultanate.

My work with the now named Internal Security Service was interesting and enjoyable. I was back in my old stamping ground and, I hoped, helping in the progress of the country. I had encountered (and I use the word advisably) some of my colleagues before. Said Hoff, who had once commanded the Ho Chi Minh Unit opposite SAF in the Hornbeam Line, returned to the Sultanate and Islam and fought for the Sultan in the *firqa*. He became a good friend. Also working with me was Salim Khozay Salim of the Mahra. He was also known as Abu Fass (Father of the Axe). One day he mentioned that he had been wounded fighting for the Front in the Dhofar War, but had later returned to fight for the Sultan. He showed the the scar on his shoulder.

'Where did you get it?' I asked.

'In Habarut,' Salim replied. 'I was firing a mortar at the Fort and the *jaysh* replied with theirs. It killed one man and wounded me.'

I told him that I was at Habarut that day and we looked at each other and smiled. Life is strange. Salim too became a good friend. Some years later Salim invited my wife and I to a traditional *jebali* meal on the Jebel Samhan, overlooking Marbat. With us was one of those who had climbed down that precipitous 5,000 feet to attack the town below. I looked over the edge. Even as a youth I could never have attempted it.

My boss in my work was Yahya bin Nasser al Fahdy, who had once been a corporal in NFR, and had come before me for consideration for a commission in the Regiment. I recommended him and he attended the Officer Training School in Jordan. He became a brilliant officer in SAF and later in ISS where he was promoted to Major General. The position was reversed now, but it was easy. There was mutual respect and I like to believe we were a good team. He and his wife Asya and children are close friends and have stayed with my wife and I in Somerset, and we with them in Oman.

Mary and I spent seven very happy years in Dhofar and during this time the country continued to develop at an amazing pace. Before we left we gave a party for our friends. Ninety-eight people attended, half of whom were Omanis including Yahya, Said Hof and Abu Fass. Salim Ghareeb, who commanded the Firqa al Nasser at Mughsayl was also there. We drove back to England by Landrover and stayed our last night in Oman with Medhi, now a Colonel, and his wife Santi in Muscat. That evening we were invited to dinner by the Director General of the Service, Alec Macdonald. He asked us to choose the other guests. We asked Roddy Jones and his wife Gi-Gi, Courtenay Welch from the Muscat office and three Omani friends. Roddy had worked with me in Dhofar, but was now working in the head office in Muscat. The Omanis, who all brought their wives, were Mohamed Said Raqaishi, now a Brigadier and the first Omani officer to command NFR, General Hamed Said al Awfi, my former Adjutant who now commanded all the Sultan's forces – land, sea and air – and General Yahya bin Nasser. It was a great evening but, for Mary and me, tinged with sadness at leaving. The next morning we said farewell to Medhi and Santi, and their two sons, Gunajit and Roon, and departed in our Landrover. We took time on our journey home, passing through the United Arab Emirates, Saudi Arabia, Jordan and Sinai. In Egypt we diverted to do the Nile trip from Luxor before embarking on a ship at Alexandria for Italy. We then drove across Europe and home.

Mary died in 1994. She too was far too young to go. I did not want to spend Christmas in England that year and flew back to Oman. I drove down the tarmac road to Dhofar. On my return to Muscat, Yahya, who at this time was the equivalent of Honorary Colonel of the Northern Frontier Regiment, kindly invited me to a ceremonial parade of NFR to mark the 42nd anniversary of the raising of the Regiment, which took place at Ibri in northern Oman. The parade included soldiers marching past in the regimental dress of past years. First a group rode by on camels, then soldiers in the uniform of the Field Force which fought in the Jebel al Akhdar campaign marched past. They were followed by men in the camouflaged uniform of the Dhofar War. Finally the whole Regiment was drawn up in their modern ceremonial uniforms. They were exceedingly smart.

A surprise was in store. Yahya addressed the parade and told them of the fine work in the past, and during the war, performed by Major Saif Ali. Saif was then called forward and presented with a regimental crest. To my embarrasment my name was then called and, after some words were spoken, I too was presented with a crest. As he handed it to me, Yahya said, 'You see, Bryan, we do not forget.' It was a memorable moment for me, and neither will I forget.

Back in England I continued with my consultancies for NGOs, visiting a number of countries with security problems. There was no shortage of those. Whilst in England I was asked to speak at a conference on Afghanistan in London, and as a result of that met Harriet Sandys who had worked in that country privately for a number of years during the 1980s. She had also worked there as a consultant for UNESCO. We married and on my future visits to Oman I was again accompanied by my wife.

In October 1999 Medhi asked us both to the wedding of his son Gunagit in Guwahiti, Assam. We went and had a wonderful time. Medhi had also invited Audrey and Duncan Rae to attend. They were the parents of Captain Stuart Rae, Royal Marines, who had been killed fighting the *adoo* with NFR before my arrival in 1972. Medhi had looked after Audrey and Duncan when they had visited Oman following the death of their only son. He was a kind and thoughtful man.

In May 2004, Harriet and I hosted a reunion dinner at our home in Somerset for the Northern Frontier Regiment officers who had served with me in 1972 to 1974. Wives were also included. Twenty-six of us sat round the table. It was wonderful to see those familiar faces, all together after thirty years. When I last had dinner with those same officers in NFR mess in Oman I had been the senior in rank, but not any more. General Yahya, who had flown from Oman with his wife Asya, was present, as was General Angus Ramsay DSO CBE, Brigadier Tresham Gregg, Brigadier Ian Gardiner and Brigadier David Nicholls. Mike Kingscote, now a Colonel was there, and so were Christopher Kemball, Viv Rowe, Peter Tawell, Christopher Barnes, who flew in from California, Charlie Daniel, Tony Willis, Nick Knollys, Charles Ogilvie-Forbes and Bob Hudson. A good turnout! Victoria Blashford Snell, John's daughter, did the catering and we drank the health of Her Majesty the Queen, His Majesty the Sultan of Oman and to absent friends – British, Omani and Baluch. To round off a great evening Ian Gardiner and Nick Knollys showed slides of the bearded warriors of long ago for the benefit of their wives!

Sadly the Second in Command, Arthur Brocklehurst, was not there; he died following his return to England after twenty-five years in Oman. Tragically, too, David Nicholls died suddenly in 2006. It was a shock as he was a noted mountaineer, a popular man and always very fit.

My association with Oman has continued. It is a country which has prospered under Sultan Qaboos, the people are happy and there are good opportunities for women as well as for men. There are female doctors, police officers and teachers, with plenty more ladies in the universities eager to graduate and take up their professions. A Western-style democracy in this country is neither sought nor would it be appropriate. Oman's own system of government works. Long may it last.

Appendix 1 to Part 2

An English Translation of the Speech Broadcast over Radio Oman

by His Majesty Sultan Qaboos bin Said on 28 May 1972

(Following the Bombing of the PFLOAG School in Hauf and the Battle at Habarut)

In the name of God, most gracious, most merciful.

Praise be to God, the Cherisher and Sustainer of the worlds – and His aid we seek.

My Beloved People – At this stage of our historical phase, it is imperative that I speak to you about what is actually happening at our border with South Yemen, with all its misunderstandings and what they involve in provocation against us. We tolerated the situation for a long time until it reached a point when it could no longer be tolerated. It pains us to find that our forces have found it necessary to resort to the use of arms.

But what was there for us to do when we found the lives of our soldiers being lost and the sanctity of our land being violated? There is no doubt that you have heard the news of the repeated attacks which the forces of South Yemen made at our border, and the different stories and rumours which have spread about these regretful incidents. We thus felt that it would be expedient that we should address you on this subject, to acquaint you with the facts of what happened and what is happening.

Beloved Citizens – the Government of Aden always confesses and declares through its mass media and through its responsible representatives that it places all that is within its means at the disposal of the so-called 'National Front for the Liberation of the Gulf'. In fact there is an office of the 'Front' in Aden itself, and South Yemen Radio has a daily programme which broadcasts false and distorted information spreading propaganda against neighbouring countries. In Mahra, or what is known as the Sixth Province, a part of South Yemen, is a place called Hauf, approximately four miles from our Southern border. This place has been adopted by the Communist terrorists as a centre from which their terrorist activities are operated, as well as an ammunition and a supplies dump. In addition it is used as a training camp for terrorist activities. The Communist terrorists also use this place as a centre for spearheading their intrusion across the border into our land for purposes of perpetrating their criminal activities. We knew all about this. But in order to avoid a clash or involving ourselves in an armed struggle we exercised self-restraint and confined ourselves to combating the terrorists inside our boundaries. Then came Friday the 5th of May, when the fort of Habarut was subjected to enemy fire by the forces of South Yemen without justification. Here, we thought it was our duty to prepare a memorandum on the incident which we did and which we submitted to the Arab League on the 6th of May 1972. And after dropping leaflets on the aggressors urging them to stop firing without avail, our aircraft silenced the enemy firing positions. On the 16th of May, we explained to the Arab League the details of the aggression. We also sent an urgent cable to the League on the 23rd of May, in which we explained the latest act of aggression by the Aden forces. At the same time we informed the United Nations of all the enemy activities against our Territory and of the death of six members of our forces. May they rest in peace.

Citizens – our desire for good neighbourly relations resulted in disdainful reaction from the other side, and also in repeated aggression. Thus we wanted the aggressors to understand that there are forces in Oman which can repulse aggressors and an Omani army which will sacrifice all that is precious and dear to them for their country; and that our silence was the silence of a powerful peace lover and not that of a weakling. We want those who hold the reins of power in Aden and their terrorists to understand that their neighbour is an Arab Government which is historically long established, capable of repulsing enemy encroachment. We also want them to understand that no crime goes without punishment – as the Holy Qoran says: 'If then any one transgresses against you transgress ye likewise against him.' We chose an appropriate line of retaliation so that the counter-attack should be effective and painful which we directed against the main terrorist centre at Hauf on the 25th of May, 1972, where our air force bombed the Communists post and their supply and ammunition dumps which act as rear supply bases for the Communist terrorists inside the boundaries of South Yemen. Therefore the enemy came to realize that they could not stand against the onslaught of our armed forces and that one reaps as one sows.

When we made this sudden attack on Hauf we exercised our right of self-defence and discharged our duty in safeguarding our country and our religion. We are a people who work quietly building our country with determination without recourse to empty boastfulness, the like of which course of action is taken by those who wish to cover their faults by fabrication, and who accuse others of what they themselves are guilty of.

They have stated that Great Britain wages war against them with its air force and navy. They have spread these fabrications in Arab and world nations; but everyone knows that the air force is an Omani Air Force, and that the navy is an Omani Navy, and that our Omani Army is the only force which protects the land of our Nation and safeguards its prestige.

I as the Commander-in-Chief of the Armed Forces say to you that your brethren in uniform all over the Sultanate have pledged to sacrifice their lives by acting as a formidable shield in the protection of this dear land. We do not accept any other mode of life except that we should live as free men in this country and that we live with our heads up. We in this country fought against invaders and colonialists throughout history. The plains, the mountains and the seas bear witness to the fact that every period of our history has its heroes and heroic dead; and we today are the protectors of this deep-rooted heritage.

Citizens – we view Arabism from a wider and more refined and honourable angle. We do not use methods which our enemies use. We do not set one people against another. We do not provide explosives. We do not plot assassinations. Such acts are not in keeping with Arab traditions. We have never evaded our responsibility towards our nation. We have always adhered to the tenets of our Islamic Religion, and it is impossible for anyone to divert us from the path which we have laid down for ourselves. If our Lands are subjected to any interference, woe betide to the aggressor. Our people are pure Arabs, sincere and honest; no one can live within their midst who is not endowed with these qualities. Our people are peaceful, they are not aggressors and will not submit to aggression from anyone. Our people are firm believers in God; they do not accept atheistic ideologies. He who is an atheist is an outcast in our society and will be trampled upon by those who proceed towards prosperity.

Noble Citizens – the method of misleading people, fabrication of falsehoods and the language of abuse and insults which are used by the rulers of Aden and their paid terrorists, all go to indicate the bankruptcy of their thinking and their failure in bringing about a civilized way of life among their people. In the same way imported ideologies and empty slogans which they use have failed completely in satisfying the hungry masses who are in dire need of a piece of bread more than anything else. As for us we shall go on with building and development and shall remain Arabs and Muslims in our noble efforts to build our country. Here we extend our hand to clasp the hand of every Arab which is free from evil. Let us form a united front and go forth with the blessings of God. Destructive elements have no place in our midst and the aggressor is doomed to failure. May God grant us success in all that is in our interests in our life and our religion. MAY GOD SHOWER HIS BLESSINGS UPON YOU ALL.

Appendix 2 to Part 2

Enemy Tactics in Dhofar

(Included in the Northern Frontier Regiment's Operation Order,
24 October 1972)

1. The enemy are capable of moving very quickly over the difficult terrain of the area and will always try to occupy the dominating features. They can redeploy or reinforce their forces within a very short period of time. Basically, the enemy will wait to assess the strength of the force which is confronting them and try to discover the aim of that force before they commit themselves.
2. If the opposing force is superior in numbers to the enemy in any one area, then the enemy will split up into small groups of 10–15 men, avoid contact with large numbers of troops and try to harass patrols by ambushing from close quarters and then running away. Static bases become the target for heavy weapons stand-off attacks.
3. Should the enemy estimate the opposing force to be of equal numbers or smaller than their own immediate force, then they will try to outflank and cut off the opposing force. The enemy know their own areas intimately and are highly efficient in their use of cover both within the treeline and when using dead ground; however, whenever possible, they prefer to fight within the treeline as this provides better cover both from ground observation and from the air. A camel train caught out in the open of the Corridor would have no option but to stand and fight, but it should be remembered that the vanguard would be deployed ahead of the convoy, following the high ground either side of the track.
4. Early Warning. The enemy rely on the Militia, women and children to give them early warning of the approach of Government forces. Past experience has shown that it is very difficult to maintain even a small ambush position for more than twelve hours without discovery.

5. Patrols. The enemy patrol in groups of 15–20 or 6–8 men and when the presence of Government troops is suspected but not confirmed, they will advance with extreme caution. If the patrol is fired on, the enemy will roll into dead ground, retreat and then return fire from long range. They will always attempt to recover their dead and wounded before withdrawal.

6. Ambushes. The enemy will ambush known tracks and, sometimes, waterholes. The ambush normally consists of 3 or 4 small groups of men deployed at staggered intervals along a track, supported by medium or heavy machine guns, with perhaps a light mortar located on high ground overlooking the killing area. In the barren country of the Corridor, ambushes are often laid where tracks pass over the aqabats or watersheds.

Glossary

Somaliland

Askari	Soldier
Bulawi	Large dagger as worn by the Gadabursi and Esa tribes
Chaplis	Leather sandals
Chokra	Bearer's assistant. Usually a young boy.
Gerenuk	Long-necked gazelle
Ghee	Clarified butter
Ghurgie	Somali nomad's hut
Illalo	Armed tribal police
Jowari	Similar to maize. Used as horse feed.
Jumaa	Friday
Kullah	Conical shaped cap. Normally worn with a puggaree.
Magalla	Town
Midgan	Tribe of hunters and craftsmen
Oryx	Large antelope with long straight horns
Puggaree	Narrow length of material worn as a turban
Qarya	Village
Qat	Mild narcotic leaves
Rer	Tribal sub-section
Shifta	Somali raiding party
Tobe	One-piece robe
Tug	Dry river valley. Liable to spate in rainy season.
Ugaz	Chief, Sultan
Wob	Hut formed from branches placed round a mushroom-shaped tree
Zariba	Protective thorn fence

Oman

Adoo	Enemy
Askar	Tribal guard employed by the Government
Bait	House
Barusti	Hut made from palm fronds over a wooden frame
BATT	British Army Training Team
Blind	Unexploded bomb, shell or projectile
Burmail	Large oil drum. Derived from words 'Burma Oil'.
Cardamom	East Indian spice much used in Arabia
Dishdash	Long shirt-like garment worn in Arabia
Falaj	Water channel
Firqa	Military unit or tribal warrior group
FOO	Forward Observation Officer
Ghee	Clarified butter
Image Intensifier	Night-viewing equipment
Imam	Religious leader
ISFU	Iranian Special Forces Unit
Jaysh	Army
Jebel	Mountain or hill
Jebali	One who dwells on the mountain
Khor	Wadi mouth, small bay
Khareef	Monsoon
Loomi	Drink made with fresh limes, served ice cold
Majlis	Meeting room. Conference group.
PDRY	Peoples' Democratic Republic of Yemen
PFLOAG	Peoples' Front for the Liberation of the Occupied Arabian Gulf
PFLO	Peoples' Front for the Liberation of Oman
Qaa'id	Leader
Sangar	Ad hoc defensive emplacement built of stones
SEP	Surrendered Enemy Personnel
Shemagh	Headcloth
Shimaal	Literally 'North'. Also used to describe bitter wind blowing from the north.
Shuyueeyeen	Communists
Siarsee	Intelligence Officer
Suk	Market
Sunray	Leader. Army code name.
Sura	Koran verse
Topkhana	Gunners (Urdu)
Wadi	Dry river bed
Wali	Headman or Governor
Wazr	Sarong-like garment similar to Indian lungi

Index

Note: Where military ranks are shown they are applicable to the period of the narrative.

SOMALILAND & SOMALIA

OMAN

213